ENVIRONMENTAL POLITICS

CONTEMPORARY POLITICAL STUDIES SERIES

Series Editor: John Benyon, *Director, Centre for the Study of Public Order, University of Leicester*

A series which provides authoritative yet concise introductory accounts of key topics in contemporary political studies.

Other titles in the series include:

Pressure Groups, Politics and Democracy in Britain, 2nd edition
WYN GRANT, *University of Warwick*

UK Political Parties since 1945
Edited by ANTHONY SELDON, *Institute of Contemporary British History*

Politics and Policy Making in Northern Ireland
MICHAEL CONNOLLY, *University of Ulster*

Local Government and Politics in Britain
JOHN KINGDOM, *Sheffield Hallam University*

British Political Ideologies
ROBERT LEACH, *Leeds Metropolitan University*

British Government: The Central Executive Territory
PETER MADGWICK, *Professor Emeritus, Oxford Brookes University*

Race and Politics in Britain
SHAMIT SAGGAR, *Queen Mary and Westfield College, University of London*

Selecting the Party Leader
MALCOLM PUNNETT, *University of Strathclyde*

Does Parliament Matter?
PHILIP NORTON, *University of Hull*

The President of the United States
DAVID MERVIN, *University of Warwick*

The Politics of Economic Policy
WYN GRANT, *University of Warwick*

Introduction to International Politics
DEREK HEATER, *formerly of Brighton University* and
G.R. BERRIDGE, *University of Leicester*

Elections and Voting Behaviour in Britain, 2nd edition
DAVID DENVER, *Lancaster University*

The Law and Politics of the British Constitution of the United Kingdom
PETER MADGWICK and DIANA WOODHOUSE, *Oxford Brookes University*

The British Civil Service
ROBERT PYPER, Glasgow, *Caladonian University*

ENVIRONMENTAL POLITICS

ROBERT GARNER

University of Leicester

PRENTICE HALL
HARVESTER WHEATSHEAF

London   New York   Toronto   Sydney   Tokyo   Singapore
Madrid   Mexico City   Munich

First published 1996 by
Prentice Hall/Harvester Wheatsheaf
Campus 400, Maylands Avenue
Hemel Hempstead
Hertfordshire, HP2 7EZ

A division of
Simon & Schuster International Group

Typeset in 10/12pt Times
by Dorwyn Ltd, Rowlands Castle, Hants.

Printed and bound in Great Britain by
T.J. International Ltd, Padstow, Cornwall.

Library of Congress Cataloging in Publication Data

Garner, Robert, 1960–
Environmental politics / by Robert Garner.
    p. cm. — (Contemporary political studies series)
ISBN 0–13–353848–6
1. Environmental policy. 2. Environmentalism. 3. Sustainable
development. I. Title. II. Series: Contemporary political studies series
(Harvester Wheatsheaf (Publisher))
GE170.G37 1996
363.7—dc20   95–37427
CIP

British Library Cataloguing in Publication Data

A catalogue record for this book is available from
the British Library

ISBN 0 13 353848 6 (pbk)

---

2 3 4 5 00 99 98 97 96

CONTENTS

Preface   ix

Introduction   1
   Radical and reformist versions of environmentalism   2
   The environment as a political issue   4
   The political response   11

1 THE ENVIRONMENTAL CRISIS   13
   The interdependence of environmental problems   13
   Environmental issues   15
   Further reading   27

2 SUSTAINABILITY AND ENVIRONMENTAL IDEOLOGY   29
   The core ideas stated   29
   Environmentalism and the economy   30
   Science and technology   36
   Decentralization   38
   Nature and value   41
   Animals and morality   47
   Further reading   50

3 GREENS AND THE WESTERN POLITICAL TRADITION   51
   Conservatism   52

Fascism/authoritarianism   52
Liberalism   54
Marxism   55
Feminism   58
Anarchism   59
Conclusions   60
Further reading   61

4 THE ENVIRONMENTAL MOVEMENT   62
Origins and evolution   62
Explaining the growing concern   67
Classifying the environmental movement   71
The pressure group perspective   78
Further reading   85

**5 POLITICAL INSTITUTIONS AND ENVIRONMENTAL
POLICY IN BRITAIN**   87
Environmental legislation   87
Development and conservation   91
Pollution control   96
Pollution control debates   100
Further reading   109

6 THE INTERNATIONAL POLITICS OF THE ENVIRONMENT 110
The drive towards internationalism   110
The nature of international environmental regimes   111
International treaties   113
The difficulties of inter-state co-operation   115
The European dimension of environmental politics   119
Third World development and the environment   124
Further reading   127

7 ENVIRONMENTALISM AND POLITICAL PARTIES   128
The Green Party   129
Greening the major parties   139
Further reading   147

8 THE POLITICAL PROCESS AND THE ENVIRONMENT   148
Approaches to policy-making   148
Agriculture, the countryside and the environment   156

CONTENTS

The politics of pollution 163
The politics of wildlife conservation 168
Further reading 177

CONCLUSION: TOWARDS A SUSTAINABLE FUTURE 179
Faltering steps 179
Ecological modernization, sustainability and democracy 181
Lifestyle changes 182
Communities and class 184

Bibliography 190

Index 201

PREFACE

The aim of this book is to convey the scope of environmental politics by identifying and exploring its major dimensions and by indicating the range of published material in what is a rapidly expanding academic discipline. It is therefore intended primarily as an introductory text, providing a framework for those taking undergraduate courses in environmental politics. It is hoped, too, that the material will be useful for students and teachers of political theory and public policy. Last but not least, the aim is also to produce a book which is accessible enough to be of interest to the general reader.

I have incurred numerous debts during the process of researching and writing this book. I wish to express my gratitude to Stephen Young, who provided gratefully received advice, and Clare Grist, who enthusiastically supported the project from the outset and listened with patience to my lame excuses for the late arrival of the manuscript. An anonymous reader also provided a great deal of useful comments, many of which have been acted on. Most of the work for this book was done during my occupation of a lecturing post in the Politics Department at the University of Exeter. My colleagues there provided a conducive environment for academic study and I cannot think of a more appropriate place to write a book on the politics of the natural environment. My biggest thanks go to my mother and father, John and June Garner, who have supported and encouraged me over the years. Finally, the book is dedicated to Rhonda Lovell who helped me to love the beauty he is. None of the above, of course, bears any responsibility for the mistakes and omissions made nor for the opinions expressed in the pages that follow.

Robert Garner
Leicester, October 1995

INTRODUCTION

Thirty years ago, the topic covered in this book would not have been included in a popular series providing introductory accounts of political issues and processes. This is not to say that people were not concerned about the environment then. Many of the major environmental groups in Britain and the United States were well established by the 1960s, but it was not until the 1970s that the environment became an important political issue and not until the latter half of the 1980s that it became a mainstream one. As a consequence, the study of environmental politics has discarded its Cinderella status.

Indeed, by the late 1980s, we seemed to be entering a new Green era, where environmental concern had become the height of fashion. Opinion polls revealed mounting public concern for the state of the environment; consumers demanded environmentally friendly products, and producers, with varying degrees of honesty, sought to provide them; recycling centres and bottle banks flourished. Even more remarkably, the then prime minister, Mrs Thatcher, became a convert. As recently as the early 1980s she had described the environment as a 'humdrum' issue, and no doubt would have included many environmentalists with the miners as the 'enemy within'. By the late 1980s, though, she was regarding the environment as 'one of the great challenges' of the late twentieth century and, moreover, claiming that it was safe only in the hands of a Conservative government (McCormick, 1991, pp.1–2). As if to confirm that Thatcher's political antennae were working effectively, the Green Party came from nowhere to win 15 per cent of the vote in the 1989 European Parliament elections, pushing the newly formed Liberal Democrats into fourth place. Since then, the environment has slipped down the issue agenda a little, overtaken by dramatic political and economic events in Britain and elsewhere, but it remains a permanently important feature of political and academic discourse.

Radical and reformist versions of environmentalism

So, what is the stuff of environmental politics? An appropriate starting point is a definition. The common-sense definition of the term 'environment' – constituting our surroundings – would seem to be hopelessly broad, although it does reveal a sense of how all-pervasive the subject is. In practice, we can impose a limitation by focusing on the 'natural' environment, so that environmental politics becomes a study of human impact on the natural environment. But even this is insufficient, because it fails to distinguish between the scientific and the social scientific study of the environment. To understand the *politics* of the environment, some knowledge of environmental problems is necessary, but we must go further than this. We must also seek to explain why it is that the environment has become a political issue, what impact political decisions have had on the environment, why some decisions were taken rather than others, and, finally, what political structures are best able to protect the environment. It is with these themes that this book is concerned.

The terminology used in the environmental literature can be confusing, so it is worthwhile clarifying some terms at this early stage. The word 'Green' has been used since the 1950s to indicate concern for the environment and is now used in a blanket fashion by most casual observers. For others, the label Green is associated with the radical ideas and policies of Green political parties. Whatever terms we use, it is important to recognize the key division pervading the environmental debate, between radical approaches at one end of the spectrum to a moderate reformism at the other.

Various terms have been utilized to distinguish these two positions. Dobson (1990) and Porritt (1984) refer to dark and light green approaches (only the former justifying the label 'Green');

Stephen Young (1993) prefers to use the terms radical environmentalism and weak or refo.nist environmentalism; Arne Naess
(1973) coined the terms deep ecology and shallow ecology; Robyn
Eckersley (1992) distinguishes between ecocentric and anthropocentric approaches, while to add to the confusion, both Tim
O'Riordan (1976) and David Pearce *et al.* (1993) distinguish between ecocentric and technocentric approaches.

The term ecologism is preferred by some radicals because it
signifies the interrelationship between the human species and
nature, and implies a non-hierarchical order displacing man from
his dominant position, both key characteristics of the radical approach. Use of the label ecologism, however, can lead to confusion
since the term ecology – first used by the scientist Ernst Haeckel in
the 1850s – also describes a branch of biology which studies, in a
neutral fashion, the relationship between living organisms and
their environment (Heywood, 1992, p.247).

The differences between the radical and reformist positions is
more easily definable than the terminology would suggest. Put
simply, the latter position holds that environmental protection can
be effectively incorporated within modern industrial society, without fundamentally threatening economic growth and material
prosperity. Economic development, according to this position,
must be sustainable; it must, that is, be 'development that meets
the needs of the present without compromising the ability of future
generations to meet their own needs' (World Commission on Environment and Development, 1987, p.43). Put crudely, then, this
position is the politics of catalytic converters, power station scrub-
bers and bottle banks. It is an optimistic approach, which puts faith
in the ability of science and technology to solve environmental
problems without fundamentally challenging our institutional and
value systems.

Many would regard this as the totality of what is involved in
being Green or environmentally aware, but a great deal of the
available social science literature on the environment focuses on
the radical dimension. Here there is a consensus that mere tinkering with the structures of modern industrial society – a few pallia-
tives to mitigate the worst effects of industrial society – is not
enough to forestall environmental catastrophe. Rather, fundamental economic, social and political change – nothing less, that is, than
the creation of a new kind of society with different institutions and

values – is required both to deal with the severity of the crisis and
to enable people to live more satisfying and fulfilling lives.

Radical environmentalists, following Naess, have contrasted
their 'deep' position with what they regard as the 'shallow' approach of environmental reformism – the latter label used in a
derogatory sense to illustrate how it falls far short of the radical
measures needed to deal with the environmental crisis. This polar-
ization is arguably unhelpful (see Barry, 1994), not least because it
tends to belittle, or direct attention away from, the important task
of developing a theoretical perspective which can help us to understand the nature of environmental politics in the present, thus
enabling us to chart a course which recognizes the many obstacles
standing in the way of sustainable development.

One such perspective is the approach known as 'ecological modernization' which argues, from within the reformist position, that
ecological and economic imperatives are not necessarily incompatible (Weale, 1992). A great deal of attention in this book, therefore, will be devoted to the reformist part of the spectrum, since
this is the context of the 'real' world in which government re-
sponses to environmental problems are located (the subject of
Chapters 5, 6 and 8 in particular) and in which environmental
groups must operate.

No book on environmental issues, and still less one that focuses
on environmental *politics*, can ignore the radical challenge to environmental reformism. This is in part because of its empirical claim
that environmental catastrophe faces us unless we take radical steps
to limit production and consumption levels. Equally, the radical
approach offers a challenge to Western political thought since its
claim is nothing less than that the Green approach to politics represents an entirely comprehensive and distinctive ideology, justifying a
separate political party whose role is to articulate a programme of
policies based on it. The competing claims of the radicals and reformists are considered in Chapter 2, and in Chapter 3 dark Green
ideas are discussed in relation to mainstream political thought.

The environment as a political issue

A central feature of a book on environmental politics must be a
consideration of three related questions. First, why has the

environment become an important political issue? Second, what distinguishes the environment as a political issue? And third, what has been the political response to its arrival on the agenda?

The simple answer to the first of these questions is that the environment has become an important political issue because enough, or the right, people perceived there to be a problem that had to be tackled. This, of course, is to beg the question why did this happen? A number of answers suggest themselves. We shall start by looking at the impact of environmental problems.

Environmental degradation

Obviously, the raw material of the environmental debate is the deleterious effects of human activity on the planet; Chapter 1 seeks to outline the nature and consequences of this activity. Information on environmental degradation is readily available, and one could be forgiven for concluding that the rise of the environment as an important political issue is related to lay observations and scientific evidence concerning such 'invisible' phenomena as global warming and ozone depletion. Indeed, one factor which ostensibly distinguishes the environment from many other issues is the extent of objective measurement involved. Thus, there is a crucially important technical core to the study of the environment, providing a key role for engineers, scientists and technicians (Weale, 1992, p.10). Put simply, if there is a hole in the ozone layer and this is dangerous to all people, then we need to do something about it. And if something needs to be done, then we need to decide what is causing it and do something about preventing it.

The growing sense of an objective environmental crisis, therefore, is an obvious reason for heightened concern. One can point here to the well-publicized environmental disasters of the past thirty years or so – the slag heap slip at Aberfan which buried a school, with great loss of life, in 1966; the oil pollution caused by the stricken tankers *Torrey Canyon* (in 1967) and *Exxon Valdez* (in 1988); industrial accidents at Bhopal in India, which killed over 3,000 people and injured many hundreds of thousands, and at Seveso in Italy; the near-thing at the Three Mile Island nuclear facility in the United States in the late 1970s and the real thing at Chernobyl in the 1980s – to name but a few. One can point, too, to important books, conferences and scientific research – Rachel

Carson's *Silent Spring* (1962), which documented the effects on the countryside of pesticide use; the *Limits to Growth* report (Meadows *et al.*, 1972); the UN Conference on the Human Environment convened in Stockholm in 1972 (proceedings published as B. Ward and Dubos, 1972); the Bruntland Report (World Commission on Environment and Development, 1987); and various scientific papers relating to global warming and ozone depletion – which have had the effect of informing decision-makers and the wider public about environmental problems.

This evidence indicates not only that environmental problems have increased quantitatively, in the sense that the number of environmentally damaging incidents have risen markedly, but that there has also been a qualitative shift. Environmental problems are no longer perceived as localized concerns affecting relatively few people and having few long-term consequences. Instead, the central concern has become nothing less than human survival on a planet which, it is now recognized, cannot continue indefinitely to cope with the consumption of non-renewable resources or the absorption of waste products from industrial processes at the levels which it is presently asked to do. The following information tells its own story:

> Since 1900, the world's population has multiplied more than three times. Its economy has grown twentyfold. The consumption of fossil fuels has grown by a factor of 30, and industrial production by a factor of 50. Most of that growth, about four-fifths of it, occurred since 1950. Much of it is unsustainable. (MacNeil *et al.*, 1991, p.3)

Of course, as Young (1993, p.4) points out, environmental problems do manifest themselves at the local level, but 'what appear to be little local difficulties are the visible parts of much more complicated sets of inter-related problems', with regional, national and even international aspects. Thus, for many people, the increasing volume of traffic and the building of more roads to meet rising demand cause readily visible congestion and damage to the countryside. It also, though, causes less visible health problems and, even further removed, it contributes to acid rain, increases the level of carbon dioxide in the atmosphere thereby adding to the threat of global warming and, last but not least, uses up more of the world's precious oil reserves (Young, 1993, pp.5–6).

These observations lead us to identify two further features which distinguish environmentalism from many other issues. In the first place, present practices will have long-term consequences affecting the fundamental interests of future generations. This, of course, raises practical questions about the representation of future generations in our decision-making arenas as well as philosophical questions concerning inter-generational justice (Weale, 1992, pp.8–9). Second, and more important, is the increasingly international character of environmental decision-making.

Co-operation between states to achieve environmental objectives has a long history, but three post-war developments have markedly intensified the shift in focus. First, a great deal of Britain's environmental policy-making is now made in the context of EU legislation. Second, the identification of global environmental problems has not only increased the urgency for nations to act concertedly because they are potentially so serious, but it has also been recognized that they are problems that can *only* be dealt with by global co-operation. As List and Rittberger (1992, p.108) point out: 'Ecological policy, like charity, begins at home, but, unlike the latter, stopping there is often immediately self-defeating.' Put simply, all countries stand to suffer from the depletion of the ozone layer but it is little use for one country, or a handful of countries, to act by banning the production of chlorofluorocarbons (CFCs) if other countries do not follow suit. Third, there is the related problem of Third World development since one, if not *the*, main threat to the environment is the rapid development of the Third World eager to replicate the material quality of life in the West.

While the focus of this study is Britain, the growing internationalization of environmentalism will not be neglected. Thus, the global nature of the problems is discussed in Chapter 1, while Chapter 6 is devoted to an examination of the character and effectiveness of international organizations designed to protect the environment. Moreover, the impact of internationalization is also recognized in the discussion of the British environmental movement (Chapter 4) and in the environmental case studies examined in Chapter 8.

The limits to an issue-based approach

We should not overexaggerate the importance of objective environmental problems as an explanation for the existence of a politics of the environment. These objectively defined problems can, of course, be distinguished from a subjective awareness of, and concern for, such problems so that the existence of the former does not necessarily by itself explain why the environment has become an important issue. This is why the social sciences can make an important contribution to the environmental debate, and why it is not merely the preserve of scientists, technocrats or even philosophers, important though their contribution might be (Yearley, 1992, pp.49, 184–5). Indeed, it has been suggested that the objective conditions are not at all important in explaining the rise of a social problem such as the environment (Kitsuse and Spector, 1981).

As Chapter 4 illustrates, some of the standard explanations for the rising popularity of environmental protection – based on an affluence-induced post-material culture and a post-war occupational shift – do come close to denying the social importance of the increasing severity of environmental problems. While we might not want to ignore completely the explanatory capacity of objective environmental problems, the opposite extreme – that there is a simple relationship between identifying environmental problems, providing remedies for them and the generation of widespread popular support for their implementation – is surely equally simplistic.

There are a number of arguments which, at the very least, throw doubt on the 'objective problem' explanation. In the first place, many environmental problems are not directly observable or, in the case of natural resource depletion – not easy to visualize. Thus, problems are mediated through scientists – whose conclusions are rarely universally accepted within the scientific community – the media and pressure groups. Second, even though most people have indirect experience of environmental problems and disasters, many of them still remain distant affairs with few immediate effects. For example, even though we have been told that the Chernobyl nuclear accident has affected us – in terms of an increased incidence of cancer in the future – the effects remain imperceptible and we can comfort ourselves with the somewhat complacent thought – encouraged, rightly or wrongly, by nuclear scientists with a vested interest in the continuation of the industry – that our own nuclear safety record is such that a similar accident could not happen here. (The relationship between scientific evaluation of risk and the 'real' world inhabited by the general public is discussed by Beck, 1992.)

A final point is that, even when environmental problems are recognized, it does not automatically follow that remedial action will follow. For the causes of a particular visible problem may be disputed and this may delay action. For example, the British government refused for a long time to accept that the damage caused to Scandinavian forests and rivers by acid rain was primarily caused by emissions from British power stations. The government's reluctance to act was mainly a product of political expediency but there may also be genuine doubts as to the effects of particular practices as well as the causes of, and therefore the most appropriate remedies for, environmental problems. The unwillingness to act when there is doubt will be compounded where proposed solutions involve considerable sacrifices, as in the case of action to minimize the relatively little understood phenomenon of global warming.

Reluctance to act may also be caused by the costs of solutions which people are unwilling to accept, coupled with a perception that a certain degree of environmental degradation can be accommodated. Even if this causes long-term problems, it may be decided that passing on these problems to future generations is preferable to making sacrifices now. To some degree, then, there are choices to be made in the environmental debate and, as a consequence, it is a debate that is often more concerned with values, ethics and interests than with objective facts. This perception is confirmed by the changing nature of the case put by environmentalists. In the 1970s, their case was structured by warnings of imminent catastrophe encouraging, as one stream of thought, a survivalist mentality where the objective imperatives – act now before it is too late – predominated (Hardin, 1968; Ehrlich, 1972; Goldsmith *et al.*, 1972; Heilbroner, 1974; Meadows *et al.*, 1972). More recently, however, radical Greens have put greater emphasis on the desirability, as opposed to the necessity, of change. Thus, a doom and gloom scenario has been discarded in favour of promoting a society which places a good quality environment above one that worships material consumption.

One can see the advantage of such a position. The Green case is, as Robyn Eckersley (1992, pp.17–21) points out, driven above all by an 'emancipatory' ethos, since it is not just telling us that we have to give up our present material standard of living, leaving us to mourn our loss, but it is also telling us how our lives can be enriched by adopting a set of values and institutions which will make us happier and more fulfilled (*ibid.*, p.21). This appeal to self-interest is coupled with an appeal to our altruistic nature since a central feature of the radical Green approach is an ethical case for discarding an anthropocentric approach to the natural environment in favour of an ecocentric one, which recognizes the inherent value of nature.

Quite clearly, then, it is simplistic to equate the rise of the environment as a political issue with the mere existence of environmental problems. Convincing scientific evidence, particularly if backed up by clearly observed environmental deterioration, makes a social problem claim more robust, adding credibility to campaigns mounted by environmentalists (Yearley, 1992, p.75). Of equal if not greater importance, though, are the social, economic and political processes involved in placing the environment near the top of the political agenda. Of prime importance is the role performed by the environmental movement in raising the profile of the issue and generating concern, whether justifiable or not. But this is to jump one step ahead of ourselves. For the significant growth of the organized environmental movement in the 1970s and 1980s, and the greater public receptiveness to its campaigns, was itself the product of a shift in public attitudes which can, at least in part, be explained by important social and economic change. These issues are discussed particularly in Chapters 4 and 8.

The distinctive nature of the environment as an issue adds weight to the claim that public desire for its protection does reflect something more than a recognition of objective problems. For it might be argued that increased support for environmental protection represents a paradigm shift in post-war politics. In the first place, the emphasis on the empirical and normative limits to economic growth challenges the goal of every post-war government, whose major objective has been to find the best means of increasing material prosperity. Furthermore, as Weale (1992, p.7) points out, the environment is a post-welfare state sector of public policy in that it 'does not use public spending as its primary policy instrument' because it is not concerned with arriving at the correct formula for distributing the fruits of economic growth. Indeed, as Beck (1992) has pointed out, the environment may be more correctly seen as a matter of being concerned with the distribution of the 'bads' or 'risks' of economic growth. Finally, a quality environment is a public good and not a narrow sectional interest. Since the benefits of action to protect the environment will usually be widespread, distinctive problems of collective action bearing on the behaviour of groups and individuals occur. These will be considered in the chapters that follow.

The political response

The relationship between public concern and the responsiveness of political institutions is critical to a study of environmental politics. It is clear that widely perceived 'problems', however much scientific expertise has been utilized to identify them, do not always result in positive and sustained political action. It is precisely for this reason that the social sciences are able to make a contribution to a study of the environment. Thus, Chapters 5 and 6 examine the structure of environmental decision-making in Britain and internationally, focusing on the institutions responsible for making and enforcing policies which have an impact on the environment. The changing nature of British environmental policy is documented and its effectiveness assessed.

The character of environmental policy is the product of political processes, which need to be explained. Thus, despite the enormous growth of the environmental lobby in recent decades, successive UK governments have not been noted – at least before the late 1980s – for their concern with the natural environment and still less with action to remedy environmental problems. It is, of course, a flawed approach to explain this by reference to the attitudes of governmental actors alone, although such attitudes can play an important role in policy outcomes (Nordliner, 1981). Rather, environmental decision-making, like other public policy issue areas, is a complex matter involving a wide variety of actors, interests and considerations.

Thus pollution as a technical problem does not raise insurmountable difficulties, but it enters the realm of politics precisely because it is not merely a technical problem, but one which causes conflict between competing interests – motorists, oil companies and road builders versus cyclists, pedestrians and wildlife – which governments must seek to resolve. The way in which they do so will reflect the nature of power and representation in the political system, both central concerns of the political scientist. The nature of the political processes involved in environmental policy-making is a recurrent theme in this book. Chapter 4 examines the political impact of the environmental lobby and Chapter 7 considers the impact of the Green Party and the extent to which environmental concerns have permeated the mainstream parties. Chapter 8 outlines various approaches to decision-making and, through a case study approach, assesses their relevance to environmental policy-making.

A distinguishing feature of environmental policy-making is the potential for conflict between the many competing interests. This is because environmental issues cross-cut a huge variety of governmental activities – transport, agriculture, trade, and so on – and these separate policy areas, centring on a particular government department, tend to provide a great deal of influence for development-oriented interests. As we shall see, a truly sustainable policy requires the integration of environmental policy to ensure that problems are not merely displaced (from air to water, or from one government department to another, or, indeed, from present to future generations) but are genuinely resolved (Dryzek, 1987, pp.10–13). This book reveals that Britain, for a variety of reasons, has only partly developed an integrative approach and that sustainable development is unlikely to be achieved without a concerted attempt to mobilize popular support for environmental goals outside the existing political–institutional system.

I

THE ENVIRONMENTAL CRISIS

One reason for the growing importance of the environment as a political issue – albeit not the only or even the principal one – is the existence and recognition of severe environmental problems. This chapter seeks to explore the nature and scope of these problems. It is not meant to be a definitive or particularly technical account but aims rather to provide a guide for those interested in the politics of the environment who have no background in science in general or environmental science in particular. We shall be focusing, of course, on the effects of human (or anthropogenic) influences on the natural environment, although it should be noted that natural phenomena – earthquakes, volcanoes, landslides, cyclones, droughts, and so on – can have a devastating impact too (Pickering and Owen, 1994, ch.8).

The interdependence of environmental problems

Utilization of the Earth's natural resources stretches back many centuries (Goudie, 1989; Mannion, 1991), but the crucial turning point was the industrial revolution, which led to fundamental changes in manufacturing activities and resulted in far greater stresses on the natural environment. Industrial expansion caused rapid investment-led technological innovation, unprecedented population growth and the large-scale movement of people from rural to urban areas and from towns to cities (Young, 1992, p.11). Economic expansion has continued apace and received a further boost after 1945 when rising expectations demanded greater material prosperity, and a new financial system was designed to meet them (McCulloch, 1991, p.10).

Although convenient, it is somewhat artificial and misleading to consider different forms of environmental damage in isolation from others, since the problems are interdependent, a fact illustrated by the 'Limits to Growth' report discussed in Chapter 2. Thus, one particular process has multifaceted consequences, and actions to deal with one specific consequence often has knock-on effects causing unintended, and often undesirable, by-products. Both the inputs and the outputs of the industrial process cause environmental damage (Georgescu-Roegen, 1973). Raw materials are transformed into finished products by processes requiring energy. The inputs of raw materials and the energy sources required to transform them are usually non-renewable, leading to potential problems of resource depletion. Moreover, the extraction of raw materials and the extraction and use of energy sources may well cause pollution. The manufacturing process not only causes pollution but also land-use problems. In addition, by creating a large urban population, industrialism also requires an efficient, intensive and environmentally (and ethically) dubious farming sector to provide adequate food supplies.

The end-products of the industrial process have to be transported by road, air or sea, and this has implications for energy consumption, pollution and the fate of the countryside (not to mention the species of flora and fauna residing there) parts of which may have to be destroyed to build the necessary transport infrastructure. Once these products have outlived their usefulness, they have to be disposed of. This again raises issues of land-use, water and air pollution, and the fate of the human and non-human species who inhabit the areas utilized.

Many of the products of the industrial process are damaging to the environment when in everyday use, and none more so than the symbol of the modern environmental crisis, the motor car. It is easy to see why the motor vehicle has become such a symbol. Above all, it helps to illustrate why many environmentalists argue that there are no small-scale, piecemeal solutions to the crisis. Producing motor vehicles uses valuable raw materials and energy; vehicles consume energy and pollute the environment while in use; they require roads to run on; they cause urban congestion, thereby reducing the quality of life for many; and, finally, they must be disposed of when no longer needed. Seen in this context, the solutions proposed and acted on seem entirely inappropriate. Thus, while the use of lead-free petrol and the fitting of catalytic converters do stop some of the worst emissions, they do not deal with the other consequences of car use. While cars continue to be produced, they still consume energy and still require roads. What is more, they continue to emit carbon dioxide, the gas which is regarded as a primary cause of global warming. The only solution, therefore, would seem to be a drastic reduction of road vehicles rather than more environmentally friendly ones.

Environmental issues

The rest of this chapter will document in some detail the nature of specific environmental problems. A consideration of air and water pollution issues is followed by sections on global atmospheric changes, biodiversity and resource depletion. Development issues are central to much of the discussion and their relevance is briefly indicated before being examined more fully in Chapter 6.

Air and water pollution

The issue of pollution is in itself an enormous topic. To some extent, what is covered under the heading depends on the definition used. Albert Weale (1992, p.3), for instance, defines it as 'the introduction into the environment of substances or emissions that either damage, or carry the risk of damaging, human health or well-being, the built environment or the natural environment'. This is a very broad definition and, for our purposes, it can be made more manageable by the introduction of three caveats. In the first place, following the earlier limitations imposed on the subject area, we can exclude the built environment. Second, it is appropriate to exclude the issue of global atmospheric change here also, since global warming and ozone depletion are such distinct issues, with such potentially devastating consequences, that they deserve to be considered separately. Third, as we intimated earlier, only anthropogenic pollution will be considered.

The existence of other materials in the air and water does not necessarily cause environmental hazards. Problems are caused by the quantity of a substance or the nature of the impurity (Harvey and Hallett, 1977, p.50). In the latter case, the nature of the impurity can be such that its introduction into the air or water can be devastating. Radioactive material and some pesticides fall into this category. In the former case, problems can arise either if the impurity cannot be diluted – the classic examples being oil spills and the chemicals implicated in the production of smogs – or if an additional small quantity of an already existing substance is introduced. In some cases, such as zinc and copper, a small amount of a substance is beneficial to living organisms but becomes toxic when this limit is exceeded (*ibid.*, p.53). For some substances, such as mercury and lead, a moderate amount may be benign but is deadly in increased quantities. Finally, the introduction of large quantities of a naturally occurring substance (the classic example being the use of nitrogen fertilizers) can upset the natural balance and cause great environmental damage.

Mercury is a substance used in various manufacturing processes and excessive long-term exposure to it causes severe health problems including impaired vision, speech and movement. It was once used in the hat industry to cure felt and, before mercury poisoning was recognized, the symptoms were associated with madness – hence the Mad Hatter in Lewis Carroll's *Alice's Adventures in Wonderland* (Harvey and Hallett, 1977, p.51). A primary source of lead today is from car exhausts. Lead was first added to petrol in 1924 to improve engine performance but evidence that it can cause severe damage to the central nervous system led in 1988 to the introduction of a tax incentive to encourage motorists to use lead-free petrol.

The substances discussed above constitute a fraction of the twenty-five harmful chemicals, gases and particulates which are regularly emitted into the atmosphere during various stages of the industrial process, ranging from arsenic (emitted through oil and coal combustion and glass manufacture, and linked to lung and skin cancer) to manganese (emitted from power stations and during smelting, and linked to Parkinson's disease) (Simpson, 1990, p.56). Of these, nine – most notably carbon dioxide and chlorofluorocarbons, or CFCs – are climate and atmosphere-modifying gases.

A high proportion of the total number of harmful substances are emitted from fossil-fuelled power stations and vehicle exhausts. In combination, these are responsible for so-called photochemical smogs and acid rain (McCormick, 1989). Smogs in the major cities of the world are commonplace. One of the best known was the infamous 'pea-souper' which engulfed London in December 1952. Lasting about five days, the smog was held to be responsible for almost 4,000 deaths as people inhaled acidic water droplets. This was the necessary stimulus for the passage of the Clean Air Act 1956, but although this legislation helped to end much of the pollution caused by the domestic burning of coal, by no means has it solved the problem. Indeed, in December 1991 a severe smog occurred again over London with high recorded levels of nitrogen dioxide. In other parts of the world – particularly in huge urban conglomerates such as Mexico City, Los Angeles and Athens – the problem is far worse with smogs, and the consequent health problems, a regular occurrence (Pickering and Owen, 1994, pp.107–8).

Acid rain has become an increasingly important issue since the 1980s, although the phenomenon was first recognized in the middle of the nineteenth century. It is caused when certain chemicals combine with rainfall, turning the latter literally to acid. The principal culprit is sulphur dioxide (SO^2), although nitrogen oxides and hydrocarbons are also implicated. The most visible effect is the devastation caused to trees and water courses, vegetation becoming seriously affected because of the level of soil acidity. Acid rain is a problem which occurs throughout the world with the former Soviet Union and the United States being the biggest emitters of SO^2. In Europe, it is the Scandinavian countries that have borne the brunt of the damage, much of it deriving, due to prevailing airflow patterns, from power station emissions from the United Kingdom (Schoon, 1990). By 1986, 13 per cent of all forest cover in Europe had been badly affected, an area equivalent to the size of the United Kingdom (Myers, 1989, p.35; Pickering and Owen, 1994, ch.4).

There is some good news on SO^2 emissions. Due to a variety of factors – international agreements, the recession, less reliance on coal-fired power stations and technological developments making for cleaner power stations and cars – SO^2 emissions actually fell in

OECD countries by a quarter in the two decades from 1970. In the same period, however, nitrogen oxide emissions increased by 12 per cent (Weale, 1992, pp.25, 23).

Over two-thirds of the earth's surface is covered by water and, as it is essential to human life, protecting it against pollutants is crucially important. Initially, the most serious pollutant was human waste, but laws passed since the nineteenth century and, in more recent times, especially at the instigation of the European Union (see Chapter 5) have resulted in rigorous water quality standards (Pickering and Owen, 1994, pp.137, 142).

Organic waste still, however, constitutes a problem. In many developing countries water quality remains poor and diseases such as cholera and typhoid are common. In addition, the dumping of sewage sludge in the sea remains a problem for industrialized countries which has only recently begun to be tackled (Pickering and Owen, 1994, pp.136–44). Finally, there is the problem of the disposal of animal waste. In reasonable quantities this can be used as fertilizer to enrich the soil, but the colossal amount of slurry produced often means that large quantities of nitrates, ammonia and bacteria are leached into streams and rivers. An additional problem is the use of large amounts of antibiotics which intensive animal farming often requires. Antibiotic residues also get into water courses, with consequences that are not yet fully understood (Mason and Singer, 1990).

In industrialized countries, the biggest water pollution problem now is not organic wastes but industrial and agricultural wastes, including radioactive chemicals, nitrates, heavy metals and oil. Pollution from these sources in British rivers has increased significantly in the past decade or so with the doubling of reported pollution incidents (Pickering and Owen, 1994, p.137). The main problem areas are: (1) nitrates and phosphates caused by the use and disposal of fertilizers and detergents; (2) dangerous organic chemicals, most notably polychlorinated biphenyls (PCBs), involved in the manufacture of paints and plastics, and pesticides; (3) heavy metals such as mercury, lead, arsenic and aluminium; and (4) oil.

The main consequence of excessive use of nitrates and phosphates is that, when deposited in water, it produces an explosive growth of algae, which in turn dies and decays gradually depleting the water of oxygen (see *Guardian*, 6 January 1995). This kills the fish and seriously affects aquatic animal species. This process, known as eutrophication, is particularly common in the Great Lakes of the United States. Nitrates are a particular problem since the relatively recent shift towards intensive agriculture has resulted in chronic nitrate depletion, thus requiring a massive increase in artificial sources in the form of fertilizers. There are also some direct human health consequences from excessive amounts of nitrates in water. In particular, it is associated with a blood disease in very young children, the so-called 'blue baby' syndrome, and with stomach cancer (Harvey and Hallett, 1977, p.32; Pickering and Owen, 1994, p.145).

Dangerous organic chemicals can have a devastating impact on marine life with consequences for those higher up the food chain. PCB residues, for instance, have been found in polar bears (Pickering and Owen, 1994, p.147). Equally, some pesticides are extremely dangerous to living organisms. The first generation of pesticides was introduced after the Second World War as part of the effort to maximize food production. These were based on chlorinated hydrocarbons and included the now infamous DDT. This category of pesticides was comprehensively banned in the West from the 1970s but their use continues in developing countries. Now, pesticides tend to contain less dangerous compounds, but they still cause ecological damage and their continued use may owe more to the power of the agrochemical industry (world sales of pesticides are thought to be around $50 billion a year) than their intrinsic value. Insects can, of course, devastate crops and, in developing countries, the control of mosquitoes and locusts is vital for human health as well, malaria in those countries remaining a big killer. Nevertheless, there is a mass of evidence to suggest that the long-term use of pesticides results in resistant strains of insects and it may be that the future lies in 'integrated pest management systems'. This involves, among other things, the breeding of resistant plant varieties and the utilization of natural pest predators (Simpson, 1990, pp.71–4).

Heavy metal residues in water pose severe health problems for humans. Mercury, lead, arsenic, tin, cadmium, colbat, copper and manganese are all regularly used in industrial processes and all are linked to brain damage and, in the event of excessive exposure, death. A special mention should be made of aluminium, which is being increasingly linked with Alzheimer's disease. High levels of aluminium have been found in some drinking water supplies, but the most dramatic illustration occurred in 1989, in the Camelford area of Cornwall, when a lorry driver mistakenly dumped 20 tonnes of aluminium sulphate into a water tank which was then released to the mains supply. Local people subsequently reported illnesses ranging from diarrhoea to mouth and nose ulcers and some began to suffer from memory loss – a symptom of Alzheimer's disease (Pickering and Owen, 1994, pp.148–50). The subsequent government inquiry, however, found no scientific evidence to support the residents' claims.

Oil spills are one of the most visible signs of pollution, but the spectacular accidents widely reported in the media account for a relatively small amount of the total quantity of oil deposited in the sea, the rest coming from routine discharges from ships cleaning out their tanks, natural seepage, industrial effluents and the consequence of war, most notably the deliberate sabotaging of Kuwait's refineries by Iraq in the 1991 Gulf War. When the *Torrey Canyon* ran aground in 1967, it deposited 117,000 tonnes of oil off the coast of south-west England, but even though it was enough to kill between 40,000 and 100,000 sea birds, the spill rather pales into insignificance when one contrasts it with the total annual spillage of about 3.6 million tonnes (Simpson, 1990, pp.112–15).

It goes without saying that oil pollution can have a devastating impact on marine life. It kills fish by depriving them of oxygen and birds and other sea mammals die, either because of the indirect effects of a reduction in fish stocks or directly through poisoning or because of the effects of oil on their buoyancy and insulation. There can be fewer distressing and emotive sights than a dying bird seeking desperately but hopelessly to clean itself. As a symbol of human disregard for the natural environmental in the pursuit of material comfort, it cannot be bettered. In reality, some oil spills have little long-term damage on the ecosystem. Whether or not we should still regard the suffering and death of many thousands of animals and birds in such circumstances with equanimity is an ethical question to which we shall return in Chapter 2.

Global atmospheric change

As if the long-standing problems of pollution discussed above are not bad enough, in recent years evidence has emerged that human activities have damaged the environment in much more sinister ways. We refer here to ozone depletion and global warming. They are more sinister developments for a number of reasons. In the first place, both are invisible and affect life only indirectly. The scientific community disagrees over the extent and likely consequences of both phenomena. The problem here, of course, is that should we wait until a scientific consensus about causes, scope and consequences emerges (which is unlikely) it may be too late to take any effective action. Second, both ozone depletion and global warming are truly worldwide problems. Up to now, the developed world has caused the lion's share of the problems and fairness suggests that it ought therefore to bear the bulk of the costs of dealing with them. The biggest future threat, however, comes from the prospect of increasing industrial development in the Third World. As a consequence, only effective global action can hope to deal satisfactorily with them. Such global co-operation, as Chapter 6 will illustrate, is not easy to achieve. Finally, of course, the consequences of failure are profound because, if the scientists are right, we do not have the option of continuing with present practices.

The ozone layer first became an issue in 1977 when the British Antarctic Survey discovered a significant depletion in the stratosphere, but it took another decade for this finding to be confirmed independently (Pickering and Owen, 1994, pp.67–8). By the 1980s, the threat posed by ozone-depleting chemicals was generally accepted, as evidence of substantial thinning over the polar regions, and the existence of large quantities of ozone-depleting chemicals over major cities, was discovered. As a result, action was taken (see Chapter 6).

Ozone (O^3) is a naturally occurring and highly reactive gas made up of oxygen atoms. In the stratosphere, 20–30 kilometres above the Earth's surface, a band of ozone exists which operates to exclude ultra-violet radiation from the sun. This radiation is extremely damaging to living organisms and it is predicted that the consequences of a reduction in the ozone layer, allowing more radiation to reach the Earth, will be an increased incidence of skin cancer, an increased risk of crop failure and, some scientists have suggested, global warming (the following is based on the excellent account in Yearley, 1992, pp.12–16; see also, Gribben, 1988; Booth, 1994).

The phenomenon of ozone depletion is rare, in environmental terms, for its unicausal nature. Although compounds such as carbon dioxide and methyl bromide have been implicated, as have changes in sea surface temperatures, by far and away the main culprit is held to be chlorofluorocarbons (CFCs). CFCs are a product of the industrial age, developed early in the twentieth century for use in aerosols, as coolants in refrigerators and in air-conditioning systems, foam-filled furniture, fast-food packaging and as cleansing agents in the electronics industry. CFCs do not break down easily and reach the stratosphere largely intact. High-energy radiation does, however, cause CFCs to break up and the chlorine then released destroys the ozone.

The damage caused by CFCs has been addressed by governments and, although the agreements reached are far from perfect, it would not be premature to say that a potential crisis has been averted (see Chapter 6). It is equally fair comment to add, though, that it is a relatively easy problem to solve. Not only is it possible to identify a single major cause of ozone depletion, but, in addition, substitutes to CFCs are readily available and relatively inexpensive. Crucially, solutions to the problem do not involve significant cuts in industrial production. The same fortuitous set of circumstances does not apply to the phenomenon known as global warming.

Global warming was first observed in the nineteenth century. It refers literally to an increase in the temperature of the Earth and is widely thought to be a product of the changing balance of oxygen and carbon dioxide (CO_2) in the atmosphere – other so-called greenhouse gases making a smaller contribution to global warming are methane, nitrous oxide and tropospheric ozone. Like the glass in a greenhouse, CO_2 acts as an insulator and the more of it there is, the more difficult it is for the sun's warmth to escape.

The process of photosynthesis, whereby plants absorb CO_2 and release oxygen, helps to ensure that a balance is maintained. Human activities, however, have put increasing stresses on this natural mechanism. Population growth, thus increasing the demand for oxygen, has been one factor at work, but the major problem derives from the additional CO_2 in the atmosphere. This has been caused partly by deforestation, reducing the availability of natural 'sinks' for CO_2 – thereby making the preservation of the rainforests a crucial issue. Most important of all, however, is the additional CO_2

released through the burning of fossil fuels (Yearley, 1992, p.17). In the absence of human activity, the carbon in fossil fuels would remain unused, out of circulation under the Earth's surface, but fossil fuels, in the form of coal, oil and natural gas, are the mainstay of industrial society and their use has dramatically increased. Thus, it is estimated that the total annual emissions of CO_2 have increased from 1.5 million tonnes as recently as 1950 to almost 6 billion tonnes in the 1990s, and it is further predicted that CO_2 concentrations will double by the year 2050 unless action is taken (Simpson, 1990, p.58; Pickering and Owen, 1994, p.72).

It is argued that the effects of global warming are considerable although there is still a heated debate in the scientific community about the extent of increases in global temperatures, the predicted rise of sea levels and even the link between greenhouse gases and the global climate (Pickering and Owen, 1994, pp.88–91; see also Beckerman, 1992, for an optimistic view). Rising sea levels are regarded as a key consequence caused by an increase in the volume of sea water as the polar ice caps melt, and the expanding of warmer oceans. Since the early 1970s, ice and snow cover has decreased by about 8 per cent and recent evidence shows an increase in plant growth in the Antarctic. The result of rising sea levels will be flooding, initially of low-lying areas. In addition, increases in temperatures will affect vegetation and agriculture and, of course, there is a limit to the amount of heat which living organisms can cope with.

The lack of precise evidence about the causes and consequences of global warming, and the extent of the sacrifices that will have to be made in order to deal with it, have hindered attempts at containing the problem. Beckerman (1992, p.260) argues that the costs of dealing with global warming outweigh the benefits. 'Whatever one does with the estimates', he writes, 'they are unlikely to demonstrate that the present state of scientific knowledge justifies great trouble and expense to cut CO_2 emissions by very large amounts.' Nevertheless, if the finger is to be pointed at CO_2 emissions, the solutions are clear-cut. One is to use other sources of energy, including nuclear power (which, whatever else may be said about it, does not involve the use of fossil fuels) and 'Green' alternatives based on wind, water, waves, and so on. Another is to use existing sources of energy more efficiently through better insulation of homes and workplaces and restrictions on car use.

Finally, as indicated above, the conservation of forests, and particularly the tropical rainforests, is also crucial.

The preservation of the rainforests illustrates well the interdependence of environmental problems. Not only do they provide habitats for a huge variety of animal and plant species as well as protecting against soil erosion and the silting of rivers and lakes, they also perform a vital function as 'sinks' for carbon dioxide. Far from being conserved, however, the rainforests are being cut down at an alarming rate, with one estimate suggesting that half the world's tropical forests had been cleared in the 1980s alone (cited in Simpson, 1990, p.134).

The problem is not just that forests are felled for timber, but they are often cleared to create agricultural land, and the burning of the felled trees releases further CO_2 into the atmosphere, thus adding to the problem. Describing the situation and offering a simplistic technical solution is, as always, to overlook the social and political context. Here, the clearing of the rainforests takes us into often intractable issues concerning Third World development and the thorny questions concerning the West's responsibility for environmental degradation and the moral legitimacy of asking already poor nations to make further sacrifices for our benefit (issues discussed in more detail in Chapter 6).

Biodiversity

The number of plant, non-human animal and insect species with which we share the planet is startling. Indeed, such is the incredible variety of life on Earth and the difficulty of determining the numbers, we simply do not know how many species there are (May, 1989). Excluding plants and vegetation, estimates of the total number of living species vary from 5 to 30 million. Only about 1.5 million have so far been identified. It is probable, therefore, that some species have disappeared (perhaps recently) without us knowing they ever existed. What we do know is that in the last 2,000 years, human activity has exterminated about 3 per cent of the world's mammal species, one half of these losses occurring since 1900 (Regenstein, 1985).

There are many threats to animal species, some of them natural, but many of them deriving from human activity. Hunting, for instance, has seriously eroded the numbers of many species of whales and poaching has done the same for African elephants and rhinoceros. The greatest threat, though, is not caused by deliberate direct attacks on non-human species but by the destruction of the habitats on which they depend. For example, agricultural practices have led to the removal of hedgerows, the draining of wetlands and the pollution of water courses – all vital habitats to one species or another (see Chapter 8). Similarly, overfishing may cause birds and marine mammals to starve and, as was intimated earlier, the destruction of the rainforests causes immense damage to biodiversity since although the tropical forests cover only 6 per cent of the Earth's land surface, they contain at least 50 per cent of all the Earth's species. Tropical forest depletion is thus far and away the main cause of species extinction (Myers, 1989, p.27).

Clearly, then, species extinction does occur as a result of human activities. The question to ask is, does it matter? The first answer is to say that it matters because nature has inherent value, which we ought to respect. This, of course, is a moral question to which we shall return in Chapter 2. More pertinent for the present discussion is the anthropocentric response – that protecting animal and plant life matters because it is beneficial to us.

Here we are on safer ground because, in many instances, this is clearly the case, although balancing the interests of endangered species with those of indigenous human populations in the developing countries is not easy (see Chapter 8). There is, first, the aesthetic pleasure we receive from experiencing the majesty and beauty of non-human nature. More instrumentally, many plant and animal species are economically valuable to us, in terms of tourism and food, for instance. There is an economic disincentive to hunting whales to extinction since, with effective conservation measures, stocks can be made to last longer. Indeed, the International Whaling Commission (IWC) was set up with precisely this intention, although in recent years it has been used for different purposes by those with a principled opposition to whaling (see Chapter 8).

Genetic variety is also important from a medical, agricultural and industrial perspective. Many commonplace medicines derive from natural sources – aspirin, the contraceptive pill and cancer treating agents, to name but a few – and there is every reason to believe that future discoveries may greatly benefit humans and other animals. Biodiversity has made these contributions with scientific investigations into only 1 per cent of plant species and a far smaller proportion of animal species (Myers, 1989, pp.30–2). Maintaining the diversity of the gene pool is also crucial in guarding against diseases which could otherwise eradicate plant species vital as sources of food for humans and other animals. Finally, there is the more general point that the workings of nature are so little understood that by destroying species, we simply do not know the full consequences of our actions. This brings us back to the interdependence of the natural world – that damage to one part of the ecosystem can have unsuspected knock-on effects – a point that was graphically illustrated by Rachel Carson's (1962) classic work on the effects of pesticides.

Resource depletion

Continuing with the interdependency theme, the emphasis on economic growth, powered by the use of fossil fuels, not only leads to pollution and atmospheric changes, but also raises questions about resource depletion. As we have seen, one of the key features of the radical Green position is the assertion that there are limits to growth, and this position is held, at least in part, because growth is predicated on the use of non-renewable resources.

Statistics on the use and lifespan of non-renewable resources are all too revealing. For example, it is estimated that humans use the same amount of fossil fuels in one year that it took nature one million years to create and, taking inflation into account, energy expenditure is now twenty times greater than it was about 150 years ago (Pickering and Owen, 1994, p.183). These raw figures disguise the shift from a primary reliance on coal by the end of the nineteenth century, to a reliance on oil, which now constitutes over a third of the world's energy supply. Oil, of course, is not only a fuel but is also, among other things, the raw material for fertilizers, pesticides and the plastics industry (Harvey and Hallett, 1977, pp.39–41). Utilization of these non-renewable resources has taken a heavy toll. Estimates of available supplies differ, and a great deal depends on what is meant by 're-coverable' reserves and future estimates of population size and demand. Taking these factors into account, proven recoverable reserves of oil and gas are expected to last just over 50 years and coal over 200 years (Dasgupta, 1989, pp.121–2).

There is thus an obvious need to focus attention on the conservation of energy and the development of energy alternatives. One answer is nuclear power which at present constitutes only about 5 per cent of the world's energy supply. Environmentalists take a dim view of the nuclear option but it does, at least superficially, seem to answer most of the problems, as it provides energy without the problem of carbon dioxide emissions. Of course, this is not the whole story. There are significant difficulties involved in the disposal of nuclear waste, high capital costs are involved in setting up and running nuclear power stations and there is the ever-present danger of accidents which, as Chernobyl demonstrated, can easily turn into catastrophes (Porritt, 1984, pp.173–4; Pickering and Owen, 1994, pp.71–4).

There are many alternative sources of renewable energy – hydroelectric power, wind power, tidal energy, solar energy, geothermal energy and biomass forms of energy. Each has its negative aspects in terms of cost or effects on the environment and, whatever else might be said, it remains the case that a great deal more research is necessary to make any one of them viable. There are other barriers too, such as the great vested interests involved in the production, marketing and retailing of fossil fuels. In addition, the large subsidies given to the nuclear industry, largely for political reasons (see Chapter 8), has created a significantly uneven playing field which makes it extremely difficult for advocates of renewable energy sources to compete effectively.

In this chapter, the major environmental problems facing the global community have been outlined. They are formidable and have increased over the past two decades or so. By themselves these problems constitute a reason for the rise of social and political concern, but there is no automatic link between the identification of problems, the rise of concern about them and political action to meet this concern. This book explores the social and political processes operating around environmental issues. We start by examining the attempt to develop a set of political and moral principles which can provide an ideological battering ram for change.

Further reading

There are a number of texts written by scientists and social scientists which provide an overview of environmental problems.

A book-length study is Pickering and Owen (1994), Mannion (1991) traces environmental problems historically, a useful collection of articles is Friday and Laskey (1989) and a very concise account of major environmental issues, specifically written for social scientists, is provided by Yearley (1992, ch.1).

There is also much useful information in Harvey and Hallett (1977), Simpson (1990) and Porritt (1984). More detailed studies of particular environmental problems are McCormick (1989) on acid rain, Mason and Singer (1990) on factory farming, Gribben (1988) and Booth (1994) on ozone depletion, Body (1982) on agriculture, Ehrlich (1972) on population and Regenstein (1985) on endangered species.

2

SUSTAINABILITY AND ENVIRONMENTAL IDEOLOGY

The emergence of environmental problems, and the corresponding rise of an environmental protection movement, has been accompanied by the development of ideas which seek, on the one hand, to justify our preoccupation with environmental issues and, on the other, to lead us to the most appropriate solutions for the problems identified. As we indicated earlier, the major dichotomy in environmental thought can be crudely defined as being between radicals and reformists – between, that is, exponents of the dark Green or ecocentric position on the one hand, and exponents of the light green or technocentric position on the other. This chapter seeks to outline the major differences between these positions and consider the competing empirical and normative claims which arise.

The core ideas stated

There is now a substantial and growing body of environmental thought, and it should be remembered that developing basic typologies inevitably leads to over-simplification. Nevertheless, while bearing this limitation in mind, it is extremely useful – if not essential – to provide a typology of the key ideas involved in the

Table 2.1 Technocentric and ecocentric approaches to environmentalism

Technocentrism	Ecocentrism
1. Modified sustainable economic growth.	1. Limits to, and undesirability of, economic growth.
2. Large role for technological development as a provider of solutions for environmental problems.	2. A distrust of science and technological fixes.
3. Environmental solutions can co-exist with existing social and political structures.	3. Radical social and political change necessary. A preference for decentralized social and political organization.
4. Anthropocentrism and a commitment to intra-generational and inter-generational equity.	4. Intrinsic value of nature or, at least, a weaker version of anthropocentrism; a commitment to social justice within human society and between humans and non-human nature.

environmental debate. Table 2.1 sets out the essential differences between techocentrism and ecocentrism and provides us with a structure which the rest of this chapter will follow.

Environmentalism and the economy

Technocentrics and ecocentrics differ first over their approach to the economy. The latter see economic growth as incompatible with environmental objectives. Their challenge to the ethos of economic growth and material consumption consists, in part, of an empirical claim; that there are natural limits to growth and that unless production and consumption levels and population size are reduced to sustainable levels, economic collapse will result. It is better then to manage this reduction, be prepared and act on it, or risk being overwhelmed by a crisis which will have unpredictable consequences. Thus, Edward Goldsmith's *Blueprint for Survival* (a text, originally published as an edition of the *Ecologist Magazine* which is often regarded as the definitive statement of Green ideas, at least in Britain) commented that continued economic growth will end 'either against our will, in a succession of famines, epidemics, social crises and wars; or because we want it to . . . in a series of thoughtful, humane and measured changes' (1972, p.15).

This empirical claim got its impetus from what is now a classic study, published in book form as the *Limits to Growth* in 1972 (Meadows *et al.*, 1972). The research for the book was undertaken by academics at the Massachussetts Institute of Technology who were commissioned by a group of industrialists and civil servants, led by an Italian management consultant, Aurelio Peccei, operating in a group called the Club of Rome. The researchers at MIT used computer modelling techniques to examine the interdependencies between a number of environmental variables – industrialization, resource depletion, pollution, food production and population – computing the likely result of changes in individual variables (the results of the research are outlined in Martell, 1994, pp.24–40; and Dobson, 1990, ch.3).

The conclusions of this study – setting the agenda for the survivalist stream of thought evident in the 1970s – were quickly grasped by environmentalists as evidence of the catastrophic fate that awaited us unless changes to existing levels of production and consumption were made. Seven different computer runs were suggested, the first assuming continued growth in all the variables at present trends and the others assuming solutions to one or more of the problems. The 'standard run' resulted in industrial collapse early in the twenty-first century due to resource depletion, but even when, in the second run, a doubling of resource availability was assumed as a result of technological developments, increased industrial output produced unsustainable pollution levels and eventual resource depletion. Even when solutions to both pollution and resource depletion were fed into the model, collapse was still predicted due to food shortages caused by an increasing population and the appropriation of arable land by industry. Solutions to this problem, the report suggested, are equally futile since they have knock-on effects. Thus, diverting capital to agriculture causes a drop in industrial output and even if a solution to food shortages could be found which did not have this effect, the result would be unsustainable population growth, pollution and resource depletion.

Seen from the perspective of the 1990s, the limits to growth thesis seems unduly pessimistic and, as we shall see, the ecocentric case is not based solely on the empirical claim that radical social, economic and political change will inevitably occur whether by design or as a consequence of the collapse of industrial society (the report was updated in Meadows *et al.*, 1992).

The MIT team's work has been criticized on a number of grounds (for a review see Martell, 1994, pp.33–40). In the first place, it is claimed that the computer model was too simplistic, omitting variables which might have produced very different results, and seriously underestimating the capacity of humans to develop technological solutions to environmental problems. The impression created was therefore too deterministic and pessimistic. Further, it has been claimed that the conclusions of the research reflected the class interests and ideological bias of the authors, since the conclusions were based on assumptions influenced by an ideological predisposition towards post-material values, which were in turn the product of the comfortable middle-class lives of the authors. A related criticism was the total absence of any recognition that economic growth in developing countries may be more desirable than in the West, thus giving the impression that the poorest peoples in the world should be asked to pay for the excesses of the rich developed world.

One of the central assumptions of the limits to growth approach is that there is an automatic trade-off between environmental protection and economic growth, so that an emphasis on one necessitates neglecting the other. Indeed, many environmentalists go out of their way to emphasize the economic sacrifices that their programme would require. Crucially, a central plank of the reformist or techno-centric position is a denial of this assumption. Indeed, reformists argue that the key challenge for environmentalists is to demonstrate that sustainable growth is possible; that an emphasis on environmental protection is not incompatible with economic growth and may even enhance it. Albert Weale (1992, pp.66–92) describes the challenge to the trade-off theory as 'ecological modernization', a position which, he argues, was accepted in the 1980s by decision-makers in some European countries, notably Germany. By accepting that the trade-off theory was, at best, exaggerated, governments were able to take action on environmental problems without fearing an economic backlash. Since it was accepted that the economic consequences would not be severe, governments were also able to be proactive and take action even when the causes and consequences of environmental problems were not entirely clear.

The ecological modernization position revolves around a number of distinct, but related, arguments. In the first place, it is argued that economic growth is not synonymous with the increased use of non-renewable resources. What is important, therefore, is not reducing economic growth, measured in terms of GNP, but in making sure that growth is sustainable. For David Pearce (1993, p.4) this means: 'making sure that substitute resources are made available as non-renewable resources become physically scarce and . . . ensuring that the environmental impacts of using those resources are kept within the Earth's carrying capacity to assimilate those impacts.'

This sustainability is to be achieved in part at least through technological developments. Thus, to give one example, although Britain's GNP has risen by over 30 per cent in the last two decades, the amount of energy used has stayed about the same (Pearce, 1993, pp.22–3). Not only does environmental protection fail to hinder economic growth, according to the technocentric view, but it can also be a source for future growth. This, it is argued, will be achieved through the production of low polluting goods – 'clean' cars, CFC-free aerosols, and so on – which consumers are increasingly demanding. In addition, pollution control technology itself has the potential to become an important source of economic wealth. As a consequence of greater environmental awareness among consumers and investors, companies are being forced to behave in more environmentally responsible ways.

A further claim of the ecological modernization position is that the trade-off theory overlooks the fact that, although failure to act on environmental problems now may save costs for present generations, these costs do not disappear but are transferred to future generations. In 1990 alone, the cost of pollution abatement in Britain has been estimated at £7.3 billion, over 1 per cent of GNP (Pearce, 1993, p.38). Similarly, it is argued, the trade-off theory too often assumes that whatever reduces the profits of manufacturing concerns (as tighter environmental measures would do at least initially) will result in an overall reduction in a nation's economic prosperity. This, though, is not necessarily the case since it does not take into account the problem of 'externalities', a phrase that recurs regularly in the environmental literature (Goodin, 1992a, pp.100–4). Thus, in the absence of any environmental regulations, factory owners can take the decision to discharge the waste their factories produce into the air and water, thereby reducing costs. For an individual businessman or woman, this may well be a rational decision. Air and water are public goods, external to the profit and loss account. However, the clean-up costs have not disappeared; they are simply transferred to someone else.

Now, it may well be that those who are affected by this pollution are prepared to put up with it in return for the economic benefits the factory provides. It may be, alternatively, that the community decides that they should clean up the pollution and/or insist on the implementation of more stringent environmental regulations so that the externalities are 'internalized' as a cost borne by the factory owner. One of the regular complaints made by environmentalists is that the GNP measure of national prosperity is too narrow and should be replaced by a broader indicator of national well-being, which includes the quality of the environment (Sagoff, 1988; see also *Guardian*, 14 December 1994). In the context of ecological modernization, though, the key point is that even if we limit our indicator of national prosperity to straightforward economic factors, allowing factories to pollute indiscriminately will still produce costs since the factories' pollution will damage the economic position of others too. It may, for instance, damage the tourist or the fishing industry and it may compromise the health of the people affected, thus diminishing the quality of the workforce and thereby reducing the competitiveness of the economy overall. The costs of acid rain to the economy in terms of the market price of the timber destroyed and the health costs amount to between £1.3 and £3.3 billion a year. Likewise, the estimated costs of unsustainable transport policies in terms of road congestion, road damage and health costs amounted to between £22.9 and £25.7 billion in 1991 alone (Pearce, 1993, pp.59, 152–8).

The ecological modernization position seems to offer a viable theoretical framework which can be utilized both as a device to persuade governments to act and as a means of judging how sustainable their response is. Advocates of the limits to growth position may still say, of course, that environmentally responsible growth is no substitute for low or zero growth. At the very least, we can say in response that in the real world such a scenario, particularly in the developing world, is flying in the face of reality. Whether sustainable growth is possible in the long term is an open question. It is clear, though, that we have more time to deal with the problem than some of the more alarmist accounts in the 1970s led us to believe.

It is important to recognize that the ecocentric case is not based solely on the empirical claims concerning the possibility of sustainable growth. It also opposes the technocratic position by challenging, in a number of ways, the desirability of economic growth, whether this growth is sustainable or not. The first argument here is that ending the perpetual search for economic growth and material prosperity is an intrinsic good because it leads to richer and more fulfilling lives. Schumacher (1973, p.26) expressed this view well when he wrote that 'prosperity . . . is attainable only by cultivating such drives of human nature as greed and envy, which destroys intelligence, happiness, serenity and thereby the peacefulness of man'.

What should we make of this claim? At first glance, to accept a less materially comfortable lifestyle – fewer labour-saving devices, fewer, if any, cars, less travel, and so on – does not seem particularly inviting. Greens would reply, though, that, divested of a desire for material acquisitions, people will find fulfilment in presently neglected aspects of life – in intellectual pursuits, in finding themselves spiritually, in enjoying work for its own sake and not for the monetary rewards, and in developing non-dependent and therefore more satisfying relationships with others.

As Martell (1994, pp.48–50) points out, however, there are problems with this. In the first place, who is to say that the pursuit of material possessions is not intrinsically satisfying for at least some people? Indeed, most of us could attest to the pleasures that material acquisitions have given us at some point in our lives, and, no doubt too, many of those without a materially comfortable standard of living would attest equally to their feelings of disadvantage. Moreover, there is a strong case for saying that a certain level of material comfort is a prerequisite for the development of an individual's spiritual and intellectual life, since many material acquisitions free people from the everyday tasks of physical survival. Thus, surveys show that one of the key reasons the environment has emerged as an important political concern is growing post-war affluence, which has enabled people to direct their attention to quality of life issues (see Chapter 4).

A number of other arguments employed by ecocentrics against economic growth can be briefly stated. First, there is the view that economic growth, by continually providing more for everyone, obviates the need for radical redistributive policies. It serves, therefore, as a legitimizing mechanism for inequality. A related objection to economic growth is Fred Hirsch's (1977) analysis of the 'positional economy'. The argument here is that economic growth increases demand for positional goods – uncongested roads, well-paid jobs, exotic holidays, and so on – whose supply cannot be increased to meet rising demand. Economic growth, therefore, fails to bring satisfaction since there are social limits to its enjoyment. The obvious method of dealing with this problem is to increase the price of positional goods, thereby reducing the benefits for many that might, superficially, have accrued from economic growth.

Another objection to economic growth involves its relationship to liberal democratic principles. It is commonly believed that governments since the Second World War have pursued a growth strategy as a direct response to the rising materialistic demands of the electorate. An alternative view is that political elites pursue such a strategy and encourage citizens to want material gains, in order to increase their own political power. Thus, economic growth, according to this analysis, is not only environmentally destructive but is also inimical to the democratic health of a society. If this is correct, liberal democratic principles, involving the tolerance of dissent and the preservation of property rights against the state, are well fitted to restrain economic growth (Lauber, 1978). Linked to this is the argument that the more individuals become passive consumers the less they will be active citizens. Indeed, the dominant empirical and, for some, normative model of democracy in the post-war period has been the so-called 'economic' variety whereby elections become simply a means by which political elites, behaving like producers in a market economy, compete with each other to offer benefits to a largely passive, consumerist electorate (Lively, 1975, pp.88–108).

Science and technology

It has been seen that the technocratic position places great faith in the ability of science and technology to aid the development of a sustainable society. Ecocentrics, on the other hand, are sceptical of science and technology's ability to perform this function. A more appropriate word here might be ambivalence. Ecocentrics do recognize, on the one hand, that science has played an important role in the identification of environmental problems, which has, in turn, put pressure on governments to act. The development of the science of ecology, too, by emphasizing the interdependence of nature, has done much to promote the idea that the human species is just as likely to suffer from environmental damage as any other. Ecology itself was greatly influenced by the work of Charles Darwin. Central to Darwin's work, of course, was the idea of the common origin of species which has revolutionary implications since it undermines the ideology which puts man on a pedestal, as separate from nature and therefore entitled to dominate it (Pepper, 1986, pp.100–3; see also Rachels, 1990).

Ecocentrics also recognize that faith in science and technology can lead to a reliance on technical fixes. This encourages the idea that we can continue to deplete non-renewable resources and to pollute because, in the end, science will come up with solutions. For ecocentrics, this is far too complacent, and only a fundamental shift in values, and more appropriate social and political institutions, will provide genuine answers to the environmental crisis. A reliance on technical fixes, then, is to leave the resolution of environmental problems to 'experts', which, in turn, has the effect of depoliticizing environmental issues thereby preventing the emergence of normative dimensions.

In addition, ecocentrics stress the point that the ideology of science has itself contributed to environmental problems. As David Pepper (1986, pp.37–52) thoroughly documents, beginning in the sixteenth century the scientific revolution replaced the medieval belief in God as the creator of the world with scientific rationalism. There was a strong emphasis within Christian belief on man's stewardship role. Thus, if God was the creator of nature, humans should respect it as a divine creation and not seek to exploit it. The central feature of the scientific revolution, on the other hand, was the separation of man from nature and the belief that humans could understand and control it. From this, it is a short step to the position, rejected by ecocentrics, that the world was made for human use; that it only has meaning and value in relation to our needs.

Decentralization

Technocentrics have little to say about the relationship between the environment and political organization. A significant feature of much ecocentric writing as well as the programmes of Green parties, on the other hand, is the claim that radical social and political reorganization is necessary. The nature of their arguments will be considered in more detail in Chapter 3. It should be noted here, though, that ecocentrics place considerable emphasis on decentralization, local self-government and egalitarianism as the key operating principles of the sustainable society (see Goldsmith, 1972; Schumacher, 1973; Sale, 1980; Goodin, 1992a, pp.147–56). Perhaps the best-known version is Kirkpatrick Sale's advocacy of bioregions, whereby self-sufficient and autonomous communities are 'determined by natural rather than human dictates, distinguishable from other areas by attributes of flora, fauna, water, climate, soils and land forms' (Sale, 1984, p.168).

The idea of a small-scale participatory democracy has had a long shelf-life in Western political thought. It is associated, above all, with the work of such luminaries as Thomas More, Jean-Jacques Rousseau, G.D.H. Cole as well as anarchist thinkers such as Godwin and Kroptkin (Pateman, 1970; Eckersley, 1992, p.160). In addition, there is a considerable literature on the general desirability and viability of this form of social and political organization (see Bachrach, 1969). Our remit, in an assessment of the Green advocacy of participatory democracy, though, is much more limited. That is, the question we need to ask is, what contribution can the existence of a decentralized, egalitarian and participatory democracy make to the realization of Green objectives?

The answer Greens give would seem to be two-fold. First, there are the direct environmental benefits. Thus, small, autonomous communities will require self-sufficiency, therefore ending the environmental damage caused by the national and international market in goods and large-scale industrial production. In addition, such communities (particularly in the case of Sale's bioregions) will foster a greater appreciation of nature's value, beauty and power. Second, there is the argument that a decentralized, participatory and egalitarian society is one that recognizes each person's value as an important and respected member of the community. Each person is entitled to participate equally in the making of laws, is not divided from others through unequally distributed material possessions and feels part of a cohesive community – all characteristics lacking in large and impersonal societies (Martell, 1994, pp.51–3). As Goldsmith (1972, p.51) argues: 'It is probable that only in the small community can a man or woman be an individual. In today's large agglomerations, he is merely an isolate.' In a similar vein, Porritt (1984, p.87) states that large-scale industrial societies take 'away our dignity, makes us passive recipients rather than active participants, makes us dependent rather than self-reliant, alienates us from the work we do and the people we live with'.

I do not intend to spend much time on the second of these arguments. Like the normative claims concerning the limits to growth we considered earlier, it is based on the assumption that the preferred social and political organization is capable of producing more satisfied and fulfilled individuals, thereby making the sacrifice of material consumption worthwhile. It is clear that the radical Green position embodies more than merely a recognition of the physical limits to growth necessary for human survival. It also involves an ethic concerned with the 'mutual unfolding of both the human and non-human worlds' and, as such, insists on the intrinsic value of nature (Eckersley, 1992, pp.128–9). Now while this rules out certain political regimes, such as those based on force and oppression, which do not treat humans as part of nature with the respect that beings with inherent value deserve, it is by no means clear that the decentralized and participatory form advocated is the only, or even the most appropriate, one to meet the inherent value criteria (see Saward, 1993a, who takes this view).

We are left, then, with the first of the above arguments which is the claim that the kind of political and institutional structure preferred by many ecocentrics is the most appropriate means of solving environmental problems. Clearly, there are difficulties with this too although, given that sovereign states have had some success in drawing up and enforcing international environmental agreements (as Chapter 6 reveals), we should not exaggerate the problems. Two of the best-known academic accounts of Green political thought, written by authors generally supportive of the radical Green position, doubt whether the small-scale autonomous community is the best model, as does Martell, in his sympathetic commentary on the Green case (Eckersley, 1992, pp.176–8; Goodin,

1992a, pp.146–68; Martell, 1994, pp.54–61; see also Ryle, 1988, p.66).

Robert Goodin, in particular, is determined to distance himself from the decentralization model. He attempts to achieve this by distinguishing between what he calls a 'green theory of value', which seeks to tell us why environmental protection is a desirable objective, and a 'green theory of agency', which is concerned with 'the nature of the mechanisms by which its recommendations (*put simply protecting the environment*) are to be given practical meaning' (Goodin, 1992a, p.113, emphasis in original). The latter, he argues, is not a central part of the Green case and any particular theory of agency should be accepted or rejected according to the extent to which it helps to promote Green objectives enshrined in the theory of value.

Now, Goodin's primary target here are the various lifestyle changes and consciousness-raising approaches which Greens are wont to espouse. By distinguishing between value and agency, he is able to recommend turning 'a blind eye' to some of the 'crazier views' or 'green heresies' since these are part of a theory of agency and not value (*ibid.*, pp.16–17). Strategically, of course, Goodin may be correct here, but for our purposes it is important to note that he also rejects the decentralization model on the same grounds, that it does not provide a means of achieving the objectives enshrined in the green theory of value (*ibid.*, pp.147–66).

The central problem which Goodin and other critics point to is the inability of autonomous communities to cope with the co-ordination that would be required to deal with environmental problems which, as we have seen, are transnational or even global in scope. Ecocentrics might answer this charge in two ways. In the first place, they might argue that the decentralized communities advocated would be much more environmentally aware and would appreciate the need to act collectively to solve environmental problems. 'Think globally, act locally' is a phrase commonly used by environmentalists to emphasize their dual conern.

It is not clear, however, why decentralized communities would be more environmentally aware. It may be the case that people in large urban areas are more environmentally enlightened. After all, it should be noted that some of the worst environmental damage has been caused by farmers in small rural communities. Even if it were to prove generally true, there would still be no mechanism whereby the occasional despoiler could be brought into line with other communities. This could prove fatal since those communities making an effort to protect the environment may well conclude that it is not worth their while continuing to pay the cost while other 'free riders' are enjoying the benefits without contributing. Finally, as Martell (1994, p.160) emphasizes, co-ordination is not just about the exercise of authority. Even if all the communities were willing to behave responsibly, there would still be a need for a body to co-ordinate their activities, identifying problems and initiating a response.

The second answer to the criticism is to point out that radical Greens are not opposed to co-ordination, the need for which appears in much of the Green literature (Goodin, 1992a, pp.151–2; Martell, 1994, p.56). The problem is they are not particularly coherent. At most, they are prepared to accept that larger co-ordinating bodies should be informal networks rather than permanent unified structures, and certainly nothing like a nation-state. The question remains, however, whether this would be sufficient. So, whichever way we look at it, there appears to be a strong case for an institutionalized enforcement and co-ordination body not dissimilar to the nation-state or even a larger entity, equivalent to, say, the European Union.

Nature and value

The final and most distinct principle of the radical Greens relates to a particular view of the relationship between people and nature. Put simply, radical Greens insist on an ecocentric, as opposed to the anthropocentric, perspective typical of technocentrics. The inspiration for this position is widely accredited to the American writer Aldo Leopold and later to the philosopher Arne Naess (Leopold, 1949; Naess, 1973). The distinction between an ecocentric and an anthropocentric approach is fairly easy to grasp. The latter position is human-centred. That is, it argues that only the human species has intrinsic value while the rest of nature (including non-human animals, living but not as far as we know sentient parts of nature such as plants and trees, and inanimate objects such as rocks, stones and mountains) only has extrinsic value. Thus, non-human nature, according to the anthropocentric position, has value but only to the extent that it is valuable to us (Passmore, 1980). By contrast, the ecocentric position holds that the whole of nature has intrinsic value and its value is not reducible to its use for humans. It is this position which represents a genuine environmental ethic. Crucially, it applies not only to the relationship between humans and the rest of the natural world but also impacts on how people should behave towards each other. This is drawn out nicely by Eckersley (1992, p.56), who points out that 'a perspective that seeks emancipation writ large is one that *necessarily* supports social justice in the human community'.

This distinction between the ecocentric and anthropocentric perspectives may seem somewhat esoteric, suitable only for the philosophy class, but it is actually of great practical relevance to the protection of nature. Thus, to take one example, if we were to ask why we should protect whales, these different approaches would produce very different answers. Thus, we might want to protect whales for a variety of anthropocentric reasons – because they have great aesthetic value to us, or because they have an economic value in terms of food or tourism – or we might want to protect them because we recognize they have value which is intrinsic and not dependent on any value they have to humans. Such considerations have led to regular arguments within the International Whaling Commission, which originally was set up by the whaling nations to conserve whale stocks for continued hunting but has been dominated in recent years by Western nations and environmental pressure groups with other motives. As a result, a moratorium on whaling has been introduced and still exists despite the growing scientific evidence that stocks of some species are now high enough for a resumption of hunting (see Chapter 8).

Attempts have been made to identify a continuum in environmental thought from pure anthropocentrism to pure ecocentrism. Eckersley (1992, pp.33–47), for instance, in a five-fold categorization, refers to three varieties of the anthropocentrism approach – resource conservation, human welfare ecology and preservationism – which differ in the weight they place on the exploitation of nature. Ultimately, though, they are all anthropocentric approaches, differing only in their different conceptions of which human values are more important. Thus, the first emphasizes conserving natural resources to enable their continued exploitation, the second focuses on the human benefits deriving from a clean and unpolluted environment, and the third stresses the aesthetic value of preserving wildernesses from development.

Only the last two positions take us beyond anthropocentrism. The fourth is described as animal liberation, which accords inherent value to non-human animals (discussed further below), and the fifth is ecocentrism. Only this final position provides the kind of protection for nature required by radical Greens, since its inherent value gives it a *prima facie* expectation of respectful treatment, thus ruling out unsustainable exploitation even if humans stand to gain by it.

Assessing the validity of the ecocentric position is an enormously complex task taking us deep into the realms of ecophilosophy and we can only touch on the major themes of the debate here. We need initially to distinguish between three inter-related but distinct themes. First, there is the question of our obligations to future generations, a crucial dimension in the case of environmental protection. Second, there is the question of our obligations to non-human animals. And third, there is the question of our obligations to nature as a whole. It will be apparent that each of these questions, if answered affirmatively, would progressively encompass a wider array of items to which we are required to accord moral standing. The second of the questions, concerning non-human animals, will be considered later in order to reflect both the extensive literature that now exists and the way in which it has arisen separately from studies in environmental ethics.

The vast majority of us would agree that humans have intrinsic value and the moral standing that accompanies it. We know from our own experience that we can be harmed directly in a way that matters to us. That is not to say that all humans in all circumstances should be treated in the same way, but it does mean that our interests should be taken into account when our actions are evaluated. More problematic is the question of our obligations to future generations, those who are not yet born.

Most of us would probably answer that we do owe an obligation to future generations but some awkward questions remain (this issue is discussed in Attfield, 1983; Martell, 1994, pp.80–5). In particular, although it is clear that what we do to the environment now will affect future generations, does that mean we should take their interests into account, even if by so doing the interests of some humans living now are harmed? This is a difficult question, and one that is particularly applicable to the environmental demands the West is now pressing on the developing world. The concept of sustainable development, vague though the term is as an operational principle, would seem to provide an answer here, reconciling the needs for present development with a recognition that this development should not deprive future generations of the opportunity to have a similar quality of life to which we aspire (Hurrell and Kingsbury, 1992b, pp.42–3).

The question of future generations is, of course, still an anthropocentric one. The real difficulty arises when we seek to justify the ecocentric position. The crucial problem should be apparent. How can we accord moral standing to non-sentient nature when it is obvious that rocks, trees and mountains cannot be harmed in the same way as sentient animals? Raymond Frey (1983, pp.154–5) puts the problem succinctly by contrasting the terms 'being harmed' and 'being wronged'. We can quite sensibly talk about non-sentient nature being harmed just as I can talk about harming my television set by kicking it! But it does not seem sensible to talk about wronging non-sentient nature. Thus, polluting a river is to harm it, but since the river only has extrinsic value for those sentient beings that benefit from it, it is only they who can be wronged by polluting the river. In this interpretation, then, sentience would appear to be the benchmark for moral standing. At the risk of labouring the point, Peter Singer (1983, p.123) expresses the same doubts when he states: 'There is a genuine difficulty in understanding how chopping down a tree can matter *to the tree* if the tree can feel nothing' (see also Wissenburg, 1993).

Before we move on to examine some attempts to rescue ecocentrism, it is worth mentioning another difficulty. Even if we have justified moral standing for non-sentient nature, to what, then, are we according this moral standing? Is it to individuals, to species, to ecosystems or to the concept of diversity itself? (Attaching moral standing to ecosystems is held by Johnson, 1991. The issue is discussed further in Martell, 1994; and Dobson, 1990.) Without an answer it is difficult to see how the principle could be made to work. The classic statement of the ecocentric position on this was stated by Aldo Leopold who, in a well-known passage, wrote: 'A thing is right when it tends to preserve the integrity, stability and beauty of the biotic community. It is wrong when it tends otherwise' (Leopold, 1949, p.217). The problem here is that, if value is to be given to collectivities, as is usually suggested, we are committing ourselves to a position which may require us to sacrifice the interests of individuals (including human individuals) in order to maintain the 'stability' of the whole. This holism has been roundly condemned by those with an individualistic bent, and not least by the animal rights philosopher Tom Regan, who describes it as 'environmental fascism' (Regan, 1988, p.362).

There have been some ingenious attempts to provide a solution to the sentience criteria problem of assigning moral standing to the whole of nature. Robin Attfield (1983), among others, has suggested an approach based on appeals to intuition. Here, it is argued that if we engage in thought experiments, it becomes apparent that we intuitively recognize the inherent value of non-sentient nature. Thus, imagine a nuclear war which eliminated everyone except one dying man and a healthy tree. Would it be right for the dying man to chop down the tree? A negative answer would reveal some acceptance of a value for the tree independent of its use for humans (see also Stone, 1974). The problem here, of course, is that appeals to intuition are easily defeated by appeals to competing intuition and are a poor substitute for substantive moral arguments.

Another approach is the development of an ecological consciousness which requires a change from a position based on a 'code of conduct' to one based on a 'state of being' (Dobson, 1990, pp.57–63). Thus, it is argued that we should seek to be at one with nature by experiencing its power and beauty since only then will we respect its value. While it is probably true that a greater appreciation of nature would emerge from such experiences, it does not provide a convincing rational justification for its protection, merely one claim to be balanced against another.

As we have seen, Robert Goodin does seek to identify a Green theory of value, to which theories of agency should conform. Put briefly, Goodin seeks to argue that the value of nature consists in its very naturalness and that we derive satisfaction from knowing that there are forces of nature operating independently of us and which have a history of their own (Goodin, 1992a, pp.26–41). The obvious response is to say that it remains anthropocentric because the value of nature still derives from the satisfaction *we* get from it and not from something internal to it. Goodin recognizes this but claims, as Eckersley does, that there can be a gradation of views from anthropocentrism to ecocentrism and that his position is towards the ecocentric end. His Green theory of value, therefore, entails the proposition that nature must have value 'in relation to us', but that this is different from saying that nature only has value 'for us'. This is similar to Andrew Dobson's weak and strong versions of anthropocentrism (1990, pp.63–72) and Vincent's distinction between a 'light anthropocentrism' and a 'hard-nosed exploitative anthropocentrism' (Vincent, 1993, pp.254–5). The weak or light version is 'human-centred' because only humans can place value on things, but this is different, Dobson argues, from the illegitimate strong, exploitative or 'human instrumental' version, which involves seeing the non-human world purely as a means to human ends.

Ingenious though Goodin's account is, there are still problems. It might be argued, for instance, that a being either has inherent value or it does not. Thus, because his argument remains essentially anthropocentric – still involving a value being put on nature by humans – it is open to competing human claims which, it might be argued, are equally valid. As Michael Saward points out, 'although Tasmanian mountains may be inspiring and uplifting, the New York skyline may be no less so' (Saward, 1993b, pp.510). So, if Goodin tells me I should not cut down trees because he derives satisfaction from knowing that they are there, I may respond simply by saying that I disagree! That is to say, without an argument to the effect that I should not cut down trees because to do so is to wrong them, then his Green theory of value would appear to have no particular advantage over mine, particularly if I can point to the advantages that will accrue to humans as a result of cutting the trees down.

As we have seen, it is extremely difficult to find arguments which can support a genuine environmental ethic. Given this, environmental protection would seem to be dependent on the strength of human prudential grounds. There are, of course, compelling reasons to suggest that these grounds *are* strong and varied enough for us to afford to jettison, or at least not be too preoccupied with, the need to show that nature does have moral standing (Kriger, 1973; see also this volume, ch.1). Indeed, in practice, radical Greens more often than not do, as a matter of strategy, appeal to enlightened self-interest – a point noted by Barry (1994). As Porritt (1984, p.117) observes: 'I do not believe that the majority of people will change until they believe it is in their own interests to do so.'

Animals and morality

A sub-set of environmental thought is the relationship between human and non-human animals. Here, much attention has been paid in recent years to the development of a radical position which grants to non-human animals a higher moral status than the one afforded by the traditional animal welfare view (see below). The radical position is popularly described as animal rights although, for reasons that will be explained, this label is somewhat misleading.

The origins of concern for animals, on the one hand, and the environment, on the other, derive from very different roots. Indeed, it is very noticeable how far apart the animal protection movement and the environmental movement still remain organizationally and ideologically. The current animal protection movement derives from the humane societies of the nineteenth century which were closely interlinked with other Victorian social reform movements concerned with slavery, child labour, women's emancipation and so on (Garner, 1993a, ch.2). The environmental movement, on the other hand, emerged to conserve the countryside as an amenity (see Chapter 4).

Humans, animals and nature

In increasing order of radicalism, it is possible to identify four main positions when discussing the relationship between humans, non-human animals and nature (adapted from Garner, 1993a, ch.1):

1. A pure anthropocentric position (associated, above all, with the French philosopher, René Descartes) which sees non-human animals as little more than machines. As such, humans owe no moral obligation to animals.
2. The moral orthodoxy position which regards humans as morally superior to animals but recognizes that, as sentient beings, we owe some moral obligations to them in terms of not inflicting unnecessary suffering. This is the standard way in which animals are treated in many European countries and North America.
3. A radical challenge to the moral orthodoxy position. Here, it is possible to distinguish between accounts based on the granting of rights to animals (most notably, associated with

Regan, 1988) and accounts based on utilitarianism, often distinguished by the term animal liberation (Singer, 1990). Although there are significant differences between these two positions (see Garner, 1993a, ch.1), both regard animals as much more important morally than the conventional view allows.
4. An ecocentric position which, as we have seen, seeks to incorporate the whole of nature into the moral community.

Points of agreement and conflict

There is one comparison that can be made between the radical animal rights/liberation view and the ecocentric view. This is that they both seek to argue that the moral universe must incorporate all sentient life, thus removing humans from the moral pedestal. The points of conflict, though, are equally significant. In the first place, ecocentrism wants to incorporate the whole of nature within the moral community, a position which, as we have seen, is very difficult to sustain.

Second, as we saw earlier, there is a tendency in Green thinking to emphasize the moral value of whole ecosystems or species rather than the individuals within them. This is anathema from an animal rights perspective. Thus, imagine a choice between saving the last few remaining members of an endangered species and, say, 20,000 from a common species. For the animal rightist, the survival of the 20,000 must come first since more individuals will be saved. The fact that the other animals are members of an endangered species is irrelevant (Regan, 1988, pp.359–61). Radical Greens and environmentalists in the reformist camp, on the other hand, are inclined to say that the endangered species must come first since it is the survival of species that matters and not individual animals.

The focus on collectivities causes problems for ecocentrics when they seek to distinguish morally between the various parts of the biotic community. A position which might be called biotic egalitarianism is clearly inadequate. To cope with this, the moral relevance of sentiency has been utilized. Thus, Warwick Fox states that:

> the central intuition of deep ecology does not entail the view that intrinsic value is spread evenly across the membership of the biotic community. Moreover, in situations of genuine value-conflict,

justice is better served by not subscribing to the view of ecological
egalitarianism. Cows do scream louder than carrots. (Fox, 1984,
p.199)

The concern with sentience allows radical Greens to object to
factory farming because of the animal suffering involved. In general, though, the differences identified between environmentalists
of radical and reformist hues on the one hand, and animal rights
advocates on the other, does have profound practical ramifica-
tions, and not just in the area of wildlife conservation (on which
see Chapter 8). Environmentalists in general have had very little to
say about the treatment of farm or laboratory animals and being a
radical Green does not necessitate being a vegetarian – let alone a
vegan – which is obligatory from an animal rights perspective (see
Garner, 1994). This explains why there is not a great deal of contact between environmental groups and animal protection groups
which, from a strategic perspective at least, is unfortunate (see
Ryder, 1992, for an attempt to bring the two sides together).

We have considered in this chapter the major differences between
the technocentric and ecocentric positions. Clearly, the latter represents the radical end of the environmental movement and as
such has had relatively little impact on the way in which the environmental debate has been couched in the mainstream political
arena. Of course, the dichotomy is not as black and white as this
chapter, by necessity, has had to paint it. Indeed, one can perceive
the two positions as either ends of a continuum or, to be more
accurate, a number of different continua each representing one of
the particular differences identified above. As we saw, not all ecocentrics accept the decentralization arguments or the view that
nature has intrinsic value. Seen in this way, the two approaches can
learn from each other. Thus, the ecological modernization position
offers environmentalists far greater opportunity to influence
decision-makers than the bleak prognosis of the limits to growth
school and, more to the point, the former analysis arguably represents a more accurate reflection of reality. Similarly, technocentrics
can take on board the radical's insistence that political structures
and the values they embody are important. Certainly, a study of
the politics of the environment cannot ignore the ecocentric claim
that ecologism represents a distinct political ideology. This claim is
further examined in the next chapter.

Further reading

There are now a number of introductory accounts of Green ideas. Dobson (1990) has become the standard text, but Eckersley (1992) is also very thorough; Martell (1994) provides an invaluable overview and a useful critical commentary and Pepper (1986) traces the historical evolution of Green ideas. Useful articles providing overviews of the debate are Vincent (1993), Barry (1994) and Young (1992). More difficult, but ultimately rewarding, are the groundbreaking articles in Dobson and Lucardie (1993), Goodin's book (1992a) which, despite its title, develops a particular point of view and assumes some knowledge, and John Dryzek's argument, linking ecological principles with the need for greater democratization, which can be found in two books (1987 and 1990).

It is important to read classic ecocentric works. The most important are Leopold (1949), Naess (1973), Goldsmith *et al.* (1972) and Schumacher (1973), but see also Sale (1980; 1984) and Fox (1984). A useful anthology of key writings is Dobson (1991). On environmentalism and the economy, the *Limits to Growth* report (Meadows *et al.*, 1972) is essential and has been updated (Meadows *et al.*, 1992). Critical commentaries are in Dobson (1990) and Martell (1994). The ecological modernization position is promoted in Weale (1992) and Pearce (1993). Finally, a summary of the animal rights debate can be found in Garner (1993a), and the two major philosophical works are Singer (1990) and Regan (1988).

3

GREENS AND THE WESTERN POLITICAL TRADITION

We saw in Chapter 2 that ecocentrics tend to say a great deal more than technocentrics about political organization and values. This reflects the fact that environmental reformists see the protection of the environment as essentially just another policy issue which the political system has to cope with. Environmental issues may cause peculiar problems which require some institutional tinkering (see Chapter 5) but no fundamental reordering of the political system is required. Seen in such a way, environmentalism is suitable for single-issue pressure groups and for absorption by the mainstream political parties. Ecocentrism, on the other hand, claims to be a self-contained, coherent set of principles which cannot merely be tacked on to an existing set of policies or incorporated within an established system of thought. Given this claim, it is important to examine the relationship between ecocentric ideology and Western political thought in general. In particular, we need to ask how, and to what extent, the ecocentric position constitutes a radical departure in political thought. A useful way of considering this question is to examine radical Green ideas in the context of the main political traditions.

Conservatism

There are surprising similarities between conservative thought
enshrined, in particular, in the work of the eighteenth-century
writer and politician, Edmund Burke, and themes that regularly
appear in Green writing (Martell, 1994, p.140). Greens, like conservatives, are sceptical of human capacity to comprehend a complex, interconnected world and are therefore persuaded to leave
things as they are. Thus, preservation and conservation are terms
equally applicable to the conservative and the Green thinker. The
appropriate image of a social reformer, then, is a gardener seeking
to prune and trim, rather than a engineer seeking to restructure
society according to a rationally thought out plan. Thus, John Gray
(1993, p.176) can, from a conservative perspective, applaud Green
theory, which he argues is 'an invaluable corrective to the Whig-
gish, anthropocentric, technological optimism by which all the
modern political religions are animated and which has, in the form
of neo-liberalism, even infected most of what passes today as
conservatism'.

There is, on the other hand, much in the conservative tradition
which is inconsistent with Green thinking. The image of a social
reformer as a 'gardener', for instance, sits rather uneasily with the
radical Green critique of 'nature as garden' with its anthropocentric overtones, and the dark Green celebration of wilderness
which implies a 'hands-off' approach (Dobson, 1990, p.69). Furthermore, conservatism does not have anything to say about the
limits to growth, at least beyond a general nostalgia for a pre-
industrial past, nor does it seek to extend moral standing beyond
humans. Moreover, the radical Green emphasis on radical social
and economic change and the interminable plans of a new society
which appear in Green literature also sit uneasily with the cautious
approach of conservatism (Martell, 1994, p.141).

Fascism/authoritarianism

In the past, the extreme Right has shown an interest in environmentalism. Anna Bramwell (1989) has documented the early interest in ecology by the Far Right and, indeed, the interest in the Far
Right by ecologists. Elements of the National Socialist Party in

Germany, for example, were interested in ecological issues from the 1920s and, having gained power, the Nazis were environmentally active, setting up nature reserves and experimenting with alternative forms of energy, among other things. There are ideological similarities between ecologism and fascism. As P.R. Hay (1988, p.23) points out: 'Use of biological metaphors, stress on the organic community and the individual's need to merge with it, elevation of ritual, intuition and the mystical, and distrust of the rational' are all elements that can be found in both Green writing and fascist ideology. However, it is wrong to take the association too far. As Andrew Vincent (1993, p.266) comments: 'Because national socialists used socialist methods or favoured ancient German traditions does not mean that either socialism or conservatism are eternally besmirched. The same qualification holds for ecology.'

When critics label Green thinking as fascist they are more often than not referring to the authoritarian strain that does exist in some Green writing. This authoritarian strand, particularly prevalent in the 1970s, emphasizes the need for drastic coercive solutions – particularly in the areas of reducing consumption and cutting population size – thought necessary to deal with the severity of the environmental crisis (Hardin, 1968; Ophuls, 1973; Heilbroner, 1974). These accounts tend to be based on a Hobbesian model of man as ultimately selfish and individualistic, requiring an authoritarian state (the Leviathan) to keep order.

One extremely well-known exponent of an authoritarian solution is Garrett Hardin, whose articles 'The tragedy of the commons' and 'Living on a lifeboat' (1968; 1977) are among the best-known environmental writings. His thesis is that, left to their own devices, people will always despoil the commons through greed and naivety and therefore access to it should be limited by a strong state to those who are best able to look after it. Likewise, he suggests that the state must intervene to enforce restrictions on reproduction.

While most environmentalists would agree with Hardin that environmental damage does come about in the ways he suggests, most would not accept his prescriptions (Hays, 1988, pp.23–4). This is particularly the case with his extremely illiberal views on the Third World, where, in the so-called lifeboat ethic parable, he argues, in a Malthusian idiom, that the West (in the lifeboat) should not give a helping hand to the Third World (drowning in the water) since to do so would encourage population growth and greater demands on natural resources, and so ultimately lead to everyone drowning. Garrett and other like-minded individuals, most notably Paul Ehrlich (1972), formed an organization called the Environmental Fund in the 1970s which, among other things, campaigns against food aid to the developing world.

Two basic criticisms of Hardin's eco-authoritarianism can be made. First, it might be suggested that his 'Tragedy of the commons' describes not a commons regime but an open access regime with no rules or codes of conduct designed to prevent unsustainable exploitation. Further, his 'lifeboat ethic' has been criticized for its unjustified pro-developed world stance. As Paehike (1989, pp.65–6) points out:

> Why does Hardin not suggest a more sensible scheme, one advocating the eviction of North Americans from the lifeboat? It would cost far fewer persons and would achieve for the species considerably more time to bring about stabilisation than would avoidable starvation in the so-called Third World.

The authoritarian theme is very much the exception in environmental literature, and was a particular product of the doom-laden 1970s when survival was the major concern; hence the title of Ophuls' work *Leviathan or Oblivion* (1973). To be fair, though, many exponents of the authoritarian position adopt it with a heavy heart, stressing, with some justification, that some coercion now is essential to avoid the much greater coercion that will be necessary later to deal with even greater environmental degradation (Martell, 1994, p.146). Finally, concern about population increases does remain central to environmentalism, but this concern is not synonymous with authoritarianism as a wide variety of non-coercive measures have been recommended.

Liberalism

There are some ways in which the liberal tradition might be regarded as an influence on Green thinking. The inclusion of non-humans within the ethical community, for instance, might be regarded as taking the liberal language of individual rights and obligations to its logical conclusion (Martell, 1994, p.141).

Certainly, as we have seen, contemporary advocates of animal rights and liberation do invoke the liberal tradition of rights and utility to justify their position. It is true that both J.S. Mill and Jeremy Bentham recognized that non-human animals, as sentient beings, were entitled to moral consideration, although neither was prepared to say (as consistency, at least for Bentham, demanded they ought) that non-human animals should have a moral status equivalent to that of humans (Clarke and Linzey, 1990, pp.135–40). Moreover, the ecocentric and holistic core of Green thinking puts it at odds not only with the failure of liberalism to countenance going beyond sentience as the grounding for moral standing (and most liberal thought is unashamedly anthropocentric), but also with liberal individualism.

In terms of economics, there is a debate about the compatibility of the free market and environmentalism (Eckersley, 1993; Vincent, 1993, p.267) and market solutions to environmental problems have been suggested (see Chapter 5). However, even if there is a case for a market approach, it is a reformist strategy designed to alleviate the worst excesses of economic growth rather than to challenge this growth head on. As such, it is not consistent with the limits to growth core of Green thinking. Liberal thought, of course, reached its ascendency in the nineteenth century, an era when economic growth, technological optimism and a belief in human ability to master the environment were guiding principles (Gamble, 1981, ch.1). One exception was J.S. Mill, who put the case for ecological diversity and a steady state economy, but he remains very much an isolated figure in the liberal tradition (Eckersley, 1992, p.23).

Marxism

Greens have rarely raided the liberal tradition for ideas but ideological links between Greens and the Left are much more evident (see Weston, 1986). This is partly because there have been political alliances between Greens and socialists, particularly in Germany, and partly because Marxism and socialism offer the kind of state or community intervention and regulation which most Greens think is necessary to deal with environmental problems. This is not to say that the relationship has been an untroubled one. Many

Greens have denied there is an ideological link between their doctrine and socialism, pointing out that the real distinction on ecological grounds is not between capitalism and socialism but between
capitalist or socialist industrialism on the one hand and the Green
approach on the other. According to this view, it is the 'super-
ideology' of industrialism which causes environmental degradation
and not a particular form of ownership. As Porritt (1984, p.43)
points out: 'The politics of the Industrial Age, left, right and
centre, is like a three-lane motorway, with different vehicles in
different lanes, but *all* heading in the same direction.' As some
members of the British Greens put it, socialism represents 'fair
shares in extinction' (Dobson, 1990, p.173).

There is some justification in the claim made by some Greens
that socialism is no more ecologically sound than capitalism. In the
first place, industrialism in the former Communist regimes of East-
ern Europe caused extensive environmental problems (see Gray,
1993, pp.125–33). Of course, socialists can retort by saying these
regimes were not really socialist at all or that environmentally
damaging industrialism was necessary because of the threat posed
by hostile capitalist enemies (Pepper, 1986, pp.172–3; Yearley,
1992, p.105). What we can say is that, in these countries, the means
of production were state-controlled and that state-directed industrialism was not environmentally benign.

Second, at a theoretical level, orthodox Marxism (or at least the
way in which orthodox Marxism is usually perceived) is inconsistent with Green thinking, since it is 'ultimately wedded to the same
expansionary ethos and anthropocentric framework as liberalism'
(Eckersley, 1992, p.24) It is anthropocentric because Marx, just as
Locke and Hobbes had done before him, regarded the non-human
world exclusively in terms of its use for humans, holding that it
only acquired value when being worked on by humans (*ibid.*, p.25).
Even a modern eco-socialist such as David Pepper (1993, pp.436–
42) accepts that socialism is not ecocentric in orientation and,
indeed, he celebrates the fact since ecocentrism, he argues, is often
translated into at worst anti-humanism and at best a disregard for
the human condition – the Gaia hypothesis of Lovelock (1979)
being a prime example of the latter. We may or may not agree with
this attack on ecocentrism. In the present context, though, this is to
miss the point since, because socialism is anthropocentric, it remains at odds with a central feature of the Green position.

Marxism is also an expansionist doctrine because, for Marx, it was not the forces of production (the raw materials, technology and labour-power that constitute the productive process) but the capitalist relations of production which provided the obstacle to social and political change. Indeed, the technological developments forthcoming under the capitalist social epoch were the precondition for a future socialist society (Eckersley, 1992, pp.77–82). Moreover, unreconstructed Marxists regard environmentalism as a peripheral issue, of concern to the middle class, who are simply defending their selfish interests (Enzensberger, 1974).

More recently, there have been attempts to reconcile Marxism with Green thinking. In part, this consists of a reinterpretation of the writings of Marx and Engels (Parsons, 1978; Benton, 1993). Particular attention here is devoted to Marx's early work in which human interaction with the natural environment is regarded as important for spiritual and aesthetic development, as much as meeting material needs is (Martell, 1994, p.149). The problem is the difficulty of weighing the importance of these earlier writings; furthermore, even this less materialistic interpretation of Marx remains anthropocentric since nature, for Marx, still exists for human purposes.

Some contemporary Marxists have also sought to adapt the doctrine in order to take account of modern concern for the environment (Redclift, 1984; Williams, 1986). Here, the focus has been on demonstrating the culpability of the capitalist system of production rather than industrialism *per se*. Thus, the competitive character of the capitalist system, the need continually to persuade us that we want new goods and the resulting wastefulness and inefficiency provide the real reason for environmental degradation. Conversely, under a system of common ownership, production can be organized more effectively and science and technology can be brought to bear in order to provide solutions to environmental problems.

Clearly, with its anthropocentric basis, its orientation towards growth (although toned down somewhat in most modern ecosocialist writing) and its faith in technological fixes, even this reformulated Marxism does not come up to scratch from a radical Green perspective. Nevertheless, there is a great deal in the Marxist and more general non-Marxian socialist tradition, which Greens can agree with and perhaps even learn from, and there is a growing body of literature which seeks to draw out these features (see, for instance, Gorz, 1982; Pepper, 1993a). Here, we can point to the vision of small-scale participatory democracies found in the writings of utopian socialists such as William Morris and G.D.H. Cole; the emphasis on egalitarianism both within Western societies and between rich and poor countries; and the socialist analysis of political power which provides Greens with a useful account of how vested interests often stand in the way of environmental improvements.

Feminism

There are growing links between the women's movement and the environment. At a practical level, it is very noticeable that a large proportion of environmental activists and, in particular, animal rights activists, are women (Garner, 1993a, ch.2). A number of eco-feminist writers have sought to distinguish between male and female relationships to the environment, concluding that women, rather than men, have a greater affinity to environmental protection (see Griffin, 1978; Merchant, 1980; Collard, 1988; Mellor, 1992).

Very briefly, women, it is argued, are more likely to have an affinity with the non-human environment for two reasons. The first relates to women's nurturing role (derived from their reproductive function), which provides for a set of values (of caring and compassion) more conducive to identification with the natural world – the so-called 'essentialist' position. Second, it is argued that women can identify with the environment since they have a mind-set adjusted to oppression – the so-called 'materialist' position (for a feminist account of animal rights along these lines, see Adams, 1990; also Regan, 1991, ch. 5). Thus, there is an identity of interests between the ending of male exploitation and the ending of human exploitation of the natural environment.

Both approaches are challengeable. In the first place, the simplistic portrayal of different male and female values is questionable, and even if it were possible to attach labels such as tough and aggressive to males and maternal and compassionate to females, it is by no means clear that these are innate as opposed to being a product of the social division of labour (Eckersley, 1992, p.66; see also Evans, 1993). Second, women are not the only oppressed groups in society and, in addition, it is not clear that patriarchy and anthropocentrism are synonymous since, as Eckersley (1992, p.68) points out; many traditional patriarchal societies did not despoil their natural environment.

Anarchism

There is a strong affinity between anarchist thought and much Green political theorizing. Andrew Dobson, among others, argues that the 'anarchist solution' is 'the closest approximation . . . to the centre of gravity of a Green sustainable society' (Dobson, 1990, p.83; see also Atkinson, 1991, p.8; and Carter, 1993). Anarchism is concerned with justifying stateless, decentralized, and self-sufficient communes where people live in harmony with each other (Heywood, 1992, pp.259–60).

Although the ecological imperative was not the major focus of classic anarchist thought, there are obvious parallels between the anarchist vision and the Green account of a post-industrial society. For example, 'on about twenty major points' there is agreement between Peter Kropotkin's *Field, Factories and Workshops* (written in 1899) and the *Blueprint for Survival*, although there is no acknowledgement, and Kropotkin himself was influenced by other anarchists such as Godwin and Proudhon (Pepper, 1986, pp.188–93).

The best-known eco-anarchist is the American Murray Bookchin (1962; 1971), although he is by no means the only author to adopt an anarchist approach to Green political thought (see Schumacher, 1973; Sale, 1984; Bahro, 1986). In a series of books, Bookchin has developed a comprehensive anarchist account (described as 'social ecology') with ecological principles at the forefront (see Eckersley, 1992, pp.146–60). He suggests that social hierarchy, based on class, race and gender, is the major cause of environmental degradation since domination over non-human nature follows from human domination over other humans.

Whether or not one accepts Bookchin's particular brand of eco-anarchism, all the varieties are based on the fundamental principles of decentralization and self-sufficiency. As such, they are all subject to the critique, examined in Chapter 2, which questions the ability of such small communities to deal with the international and global nature of environmental problems. Because of this, it is

by no means clear that a radical Green position can accept anarchist solutions, and, as we have seen, a number of Green writers have
suggested as much.

Conclusions

Our brief exploration of Green political thought reveals that it
draws its ideas from a wide variety of political traditions. As David
Pepper rightly observes, Green thinking still remains in a 'rather
muddled political state' (Pepper, 1986, p.204). In order to assess
Green thinking more coherently, we can, following Martell (1994,
ch.5), ask two questions. First, is there anything distinctive about
Green political theory which offers a challenge to mainstream
political thinking? Here, the answer must be yes. As Eckersley
(1992, p.2) points out: 'The questions raised by environmental
philosophers have exposed a number of significant blind spots in
modern political theory.'

Two blindspots are particularly important. First, the emphasis on
the limits to growth adds a new dimension which political thought
must take account of (and to a certain extent has) when arguing for
particular social and political arrangements. Further, ecocentrism –
the extension of inherent value beyond the human species to incorporate non-human nature – is a distinct departure in political thought.
All the major traditions we have considered are anthropocentric.
They 'merely promise different ways of exploiting nature for the
convenience and benefit of humankind' (Heywood, 1992, p.245). The
adoption of an ecocentric approach requires fundamental change in
the way we think about social, legal and political institutions and
practices. In the two senses described above, then, Dobson (1993,
p.229) is right to say that ecologism represents a new ideology which
cannot wholly be 'spoken in the language' of Conservatism, Liberalism and Socialism.

Our second question is to ask to what extent there are clear
ecological reasons or justifications for particular kinds of social and
political arrangements. Here, the answer is not so clear-cut. Some
writers sympathetic to the Green cause argue that ecology is consistent with a wide variety of political structures (Ryle, 1988) while
others, such as Dobson, as we noted earlier, think that particular
systems are more appropriate. Clearly, both cannot be right. The

answer, indeed, would seem to be that both are wrong, that while there are a number of political structures capable of fulfilling Green objectives, the choice is not completely open (Martell, 1994, p.160). From the analysis in this chapter, for instance, we would rule out decentralized solutions in favour of state-based ones capable of dealing with difficult environmental problems. But this state-based solution must not be authoritarian because such regimes do not give to humans the respect they deserve. It should be remembered that humans are part of nature and should not be treated with any less respect than the non-human natural world which Greens seek to protect.

Further reading

The relationship between ecology and mainstream political thought is covered admirably in Eckersley (1992), Martell (1994, ch.5), Hay (1988) and, to a lesser extent, in Dobson (1990). Gray (1993) identifies links between conservatism and environmentalism. Classic 'eco-Hobbesian' accounts are Hardin (1968, 1977), Heilbroner (1974) and Ophuls (1973). There is a huge eco-socialist literature. Eckersley (1992) should be read to provide the framework, followed by the excellent account in Pepper (1993a). Benton (1993) is a fascinating attempt to reconcile Marxism, ecocentrism and animal rights but is hard going and requires some preliminary background reading. Eco-feminism is best approached through Mellor (1992) and eco-anarchism through Eckersley (1992), Dobson (1990) and Carter (1993) before moving on to Bookchin (1962; 1971).

4

THE ENVIRONMENTAL MOVEMENT

The environmental movement has grown enormously in recent years and a bewildering array of groups of different sizes, character and importance now exists. As John McCormick (1991, p.34) points out, 'Britain has the oldest, strongest, best-organized and most widely supported environmental lobby in the world.' The major part of this chapter seeks to explore three distinct aspects of the environmental movement. First, the reasons that have been put forward for its rise; second, how we might best categorize the movement to make sense of its defining characteristics and significant divisions; and third, a preliminary investigation (to be built on in Chapter 8) into the movement's capacity to influence public policy outcomes. Before embarking on this analysis, the origins and evolution of the environmental movement are considered.

Origins and evolution

Concern for the countryside was the major impetus for the formation of the first environmental groups in the nineteenth century. From the sixteenth century, the activities of amateur field naturalists made more people aware of the beauty of the countryside and by the latter part of the nineteenth century, with the help of much improved public transport aiding access, hundreds of natural history societies existed with a combined membership of around

100,000 (Lowe and Goyder, 1983, p.18; Evans, 1991, pp.18–20; McCormick, 1991, p.29). Even though they were concerned primarily with studying and enjoying the countryside rather than conserving it, these societies drew attention to, and felt strongly about, the damage being caused (McCormick, 1991, p.30).

From its early days, the emerging environmental movement had three distinct strands. In the first place, there were those groups concerned with preserving the countryside as an amenity to which people could escape from the squalor and grime of urban and industrial Britain. This was the rationale behind the creation of the Commons, Open Spaces and Footpaths Preservation Society (1865), the National Trust (1895), the Council for the Preservation of Rural England, later the Council for the Protection of Rural England (1926) and the Ramblers Association (1935). The second strand consisted of those groups concerned with nature conservation. Thus, the Royal Society for the Protection of Birds (RSPB) was created in 1889 and the Society for the Promotion of Nature Reserves (since 1981 the Royal Society for Nature Conservation – RSNC) was set up in 1912 initially to persuade the National Trust to use some of its resources to create nature reserves. The distinction between nature conservation and amenity has been an important divide in the history of countryside politics in Britain, not least determining the division of responsibilities of the state environmental agencies (see Chapter 5). There can obviously be conflicts between the two strands since the most ecologically important areas may not be those that are sought on recreational or aesthetic grounds. With the emergence of ecology as an important scientific discipline, the conservation strand has become increasingly dominant.

The third strand in the emerging environmental movement was the growing concern for animals which precipitated the emergence of the animal protection movement in the nineteenth century, a movement which, as we saw in Chapter 2, has different organizational and ideological roots from the broader environmental movement (Garner, 1993a, ch.2). In the early part of the nineteenth century, the major causes of concern were the cruelties inflicted on animals by the urban working class such as the treatment of carriage horses and the use of animals for baiting, whereas the cruelty inflicted on animals by the aristocracy (through hunting and shooting) and the scientific elite (in animal experiments) was

Table 4.1 Increases in the membership of the major environmental groups 1971–89

	1971	1980	1985	1989
Greenpeace		10,000	50,000	320,000
FOE	1,000	12,000	27,000	120,000
WWF	12,000	51,000	91,000	202,000
Ramblers	22,000	36,000	50,000	73,000
National Trust	–	950,000	1.32m.	1.75m.
CPRE	21,000	27,000	26,500	44,500
RSNC	64,000	140,000	165,000	205,000
RSPB	98,000	321,000	390,000	433,000

Sources: McCormick (1991, p.152); Grant (1989, p.14).

by contrast largely ignored. As Harriet Ritvo (1987) suggests, this class bias was at least partly the product of a desire for social control, since animal cruelty, and baiting in particular, was associated with drunkenness and absenteeism from work.

Whatever the motive, the first law in this country (and probably the world) designed to protect animals was passed in 1822 and two years later the Society for the Prevention of Cruelty to Animals (the royal prefix was added later) was formed to police the legislation. As the century progressed, concern for animals expanded to include experimentation and the protection of wild animals and birds. Of the thirty or so major animal protection groups now in existence, no fewer than eight were formed in the nineteenth century and thirteen existed by the outbreak of the Second World War (Garner, 1993a, p.43).

The modern environmental movement dates from the late 1950s and early 1960s, a period of renewed interest in environmental issues, which resulted in dramatic increases in the membership (see Table 4.1) and income of existing groups (and the creation of new ones). In 1980, Lowe and Goyder (1983, p.1) identified nearly a hundred national environmental groups and several thousand local ones, with a combined membership of 2.5–3 million, or about 5 per cent of the total population. This membership figure was roughly double that of 1970, which in turn was double that of 1960. A more recent estimate puts the figure a decade later at about 4.5 million, some 8 per cent of the total population (McCormick, 1991, p.34). The membership of the largest group is very impressive.

Overshadowing all the others is the National Trust with more members than all of the political parties combined. Extra income means, of course, that groups can employ more and better quality staff, and this in turn leads to better organized and more extensive campaigns. Between 1984 and 1989 staff numbers at Friends of the Earth increased by 900 per cent and at Greenpeace by 570 per cent (McCormick, 1991, p.155).

In the early 1990s, there was evidence of some decline, with Friends of the Earth suffering a 10 per cent reduction in income, and similar problems besetting Greenpeace (*Guardian*, 19 October 1994), but there is nothing to suggest that this is anything more than a transitory phenomenon caused, perhaps, by the recession. Even if this decline occurs across the board, the long-term growth remains impressive (Young, 1993, p.19). The membership of the RSPB, for instance, stood at around 4,000 in the 1930s compared to nearly half a million today.

Another indicator of the rise of the environment as a political issue is the existence of a much larger 'attentive public', consisting of those who are not members of any specific group but who express an interest in the issues raised by environmental groups (Lowe and Goyder, 1983). MORI polls in 1989 revealed that 18 million people regarded themselves as environmentally conscious shoppers, while between May and June 1989 the proportion of people rating the environment as the most important issue rose from 17 per cent to 35 per cent (Ward, 1990, p.223; McCormick, 1991, p.108). Of course, the information revealed by such polls must be treated with caution (see Yearley, 1992, pp.79–80), and it is certainly the case that the environment has slipped down the political agenda since (Young, 1993, p.110). Nevertheless, such evidence, coupled with membership increases of environmental groups, does reveal a shift in public attitudes and needs to be taken seriously.

The modern environmental movement is different in at least two important respects from the first wave of environmental concern in the nineteenth century. In the first place, it is to a far greater extent a mass movement, not only because group memberships have increased but also because members of some newer groups in particular are encouraged to be more active in terms of participating in demonstrations and even various forms of direct action. Many of the older groups tend to be much more cautious, relying on their technical expertise and ability to engage in quiet negotiations with decision-makers, the wider membership only being called on in specific and limited cases to back up the leadership's position. The stress on mass activism, the rejection of hierarchical organizational structures and the old political divisions based on capital and labour evident in the modern environmental movement, are all characteristics of what social scientists have called new social movements.

Obviously, the symbol of this new activism was the formation of Greenpeace and Friends of the Earth which, as Table 4.1 reveals, secured the greatest increases in membership during the 1980s. Greenpeace dates back to the late 1960s and earned its spurs in a Canadian-based sea-bound protest against US and French nuclear testing before turning its attention to whaling (McTaggart, 1978). The organization flourished during the 1970s with a British branch created in 1977. By 1989, the worldwide membership of Greenpeace was estimated to be 3.5 million, the British section contributing over 300,000 of these (Yearley, 1992, p.72). Friends of the Earth was founded in 1969 in the United States by David Brower who had fallen out with the Sierra Club, a major US conservation group, because of his desire to adopt a sharper campaigning edge (McCormick, 1991, p.33). The British branch was set up a year later, and by the early 1980s more or less independent branches existed in twenty-nine countries (Lowe and Goyder, 1983, p.124). Friends of the Earth has moderated its image somewhat since the late 1960s (causing Brower to leave the American organization). It tends now to concentrate on working with industry and producing well-documented technical evidence of the causes and consequences of environmental degradation and possible resolutions, as opposed to encouraging confrontation with industry and mass action to highlight environmental problems (McCormick, 1991, pp.117–18). Nevertheless, it is still regarded as a radical group and as such treated with suspicion by decision-makers.

Second, there is a far greater recognition now of the interdependence of environmental problems and parochial countryside issues, for long so dominant, have declined in importance. As a reflection of this, more general groups such as Greenpeace and Friends of the Earth have emerged, prepared to campaign on many different fronts. Further, ostensibly single-issue organizations now concern themselves with a whole range of environmental issues. The RSPB, for instance, recognizes that birds can be harmed by a wide variety of human activities threatening them and their habitats.

Explaining the growing concern

Documenting the expansion of the environmental movement is much easier than explaining it. A number of possible explanations have been suggested. Adapting Martell (1994, ch.4) here, it is possible to identify three varieties. First, there are those that see growing environmental concern as a by-product of cultural and structural factors happening independently of the actual objective state of the environment (reviewed in Lowe and Rudig, 1986, pp.513–20). Second, are those that place emphasis on the mediating influences of the environmental lobby, the media and scientists. Finally, there are those that focus on the existence of worsening environmental problems as the key trigger for concern. We might be led by our intuition to assert that objective environmental problems, and the way in which these issues are mediated through pressure groups and the media, are self-evidently important explanations of rising environmental concern. Cultural and structural explanations, however, would deny this 'common-sense' view of the world and, for this reason, we shall examine their claims in some detail.

Proponents of a cultural change focus on a shift in values which, it is argued, has produced as one of its consequences mounting concern for the environment. Ronald Inglehart (1977; 1990), the best-known proponent of this type of explanation, charts the rise since 1945 of a section of the population expressing so-called post-material values (see Table 4.2). These, he argues, have arisen as a consequence of post-war affluence. As the welfare state and economic success have taken care of many people's material needs in the developed world, they have increasingly turned their attention to meeting non-material goals, one of which is the desire to live and work in a pleasant environment. These values are particularly prevalent in the generations who have grown up since 1945 and so, although post-materialist values are not yet held by a majority of the adult population, there is every possibility that they will

Table 4.2 Materialist and post-materialist value types in six Western European countries by age group, 1970

Age group	65+	55–64	45–54	35–44	25–34	15–24
%						
Materialist	48	45	36	35	31	20[a]
Post-materialist	3	7	8	12	14	25[a]

[a] The generation born after 1945.

Source: adapted from Inglehart (1990, p.49)

become predominant in years to come. Since the major political parties, based as they are on the old paradigm of economic growth and class representation, are not well suited to pursuing the new post-materialist agenda, the new social movements, including the environmental movement, have attracted support.

The development of the environmental movement does indeed seem to be linked with economic prosperity. Lowe and Goyder (1983, pp.16–17) identify four periods – the 1890s, 1920s, the late 1950s and the early 1970s – when concern for the environment was particularly evident, and these do correspond with the end of periods of extensive economic expansion. This would also seem to explain why concern arose again towards the end of the 1980s as the economy was booming and dropped off in the early 1990s when recession arrived. Clearly, then, the economic climate does have an effect on the issues people regard as salient. This is confirmed in a study by Andrew Blowers (1984) of an environmental dispute surrounding a brickworks in Bedfordshire. Blowers demonstrates how the onset of recession in the early 1980s transformed the political agenda from one in which environmental opposition to the redevelopment of the brickworks was paramount to a situation in which the desire to protect jobs became more important than environmental protection.

The specific claims made by the post-materialist school are more difficult to sustain. In the first place, it needs to be asked why the satisfaction of material needs leads to post-materialism rather than new material needs. Inglehart derives his ordering of values from Maslow, who argued that needs are pursued in a hierarchical order according to the extent to which they are necessary for survival (Maslow, 1954). Thus, once the basic physiological needs are met other higher-order needs, such as love and esteem, come into play. It is by no means clear, though, why this should be the case. For one thing, what one generation regards as essential will differ from another. At one time, televisions and cars were regarded as luxuries, now they are common and not to own one through lack of resources is regarded as a form of deprivation. In the future, computer ownership will no doubt fall into this category (Martell, 1994, p.125).

A further criticism is that we could accept the evidence about post-material values but deny that affluence has been the chief cause. This brings us to the competing explanations all of which could be held responsible for the emergence of post-materialist values. Thus, the role of the environmental movement and the media in promoting post-material issues might be responsible (Martell, 1994, pp.125–6) or, alternatively, structural changes in society may have had an effect.

The structural interpretation is associated above all with Stephen Cotgrove and Andrew Duff (1980; 1981), who argue that the rise of environmentalism as an important issue reflects the ideological disposition of a new social grouping which has emerged in the post-war period. This new fraction of the middle class consists of those who work in the non-productive service sector – doctors, social workers, teachers, and so on – a sector that has grown extensively since 1945. It is occupation as opposed to affluence, then, which, according to this view, is crucial. Those working in new middle-class occupations are much more likely to espouse post-material values than the private sector working class and middle class because, it is argued, they are insulated from the dominant values of industrial society. Thus, environmentalism is 'an expression of the interests of those whose class position in the non-productive sector locates them at the periphery of the institutions and processes of industrial capitalist societies' (Cotgrove and Duff, 1980, pp.340–1).

It is not being claimed here that environmentalism is an expression of class interests. Such a position is difficult to justify. Clearly, some environmental campaigns, particularly those that seek to prevent further development in leafy suburbs (the NIMBY syndrome), is motivated by self-interest (Lowe and Goyder, 1983, pp.28–30). But this does not account for the post-materialism of the new middle class since those in white-collar public sector jobs are far from being the most affluent part of the middle class. Indeed, psephological studies indicate that the new middle class are more likely to vote for the Liberal Democrats and Labour than for the Conservatives (Garner and Kelly, 1993, ch.9). So, rather than deriving from need deprivation or class interests, the structural explanation suggests that changing values derive from ideals.

Persuasive though the structural explanation may sound, it has a number of problems. In the first place, the link between occupation and ideals is not entirely credible. As Lowe and Rudig (1986, p.522) point out, why should those working in the public sector espouse the end of economic growth when it is precisely that which ensures the continued existence of the welfare state? Furthermore, while the social profile of the members of environmental groups does give some support to the structural explanation, with members of Friends of the Earth, the RSPB and the Conservation Society, for instance, being drawn disproportionately from the new middle class identified by Cotgrove and Duff, other groups, such as the Council for the Protection of Rural England (CPRE), draw their membership disproportionately from the more affluent middle and upper classes (Lowe *et al.*, 1986, p.115). Furthermore, the 'attentive public' is much more evenly balanced socially (Lowe and Goyder, 1983, pp.10–13; Porritt and Winner, 1988, p.182). An additional point is that, as Lowe and Goyder point out, it may be that the social characteristics of environmental activists simply reflect the greater propensity of the new middle class to join any voluntary organization as opposed to a specific characteristic of environmental concern.

A more serious objection to the structural explanation is the difficulty of determining causality. Even Cotgrove and Duff (1980, p.102) admit that 'environmentalists try to choose occupations congruent with their . . . post-material values'. If this is the case, the whole theory is devalued since post-material values can no longer be explained in terms of occupation. This, of course, takes us back to square one and our search for an explanation for the existence of the value shift! This does not mean that Cotgrove and Duff are prepared to accept the affluence argument of Inglehart after all, since their research still suggests that material conditions are not an accurate predictor of post-material values (*ibid.*, p.106).

The final point here is that both the value- and structural-based theories can be criticized on the grounds that they completely ignore the possibility that it is the deterioration of the environment, and those agents seeking to draw attention to it, which has played a key role in bringing the issue on to the political agenda. To 'effectively divorce . . . environmental concern from ecological problems' (Lowe and Rudig, 1986, p.518) is surely to lose sight of much that is important. To give one example, survey evidence demonstrates that concern for the environment manifests itself in different countries according to particular national and regional problems (see Martell, 1994, p.134).

Classifying the environmental movement

There are a number of classificatory schemes that can be utilized to help us understand the nature of the environmental movement.

Interests and causes

The most widely utilized distinction in the pressure group literature is between groups that exist to serve the often economic interests of their members – trade unions and business organizations being the obvious examples – and those concerned with promoting a cause which is not, exclusively at least, in the interests of their members. Most environmental groups can be classified as cause groups although, particularly in the United States, they are known as public interest groups (to be contrasted with sectional or special interests) as a consequence of their aim to achieve objectives which are beneficial to the wider public.

Lowe and Goyder (1983, p.35) make a further refinement to this by distinguishing between 'emphasis' groups and 'promotional' groups. Emphasis groups are those that have achieved some success and at least part of their role is concerned with defending these gains. This applies mainly to the older environmental groups such as the RSNC and the CPRE. Promotional groups such as Friends of the Earth, on the other hand, are concerned almost exclusively with promoting change. The implication here is that a group that fails over time to make some gains will struggle to survive, particularly if it relies on its membership for its income.

Not all environmental groups are concerned primarily with promoting a cause. Some, such as the British Waste Paper Association,

Environmental Resources Ltd and the Body Shop, are trade associations or companies which have a vested economic interest in promoting an environmental message. In addition, many groups concerned with their particular local environments can be described as non-economic *interest* groups, since their major purpose is to protect their own areas from development (such as the building of more houses) even if it would benefit others. Sometimes this can have an economic dimension too when, for instance, property prices could be affected.

The classic case of a successful local campaign involved the Wing Airport Resistance Association (WARA) whose opposition to the building of the third London airport near the small Buckinghamshire town of Wing is often used as a model of how to resist major developments effectively (Kimber and Richardson, 1974). Crucially in the present context, the strategy of WARA was based, not on opposing the idea of an airport *per se*, but on why it was inappropriate to build it in *their* back yard. The fact that they were happy to suggest alternative sites demonstrates that their concern was their own interests and not the environment in general. This applies equally to the dumping of nuclear waste. Even those who recognize the value of nuclear power would be none too happy if it was proposed that the waste be dumped in their own area.

Most environmental groups are cause groups, having a voluntary and sometimes also a charitable status. Such organizations, it has been argued, face problems which do not affect interest groups. These problems derive from the rational choice theory of group behaviour most associated with the work of Mancur Olson (1965). For Olson, it is against the interests of individuals to participate in the achievement of collective goals, even if they value these goals. This is because rational individuals will take a 'free ride' by calculating that it is not worth paying the costs of participation since they will enjoy the benefits gained by the group anyway. This makes the organization of a group problematic since, if Olson is right, it is not clear why anyone ever bothers to become a member. Olson's answer is that groups are able to recruit members in so far as they offer 'selective incentives' which are only available to members. The problem for cause groups is that they do not have the same capacity to provide such incentives as interest groups do.

If Olson is right, cause groups would appear to be at a serious disadvantage. At the same time, membership of cause groups, including, as we have seen, environmental groups, has greatly increased. How, then, do we explain this? One response is to point to the fact that some environmental groups do provide selective incentives. The National Trust provides access to heritage sites and RSPB membership provides free access to nature reserves. In addition, most groups provide literature to members, some of which is very well produced and by itself has some value.

Another response is to say that Olson is wrong and that other motivations underlie group membership. Thus, people may join groups because of the intrinsic satisfaction they receive from participating in group activity in terms, for instance, of the social life membership provides. Further, it might be suggested that the achievement of public policy goals is the key motivation. Whether Olson is right or wrong, he did direct attention at the issue of group mobilization (see McCarthy and Zald, 1977), a topic that had previously been taken for granted, and, in the case of environmental groups at least, one that requires a good deal of research.

Primary and secondary activity

Another useful distinction to make is between primary and secondary group activity. The former consists of those activities designed to secure legislative change through influencing decision-makers. The latter consists of those activities designed to provide a service to group members or those on whose behalf a group seeks to work (Grant, 1989, ch.1). In reality, many environmental groups engage in both types of activity but it is important to note that much secondary activity does take place.

In particular, environmental groups carry out a great deal of their own conservation work. Thus, the National Trust acquires and maintains historic buildings and scenic areas; and, since the 1920s, the RSPB has owned and maintained nature reserves of particular value to birds. Since the 1960s the RSNC has been the co-ordinating body for a country-wide network of voluntary county trusts (or wildlife trusts as they are now known) who own and manage some 1,500 nature reserves (Warren and Goldsmith, 1983, p.346; Simpson, 1990, p.165; Yearley, 1992, pp.57–9). Likewise, the British Trust for Conservation Volunteers (BTCV) was set up in 1970 to train volunteers in nature conservation who then may go on to work, in a paid or voluntary capacity, for a particular nature reserve (*Green Magazine*, March 1991, pp.54–6).

In the 1980s, too, local clean-up campaigns and waste recycling schemes were set up, often with the help of government funding through job creation schemes (Young, 1993, p.28). Thus, in the mid-1980s, the BTCV, the RSNC and Friends of the Earth linked up with the Department of the Environment, the Manpower Services Commission and the private sector to create UK 2000, an organization involved in various environmental projects at the local level (Porritt and Winner, 1988, p.163; Lowe and Flynn, 1989, p.272). Finally, some environmental groups also have a policing role. The RSPCA was created in 1824 with the primary function of policing the first animal welfare legislation carried through Parliament two years earlier, and its uniformed inspectorate is a familiar sight in Britain (Garner, 1993a, pp.183–5). Similarly, RSPB inspectors try to ensure that protected bird species are not killed or their eggs stolen. Finally, and more recently, a number of local badger groups have been created to keep an eye out for badger baiters.

Geographical sphere of influence

The third way of classifying environmental groups is in terms of their geographical sphere of influence. Here, we can make a distinction between those groups that have a national, international or local focus. This distinction is not clear-cut, of course, because many groups work in all three spheres. As environmental decisions are increasingly taken at a supra-national level, it is not surprising that environmental groups have adopted an international role. But, even though the European Union is obviously crucial and the growing number and importance of international environmental treaties makes pressure group involvement essential, groups do not ignore the lobbying of their own governments (Mazey and Richardson, 1992). This is not only because national governments still exercise a great deal of sovereignty, which they do, but also because it is necessary for groups to persuade their government to reflect their views in the international arena (Grant, 1989, ch.5). Moreover, since, as with EU directives, the implementation of supra-national decisions is usually left to national governments, there is still a need to apply pressure at the national level in order to ensure compliance.

A further point is that there is still plenty of scope for environmental groups to exercise influence at the local level. As Chapter 5 discusses, local planning authorities are responsible both for drawing up development plans for their areas and for granting consent for individual development proposals. Both provide opportunities for local environmental groups to participate in decision-making and they have grasped this opportunity. To give one indication of their involvement, the number of local amenity societies has increased rapidly from about 150 in the mid-1950s to over 1,000 twenty years later (Lowe and Goyder, 1983, ch.5; see also Blowers, 1984, for an extended case study of one particular planning decision). Local authorities have also often taken the initiative by drawing up general environmental plans, and this process was encouraged by the Rio Summit which emphasized the need for local authorities to produce so-called Agenda 21 documents detailing how they are putting the principle of sustainable development into operation (see Chapter 6) (Ward, 1993).

Despite all this, the international dimension of environmental decision-making has become more important and much contemporary environmental activity is directed at this level. One international body which non-governmental organizations (NGOs) can directly join is the International Union for the Conservation of Nature and Natural Resources (known as the World Conservation Union). Founded in 1948, the IUCN is a unique organization in that membership is open to governments and their agencies as well as NGOs, and it now boasts a membership of more than 50 states, 100 agencies and 400 NGOs (Boardman, 1981, pp.88–91). While not having any legal authority, the World Conservation Union does have influence. The joint IUCN/World Wide Fund for Nature (WWF) reports, *The World Conservation Strategy* (1980) and *Caring for the Earth: A strategy for sustainable living* (1991), for instance, are regarded as important guides to conservation issues and strategies by both governments and NGOs.

At the international level, we can make a further distinction between, on the one hand, those groups existing only in one country but which also lobby other governments and international organizations and, on the other, those groups with branches in other countries. In the former category can be included most notably the RSPB which set up an international office in 1979, employ a full-time Brussels lobbyist (McCormick, 1991, p.134) and is an affiliated member of the International Council for Bird Preservation, formed in 1922 to represent national bird protection organizations.

In the latter category come organizations such as Greenpeace, Friends of the Earth and the WWF which, as well as having branches in a number of countries, have also set up their own Brussels offices. WWF (originally called the World Wildlife Fund) was set up in 1961 as a result of a British initiative involving, most importantly, Max Nicholson and Peter Scott (McCormick, 1992, pp.41–3). It plays a crucial international lobbying role and also provides a great deal of financial resources for conservation projects throughout the world (Boardman, 1981, pp.78–86; McCormick, 1991, p.33). The existence of these kinds of federal organizations can be important in representational terms. Attendance at the meetings of the International Whaling Commission, for instance, is open only to those NGOs that have offices in more than three countries (Lyster, 1985, p.23).

A further category consists of umbrella organizations which exist only to lobby international organizations. The European Environmental Bureau, for example, liaises with the European Union on behalf of national environmental groups (Lowe and Goyder, 1983, ch.10; McCormick, 1992, pp.101–2,181–2). Founded in December 1974, the Bureau now represents about a hundred groups from all the member states, including over twenty from Britain (Lowe and Flynn, 1989, p.272). Another example is Eurogroup for Animal Welfare set up by the RSPCA in 1980, which exists to represent national animal protection groups as well as providing the secretariat for the Intergroup on Animal Welfare consisting of MEPs (Garner, 1993a, p.40).

At the national level, too, there are a number of umbrella organizations. The Council for Environmental Conservation, for instance, was founded in 1969 to coordinate the environmental lobby. After a rather troubled existence, at least in part because groups were not prepared to give up enough of their autonomy to make it viable, it was renamed the Environment Council in the mid-1980s. One of its committees, the Wildlife Link, has been reasonably successful in providing a means whereby various groups can exchange information and present a united front to government departments (McCormick, 1991, p.37). Also worth mentioning is the Green Alliance, which helps provide groups with information on the workings of the political process and how the environmental movement can use it to their best advantage (*ibid.*, p.38).

Issue concern

There is a large number of environmental groups campaigning on a wide variety of issues. Lowe and Goyder (1983, p.80) divide issue concerns into four distinct areas: conservation, recreation, amenity and resources. In addition, they identify a 'central core' of groups (the CPRE, the Civic Trust, the National Trust, the RSPB, Friends of the Earth and the Council for Environmental Conservation) which have the most extensive movement-wide contacts. The issue focus in Britain has been predominantly on wildlife and coun-tryside issues, as opposed to wider issues of pollution. Thus, the biggest and most well-established groups are those, such as the RSPB, the RSNC, the National Trust and the CPRE, which focus exclusively on conservation and amenity issues. Conversely, the National Society for Clean Air (NSCA) is the only national group which has, over the past three decades, worked exclusively on pollution issues. The NSCA, in its previous manifestation as the National Smoke Abatement Society, was regarded as a key influ-ence leading to the Clean Air Act 1956 (Kimber and Richardson, 1974).

The focus on conservation politics is not at all surprising. Damage to the countryside is much more visible than all but the worst cases of air or water pollution. In addition, improved trans-port infrastructure and the much wider ownership of cars has made the countryside more accessible for many people. Finally, the greater opportunities for environmental groups to participate in decisions affecting the countryside (compared with the secrecy with which pollution control has traditionally been associated in Britain) have also made it an issue which lends itself to group activity.

Another distinction worth making is the breadth of concern different groups have. Some groups, such as the RSPB and the Soil Association, have a fairly narrow remit, while groups such as the WWF and the RSNC have a much wider one. What distinguishes the modern environmental movement is the extent to which they are now much more ecologically informed. Thus, even groups which ostensibly have fairly narrow interests recognize the extent to which their particular concern, whether it be insects or birds, can be affected by a wide variety of activities from intensive agriculture to urban encroachment.

In the animal protection field there has always been a mixture of single-issue groups (such as the National Antivivisection Society and the League Against Cruel Sports) and more broadly based groups, most notably the RSPCA. In recent years, though, there has been a tendency for individual groups to emphasize a range of issues – factory farming, vivisection, blood sports, and so on. This has an ideological cause, deriving from the emergence of animal rights, a philosophical position which can be consistently applied to all forms of animal exploitation. Thus, if one accepts that animals have rights, it is inconsistent to campaign against hunting while ignoring the use of animals for food, clothes and as laboratory subjects (see Chapter 2).

The pressure group perspective

Most environmental groups do, at least some of the time, seek to influence public authorities, and one of the key elements of an analysis of group politics is to assess how successful they are in achieving their objectives. Political scientists have long recognized that groups play an important role in determining public policy outcomes, with the pluralist perspective in particular emphasizing their central role in democratic politics (Dahl, 1971).

It is extremely difficult, however, to determine the extent of this influence. We could, for instance, simply look at decisions made, see how far they coincide with a particular group's objectives and impute influence accordingly. This is, of course, to disguise some major problems. It is, for instance, to overlook the possibility that some issues are consciously or unconsciously excluded from the decision-making arena so that the decisions made do not involve the most important issues (Bachrach and Baratz, 1962). Further, it cannot be proved that a particular decision would not have been made anyway without a group campaigning for it because of the strength of public opinion or through the personal commitment of decision-makers (Grant, 1989, pp.114–16). We shall return to consider the political processes involved in environmental decision-making in Chapter 8. Here, the basic framework for an analysis of the influence of the environmental lobby is sketched out.

The institutional targets of the environmental lobby

Environmental groups, like all other pressure groups, have a number of targets which they seek to influence. We have seen that the nature of environmental decision-making has put a premium on the supra-national level but that lobbying government departments and agencies and local authorities is still important. Distinctive features of the British political system, of course, are the unitary nature of the British state and the dominance of the legislature by the executive. This means that gaining access to the executive, or so-called 'insider status', is crucial for pressure groups and the environmental lobby is no exception (the role of Parliament is discussed further below). Not only can the government of the day be virtually assured of getting its legislation through Parliament unamended, it is also the case that an increasing number of Acts are skeletal in nature, and authority is delegated so that the executive is able to make regulations in the form of statutory instruments. This is the case, for instance, with the Wildlife and Countryside Act 1981, which gives the Secretary of State for the Environment responsibility for deciding which species are to be granted protection (Grant, 1989, pp.63–4). Parliamentary scrutiny of such secondary legislation is so limited that it is important for pressure groups to gain access to the executive in order to influence the content of regulations.

The nature of insider status needs to be further refined. In the first place, there is a variety of different levels of access, ranging from written consultation and an occasional meeting with officials and even ministers, to regular, high-level consultation (Grant, 1989, p.60). Further, it should be recognized that access is not the same as influence. Thus, Lowe and Goyder's research (1983, pp.63–5) revealed, in the early 1980s, that while environmental groups regarded most government departments and agencies as either 'entirely accessible' or 'very accessible', many departments were regarded as generally unreceptive to their point of view.

It has also been pointed out that environmental groups risk being 'imprisoned' by the executive, forced to moderate their demands in order to gain access to decision-makers without gaining the influence that this strategy requires (Sandbach, 1980, ch.1). Thus, it might be argued that one of the main functions, or at least one of the consequences, of the state conservation agencies has been to provide a pseudo-governmental arena within which environmental groups can participate, thereby giving the impression of influence, while officials and ministers are left alone to make the major decisions (Lowe and Goyder, 1983, p.67). Nevertheless, despite these reservations about access, it is fair to say that influence without access is unlikely, not least because if the demands made by a particular group generate a significant degree of support, access of one kind or another is likely to follow.

The influence of the environmental lobby

A cursory glance at the ability of the environmental lobby to influence decision-makers reveals, from their perspective, a somewhat depressing picture. A crucial problem faced is the need to influence a number of government departments. Environmental groups have always had reasonably good access to the Department of the Environment (Lowe *et al.*, 1986, p.121) but targeting the Department of the Environment by itself is not sufficient because, despite its name, environmental issues are only part of its remit and, in addition, it is not responsible for many of the major decisions that impact on the environment (see Chapter 5). Thus, it is the development-oriented departments – in particular, Trade and Industry, Transport and the Ministry of Agriculture, Fisheries and Food (MAFF) – which hold the key to effective environmental policy, and these are the very departments which the environmental lobby has found difficulty in penetrating (Lowe and Goyder, 1983, p.63).

Access to the development-oriented departments, then, tends to be restricted to a small number of powerful interest groups which have a vested economic interest in preventing environmental protection issues from being considered. Thus, the road lobby is influential within the Department of Transport and the industrial lobby within the Department of Trade and Industry. The classic case of this type of decision-making structure, which political scientists have characterized as a policy community, is the close relationship between MAFF and the National Farmers Union. This relationship is examined in depth in Chapter 8. Here, it is worth mentioning an important illustration of the policy community at work. This concerns the Wildlife and Countryside Act 1981. Despite being one of, if not *the*, most important conservation measures passed since 1945, only one conservation group, the RSPB, was consulted thoroughly by MAFF during the formulation stage. Not even the state conservation agencies were involved until after the proposals were announced and by then it was too late to make radical changes (Lowe *et al.*, 1986; Cox and Lowe, 1983).

There is some evidence that the relationship between environmental groups and key government departments has 'improved markedly' in recent years (McCormick, 1991, p.40). Young (1993, pp.62–3) suggests that MAFF has become more responsive to environmental concerns and our case study in Chapter 8 does confirm this. As Young himself admits, however, there has not been a fundamental change in patterns of decision-making and, as Chapter 5 demonstrates, environmental policy in Britain has been cautious and, particularly if one accepts that environmental problems are severe, inadequate.

Pressure group resources

One factor, albeit not the only or even the most important one, which may explain policy outputs is the resources groups can utilize in an attempt to achieve their objectives. A number can be identified. First is a group's *expertise*. Decision-makers, other things being equal, are not interested in sloganizing or moral arguments. What they appreciate is accurate information and practical solutions to technical problems. The RSPB's great expertise in bird conservation, for instance, gives it considerable advantages when approaching government (Lowe and Goyder, 1983, p.58). Similarly, Friends of the Earth has focused increasingly on providing technical information and one would expect it to reap the benefits of this change in strategy.

Another factor is the *resources* a group can muster. Money buys not just competent lobbyists and the means to publicize a group's objectives, but also enables the appointment of highly qualified researchers to provide the expertise a wealthy group like the RSPB can muster. Resources apply not just to finance but to the advantages a group's membership can provide. This can be in terms of mobilizing the membership to put pressure on public authorities. It can also refer to the quality of the membership. In particular, articulate professionals can be a great asset. Thus, as Lowe and Goyder (1983, pp.91–6) point out, local conservation groups have predominantly middle-class professional memberships. More importantly, many can boast architects, planners and even appointed and/or elected members of local authorities among their number. Such groups are usually given consultative status because they can help a local authority meet its statutory obligations both to consult interested parties and fulfil conservation objectives (Young, 1993, p.20).

The most important resource a group can muster is its ability to exercise *sanctions*. Here the economic functions performed by interest groups, such as farmers and industry, in terms of providing employment and generating wealth, can be a crucial factor in determining how a government, ever aware of the electoral consequences of an economic downturn, will respond (Lindblom, 1977). Clearly, this is extremely relevant to environmental measures which many perceive, rightly or wrongly, to have economic costs.

Environmental groups, however, have some sanctions of their own. One is their ability to cause delays through the planning system. This is a form of influence which may be anticipated by developers who, to avoid a costly and time-consuming inquiry, may change their plans to incorporate the objections of environmentalists. A related sanction is the use of direct action, which may have the effect of delaying development projects and increasing the costs involved because of the greater security provision necessary (see below for more detail on direct action as a tactic for environmentalists).

A further sanction relates to the ability of environmental groups to generate public support for their objectives which governments may have to take into account (Lowe and Goyder, 1983, pp.59–60; Marsh, 1983, p.15). A recent example has been the highly publicized campaigns against the veal trade, which has forced a response from the government, however inadequate. The evidence does suggest that once an issue creates problems for governments, in terms of public disorder or electoral opposition, for instance, they are forced to act (Gamson, 1975). A crucial point here, though, is that public support alone is not enough since it is the saliency of an issue, or the strength of feeling relative to other issues, that matters. Thus, it might be argued that the high level of public support for environmentalism is somewhat deceptive since, when it came to the crunch, elections in the 1980s and 1990s were still won or lost on the so-called 'feel good' factor which relates to narrow material standards of living (see Chapter 7).

Outsider activities and direct action

Unable to gain regular and intense access to decision-makers, most of the environmental movement's attention is directed to outsider activity which involves campaigning to raise media and public awareness of environmental issues in order to influence public authorities directly. Thus, demonstrations, petitions, public meetings and the distribution of literature remain important activities. It might be argued too that Parliament's impotence in the British system puts the lobbying of MPs in the outsider category, although the influence of the House of Commons will vary, depending particularly on the size of the governing party's majority. In normal circumstances since the Second World War, only when no party lines are attached to a bill will significant numbers of MPs be open to persuasion. The importance of much environmental legislation, and the fact that much of it is dictated by decisions made by the European Union, means that it is extremely rare for Parliament to become a genuine decision-making arena. Environmental groups can take advantage of its scrutiny role though, and many groups do give evidence to select committees in the House of Commons (particularly the environment committee) and both the science and technology committee and the European Union committee (which scrutinizes European proposals) in the House of Lords.

It is important to distinguish between those activities that reflect a reluctant outsider status and those that reflect a suspicion of normal decision-making channels. In the latter category we can further distinguish between those that remain outsiders because they are aware of the dangers of being 'captured' by government and those that seek to bypass the public policy route entirely. This last category includes all those activities under the heading of direct action.

Direct action is an important aspect of the environmental movement's armoury. It covers a huge variety of actions and should not be thought synonymous with illegality. It includes, for instance, attempts to influence consumer behaviour and, indirectly, the behaviour of producers and retailers. The emphasis on the 'Green consumer' was an important strategy of environmentalists and in the late 1980s it began to reap dividends. Direct action also involves non-violent civil disobedience, such as sit-ins at motorway sites, sabotaging hunts and the well-known Greenpeace tactic of monitoring and disrupting whale hunts, all of which fall on the boundaries of illegality (on the recent upsurge in road protests, see *Guardian*, 10 July 1993; 7 December 1994; 13 February 1995). It is often difficult to draw a hard-and-fast distinction between direct action and more traditional pressure group activity since it is at least partly aimed at generating publicity which helps to put pressure on decision-makers. The work of the Environmental Investigation Agency, for instance, produces much valuable information which can be used by general campaigning groups.

At the other end of the spectrum are more extreme activities. The Sea Shepherd Conservation Society, for instance, was formed in 1977 by Paul Watson, who was expelled from Greenpeace for his willingness to pursue a more rigorous and aggressive form of direct action. The organization has been responsible for attacking pirate whaling ships and, in one particularly notable action, for causing extensive damage to a whale processing station in Iceland. It now claims 30,000 members worldwide, over half of whom are in the United States (Allaby, 1986, p.213; *Guardian*, 21 September 1994). Similarly, a group called Earth First! has, originally in America and now in Britain, advocated, and carried out, attacks (known as ecotage) on equipment used on construction sites. Even more controversially, activists have driven long nails into trees with the intention of, at best, deterring loggers and, at worst, seriously injuring them (Axelrod and Phillips, 1993, p.73; Young, 1993, p.22). The deep ecology focus of Earth First! has sometimes led it to anti-human conclusions, some followers advocating illiberal policies such as mass sterilization and others contemplating with equanimity the possible consequences of the AIDS virus (Vincent, 1993, p.267). There is no reason to believe, however, that such views are widely held among Earth First! activists and, in as far as they are, it tends to apply more to the movement in the United States than in Britain.

The Animal Liberation Front (ALF), too, has adopted a wide range of direct action strategies (Garner, 1993a, ch. 8). This has most notably included breaking into factory farms and laboratories where the animals may be released, equipment destroyed and evidence of ill-treatment compiled. Some animal rights activists have also been associated with planting incendiary devices in the premises of fur retailers and even seeking to target the homes of scientists engaged in vivisection. The ALF denies responsibility for much of this, and seeks to draw a distinction between harming people and harming property. Such a distinction is, theoretically at least, possible to make and it is important to note that not one person has been killed as a result of the activities of radical environmentalists/animal liberationists. The ALF, however, consists of autonomous cells of activists and, for obvious reasons, has no hierarchical organizational structure. The important fact, therefore, is that some activists are prepared, rightly or wrongly, to intimidate those involved in the use of animals and risk physically harming people.

We have seen in this chapter that the environmental movement has grown extensively in the past twenty years or so and that it has become even more complex in terms of ends and means. The vast majority of groups however, seek, at least part of the time, to influence public policy outcomes by using traditional campaigning and lobbying methods. To assess how successful they have been we need to examine how the political system has responded. It is to this we now turn.

Further reading

Not a great deal of serious academic research has been done on the environmental movement. Lowe and Goyder (1982) remains the most thorough coverage but is now somewhat dated, as is Kimber and Richardson (1974), although the latter does provide some case studies of important issues. There are chapters in Young (1993) and McCormick (1991) worth reading, Porritt and Winner (1988) is also useful, as is Grant's (1989) study of pressure groups in general. The international environmental movement is tackled by McCormick (1992), Mazey and Richardson (1992) and Boardman (1981). There are studies on particular parts of the movement. Much useful information on the conservation movement is provided in Evans (1991), Warren and Goldsmith (1983) and Lowe *et al.* (1986). The animal protection movement is examined in Garner (1993a; 1993b; 1995) and R. Thomas (1983), and the anti-nuclear lobby is discussed in Ward (1983). McTaggart (1978) is a very personal account of the development of Greenpeace. The debate about the rise of environmentalism is summarized in Martell (1994). The chief protagonists are Inglehart (1977; 1990) and Cotgrove and Duff (1980; 1981). Reference should also be made to Lowe and Rudig (1986) for a critique of cultural and structural explanations.

5

POLITICAL INSTITUTIONS AND ENVIRONMENTAL POLICY IN BRITAIN

This chapter examines environmental policy and the structure of environmental decision-making in Britain – the real nitty-gritty of environmental politics. It will describe the institutions responsible for environmental decision-making and the major pieces of legislation giving rise to this institutional structure and the way in which its constituent parts operate. In addition, some of the major issues arising from this decision-making structure are considered. In the first place, it will be asked how effective Britain's system of land-use planning is. Second, it will be asked how far Britain's pollution control system has changed from the traditional emphasis on pragmatism, flexibility and fragmentation towards a more rigorous, standardized and integrated one. Finally, the case for at least partly replacing the traditional regulatory approach with a system of economic instruments is assessed.

Environmental legislation

When considering Britain's environmental legislation, the haphazard and piecemeal way in which it has been introduced quickly becomes apparent. Indeed, at least until recently – and perhaps not even now – Britain did not have a policy for the environment, in the sense of a clearly laid out and consistent plan integrated across the whole range of governmental activities (Young, 1993, pp.65–6). Britain's environmental protection system machinery consequently is very difficult to describe.

For many centuries, attempts have been made to deal with the environmental problems that emerged from time to time. Thus, a decree issued by Edward I in 1273 to prohibit the burning of sea coal is said to be the first environmental regulation in Britain (Vogel, 1986, p.31). Modern practice, however, dates back to the nineteenth century. Since then, numerous statutes have moulded the system which exists today. In chronological order, the main measures are as follows:

1853 Smoke Nuisance Abatement (Metropolis) Act

1863 Alkali Act

1876 Rivers Pollution Prevention Act

1906 Alkali and Works Regulation Act

1947 Town and Country Planning Act

1949 National Parks and Access to the Countryside Act

1953 Navigable Waters Act

1954 Protection of Birds Act

1955 Rural Water Supplies and Sewage Act

1956 Clean Air Act

1958 Litter Act

1960 Radioactive Substances Act

1960 Estuaries and Tidal Waters Act

1961 Rivers (Prevention of Pollution) Act

1963 Deer Act

1963 Water Resources Act

1968 Countryside Act

1968 Agriculture (Miscellaneous Provisions) Act

1969 Creation of the Royal Commission on Environmental Pollution

1970 Creation of the Department of the Environment

1972 Deposit of Poisonous Wastes Act

1973 Water Act

1974 Control of Pollution Act

1974 Dumping at Sea Act

1975 Conservation of Wild Creatures and Wild Plants Act

1976 Endangered Species (Import and Export) Act

1980 Local Government, Planning and Land Act

1981 Wildlife and Countryside Act

1986 Housing and Planning Act

1986 Agriculture Act

1986 Food and Environment Protection Act

1986 Animals (Scientific Procedures) Act

1987 Creation of Her Majesty's Inspectorate of Pollution

1988 Agriculture Act

1989 Water Act (created the National Rivers Authority)

1990 Environmental Protection Act

1990 (September) White Paper *This Common Inheritance* published

The most effective way of making sense of these measures is to distinguish between the two main systems through which environmental policy is implemented (Blowers, 1987, p.279). In order to avoid complications here, I have excluded the policy machinery involved in regulating the welfare of animals (for a more detailed treatment, see Garner, 1993a; 1995). However, some reference to animal welfare policy-making is made in chapter 8, particularly in the case studies on agricultural policy making and the International Whaling Commission. In this chapter, we shall focus on development and conservation issues which are resolved through the land-use planning system and the pollution control system concerned with regulating emissions into the air, water and soil.

A number of points can be made about these two systems before we go on to describe them in detail. First, in both cases, Britain is unique in having the world's first national pollution agency and a more comprehensive system of land-use planning than anywhere else (Vogel, 1986, p.144). Second, as we had cause to point out in Chapter 4, much of the controversy surrounding the environment

in the post-war years has centred on development and conservation issues. This is a direct consequence of the greater visibility of
the issues, both in terms of the effects of decisions (or inaction)
and in terms of the ability of interested actors to participate in the
making of these decisions. It is also a product of the fact that
agriculture, protected by extensive state support, had grown
throughout the 1970s and early 1980s, whereas, in the same period,
industrial pollution and major capital projects (such as the Chan-
nel Tunnel) were constrained by the recession. Third, it should be
noted that the two systems are not entirely separate. Local authorities, for instance, will be concerned with the possible pollution
resulting from developments when they decide whether or not to
grant planning permission to them. The difference is that, once
granted, planning permission cannot be revoked and control over
emissions is exercised by the pollution control system.

A further overlap is that the Department of the Environment
(DoE) figures heavily in both systems. The DoE was created in
1970 as a result of the amalgamation of the Ministries of Housing
and Local Government, Public Buildings and Works, and Transport. Since then, transport issues have been devolved to a separate
department and the Department of Energy was abolished in 1992,
most of its environmental functions going to the DoE. Despite its
name, environmental protection has proved to be a relatively small
part of the DoE's responsibilities. Particularly in the 1980s it spent
a disproportionate amount of time and effort on more general
local government affairs and, as McCormick (1991, p.17) points
out, until the appointment of Chris Patten in 1989, no Environment Secretary had shown any particular interest in the natural
environment.

As we indicated in Chapter 4, many key environmental responsibilities remain with other departments such as Transport
(responsible for vehicle emissions and transport noise), Trade
and Industry (responsible for elements of energy policy) and
MAFF (responsible for environmentally sensitive areas, pesticide
control, farm waste management and animal welfare). Further,
the Treasury has a significant influence as the holder of the purse
strings. Moreover, there is a whole network of so-called quasi-
governmental agencies with responsibilities that impact on the
environment. As well as those specifically concerned with promoting environmental objectives (on which see below), mention

can also be made of urban development corporations, the Agricultural Development Advisory Service, British Rail and the British Tourist Authority (Young, 1993, p.57).

Development and conservation

As Figure 5.1 demonstrates, the centrepiece of the system designed to resolve development and conservation conflicts is the land-use planning system. In the nineteenth century, local authorities were given powers to clear slum areas for redevelopment, but the modern land-use planning system dates back to a series of Town and Country Planning Acts introduced since the 1920s (Vogel, 1986, p.108). There were attempts by the Thatcher governments, which were ideologically opposed to restrictions on the free market and hostile to Labour-controlled local authorities, to remove some planning powers, particularly in urban areas (Blowers, 1987), but the system remains largely intact and, as we shall see, from an environmental perspective at least, it has been positively added to.

The major piece of legislation remains the Town and Country Planning Act 1947. This effectively took the development of private property under public control. The legislation requires that all proposed development be subject to planning permission by the relevant local authority. Thus, local authorities draw up extensive development plans and will consider individual development applications in the light of the overall plan, either rejecting the proposal outright or attaching conditions to their permission. Since 1968, the public have had a statutory right to be consulted over individual applications. Although a meeting of the full council is usually required to approve decisions, the real power lies with local planning authorities, which consist of those councillors who are members and the planning officials who serve them.

Ultimate authority rests with the Secretary of State for the Environment since, if the planning authority rejects an application or insists on conditions unacceptable to the applicant, there is a right of appeal (to the DoE in England or the Welsh or Scottish Office). Only the applicant has the right of appeal so that an environmental group, for instance, cannot appeal against the granting of an application. The Secretary of State can then decide to reject or uphold

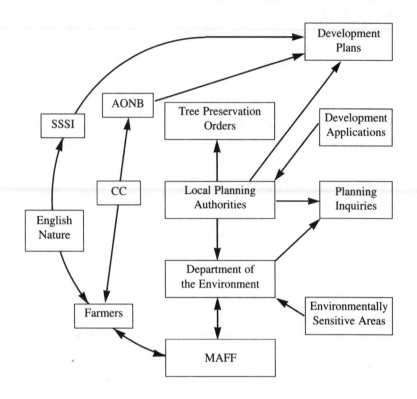

AONB = Areas of Outstanding Natural Beauty.
CC = Countryside Commission.
MAFF = Ministry of Agriculture, Fisheries and Food.
SSSI = Sites of Special Scientific Interest.

Figure 5.1   Development and conservation: institutional structure

the appeal or, which is most likely in controversial cases, order the setting up of a public inquiry. The Inspector appointed by the Secretary of State will then hold an inquiry and submit a report usually containing a recommendation which the Secretary of State can accept or reject (Vogel, 1986, pp.108–9). One other option the Secretary has is to 'call in' an application before it has been discussed by the local planning authority, thereby bypassing the usual procedure.

The state conservation agencies

In addition to the planning system, development and conservation issues are also the direct concern of the state conservation agencies, namely English Nature and the Countryside Commission (CC), responsible to the DoE, and the Forestry Commission, responsible to the MAFF in England and the Secretaries of State for Wales and Scotland. English Nature and the CC were created by the National Parks and Access to the Countryside Act 1949. The former was created as the National Parks Commission, was later renamed as the Nature Conservancy and then, in 1973, the Nature Conservancy Council (NCC). Its present name derives from changes made in the late 1980s and enshrined in the Environmental Protection Act 1990. In Scotland and Wales the NCC and the Countryside Commission were combined to form the Scottish National Heritage and the Countryside Council for Wales. In England the established division between conservation and amenity remains (Young, 1993, p.58). The motivation for these changes was in part cost cutting and in part the government's irritation at the Nature Conservancy Council's opposition to Scottish Office conservation policy. Thus, the new Scottish National Heritage could be controlled more effectively by the Scottish Office than the DoE-sponsored NCC (Ward, 1990, p.226). The criticism of the conservation community was placated somewhat by the creation (also in the 1990 Act) of a Joint Nature Conservation Committee.

The major task of English Nature is to identify areas of the country which have a particularly important flora, fauna or geology. Once identified, it then recommends to the Secretary of State that these areas be designated as sites of special scientific interest (SSSI). At present, there are 5,700 SSSI in Great Britain, covering 7 per cent of the land. It also has responsibility for creating national nature reserves, of which there are 242 in Great Britain, and, in consultation with local authorities, it may also designate areas as 'local nature reserves' (Rydin, 1993, p.127). In keeping with the historical distinction between conservation and amenity in Britain, the Countryside Commission is concerned with identifying areas which can be designated as Areas of Outstanding Natural Beauty (AONB) or as national parks. There are now thirty-nine AONBs in England and Wales, covering some 13 per cent of the land area (*ibid.*, p.122). There are seven national parks in England and three in Wales, which, once designated, are run by separate authorities. Similarly, in conjunction with local authorities, the Countryside Commission also identifies coastlines with a particularly scenic quality (designated as 'heritage coasts') and establishes 'countryside parks' (Lowe and Goyder, 1983).

The final agency with a specific conservation function is the Forestry Commission. This was set up in 1919 as a result of a post-war timber shortage and performs both a commercial and a regulatory function, existing as a nationalized forestry concern selling timber from forests it has grown on its own land, as well as regulating the private forestry sector. The Forestry Commission is responsible to MAFF as well as to the Welsh and Scottish Offices, the latter, because of the concentration of forests in Scotland, acting as the main sponsoring department (Grant, 1989, pp.140–1). The environmental effects of both deforestation and inappropriate afforestation (the planting of uniform coniferous forests and the destruction of ancient woodlands) can have severe environmental consequences (Lowe *et al.*, 1986, pp.46–50) and, although the Forestry Commission has had responsibility for recreation and conservation since 1967, critics contend that it is far too close to private timber interests and therefore pays insufficient attention to the damage caused by their activities (Grant, 1989, pp.141–5).

The planning system – pros and cons

There are two main positive aspects of the planning system. First, by allowing for a great deal of public participation, environmental groups can have a significant input into important conservation issues. As we saw in Chapter 4, local authorities will often seek the help of conservationists when taking decisions, not least during the process of drawing up their development plans. Second, local authorities must increasingly take into account environmental factors when drawing up a development plan. Thus, since 1991, the DoE has specifically instructed planning authorities to pay particular attention to the way in which local authorities can help to promote sustainable development and the effects development is likely to have on global warming and the quality of air and water. Likewise, a 1985 European directive (implemented in 1991) makes it mandatory for developers seeking permission for major projects such as oil refineries and power stations to produce an environmental statement, documenting the environmental effects of the development. This is potentially very useful for environmentalists who, as Young points out, have often been at a disadvantage because they lacked the resources to gather such information (Rydin, 1993, p.101; Young, 1993, pp.61–2). Now, they hope their opponents will provide it for them.

From an environmental perspective, however, there are still weaknesses in the land-use planning system. First, environmentalists cannot appeal against a decision to grant planning permission, nor can they insist on a public inquiry. Furthermore, not only are the terms of major public inquiries (known as public local inquiries) usually narrow – environmentalists cannot challenge the need for a motorway but only challenge the chosen route (Vogel, 1986, pp.135–7) – but also the financial resources available to developers are usually far greater than those of any environmental group (see Chapter 8). Third, in some circumstances, the element of public participation in planning decisions can work against environmentalists, since developers can draw support from the local community by pointing to the economic benefits a particular project can bring. As Vogel (1986, p.127) points out:

> In the case of pollution control, the lack of opportunities for public participation may mean that less weight is given to environmental considerations; in the case of the planning system, however, it is often precisely the relative accountability of local planning authorities to public pressures that undermines the political influence of amenity interests.

A classic instance of this was documented by Andrew Blowers (1984), who demonstrated how opposition to further development at a Bedfordshire brickworks in the late 1970s was defeated by the recession of the early 1980s which changed the priorities of the local trade unions.

An additional, and crucial, weakness of the planning system is the relative positions of the state conservation agencies and farmers. We have seen that neither the CC nor English Nature (or, prior to 1991, the NCC) have played any significant part in the formulation of conservation legislation. Likewise the planning system takes precedence over the designation of SSSIs and AONB. In other words, while there may be a presumption against development in designated areas (and such areas are marked on local authority development plans) English Nature and the CC have no statutory authority to determine land use, only the right to persuade and cajole.

By far the biggest problem faced by the state conservation agencies is their inability to control agricultural development. For reasons that are explored in Chapter 8, the Town and Country Planning Act 1947 excluded agriculture from any planning constraints and, despite attempts to close this gap since then the position is largely unaltered today (Rydin, 1993, p.117). English Nature and the CC have been given the authority to conclude management agreements with farmers and some funds to offer as compensation, but their resources are generally considered to be inadequate for the task (Vogel, 1986, pp.140–2; Pearce *et al.*, 1993, pp.111–13).

One final point is worth making here. Even if the state conservation agencies did have statutory power to insist on the protection of land as an SSSI or AONB, which they do not, this would still leave the vast majority of the countryside unprotected. As Evans (1991, p.xxiv) points out, the designated National Parks, nature reserves and country parks amount to no more than 10 per cent of the total British land area of 22.7 million ha.

Pollution control

Pollution control mechanisms have been subject to a great deal of change in the past two decades or so, and it is important to document these changes before going on to examine their character and significance.

The traditional approach to pollution control

The traditional British approach to pollution control was based on a regulatory system focusing either on particular substances (radioactive or toxic waste) or particular media (air, water, soil). As a result, a whole range of inspectorates grew up in a haphazard way to check emissions from industrial processes. The first of these was the Alkali Inspectorate set up in 1863 to enforce the Alkali Act of the same year, which sought to remove most of the hydrochloric acid emitted by alkali manufacturers (Vogel, 1986, p.32). Over time the Alkali Inspectorate became a more general air pollution inspectorate as more and more industrial processes came under its control. To reflect this wider remit, in 1982 it was renamed the Industrial Air Pollution Inspectorate (IAPI). By the early 1980s, the IAPI was just one of a network of inspectorates including the Wastes Inspectorate, the Radioactive Substances Inspectorate and the Water Quality Inspectorate (Weale, 1992, p.105). In addition, local authorities were responsible for domestic sources of pollution and those industrial processes not covered by the inspectorates. Thus, for instance, local authorities were given powers to control smoke emissions from coal fires under the Clean Air Act 1956 passed in response to the London smogs of the 1950s (Scarrow, 1961).

Despite the number of agencies concerned with pollution control, the operating procedures of the inspectorates were remarkably uniform (Hawkins, 1984). Typically, inspectors would visit factories and enter into negotiations until agreement was reached on the volume and nature of the pollution that would be permitted. Thus, the stringency of the conditions applied to authorizations would vary from plant to plant depending on the inspectorate's definition of the 'best practicable option' (BPO) operating principle established in the Alkali and Works Regulation Act 1906.

This procedure enabled inspectors to take into account the ability of the plant to meets the costs of improvement, the economic importance of the process, the environmental threat posed by the pollutant and the ability of a particular medium to absorb a particular substance (Vogel, 1986, pp.70–80; O'Riordan and Weale, 1989, pp.278–9). This negotiated consent was concluded in secret with little public access to information on the grounds that cooperation could only be sustained if confidentiality was maintained (Jordan, 1993, p.408). Moreover, formal legal action was very rarely taken, the inspectors preferring to persuade and cajole. Thus, between 1920 and 1966 only two firms were prosecuted for breaches of the inspectorate's authorization (Vogel, 1986, p.88). Finally, because the emphasis was on single medium control (air, water or soil), if an industrial process was polluting in more than one it would have to seek multiple authorization or multiple permissions (Weale, 1992, p.95).

The changing nature of pollution control

Considerable changes have occurred in the institutional structure of British pollution control in recent years, and it is worthwhile sketching out the present state of affairs (see Figure 5.2) before we move on to consider some of the key debates behind these changes. These changes have been typically haphazard and incremental but, at the very least, the traditional structure of pollution control has been at least modified if not transformed.

We noted earlier that the DoE is itself a relatively new institution dating back to 1970. Relatively new too is the Royal Commission on Environmental Pollution (RCEP), which was created in 1969 in response to environmental concern. It has no executive powers but its reports are authoritative and can sometimes, as with the 1994 report advocating measures to cut car use significantly, hit the headlines and contribute to a change in government policy (*Guardian*, 27 October 1994). Most notably, the RCEP was responsible in the 1970s for recommending the streamlining of pollution control agencies (Weale, 1992, p.102), but it was not until 1987 that this became a reality with the creation of Her Majesty's Inspectorate of Pollution (HMIP) within the DoE, and not until the Environmental Protection Act 1990 that it was given powers concomitant with the role assigned to it.

HMIP is an amalgam of the separate pollution inspectorates, with IAPI at the centre. The aim was to integrate pollution control in order to rationalize the existing system, preventing the inefficiency and the cross-media transfer of pollutants inherent in multiple permitting (see below). Thus, the aim is to introduce a system of overall site licences based on the 'best practical environmental options' (BPEO), a principle reflecting the multi-medium approach of integrated pollution control (IPC) (Ward, 1990, p.227). This will operate in tandem with the principle of 'best available techniques not entailing excessive costs' (BATNEEC), the term replacing, but meaning much the same as, BPO in the Environmental Protection Act.

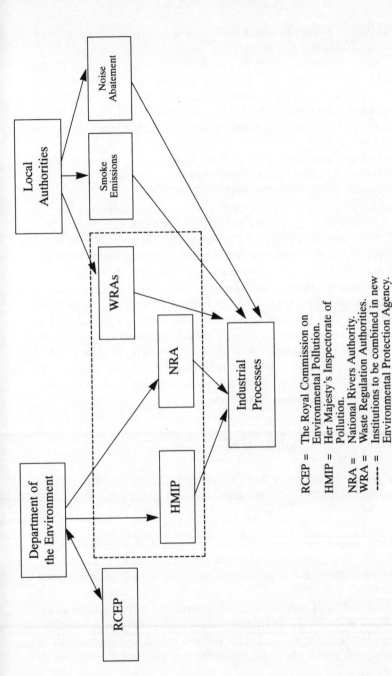

RCEP = The Royal Commission on
       Environmental Pollution.
HMIP = Her Majesty's Inspectorate of
       Pollution.

NRA = National Rivers Authority.
WRA = Waste Regulation Authorities.
----- = Institutions to be combined in new
       Environmental Protection Agency.

Figure 5.2 Pollution control: institutional structure

BATNEEC will apply where pollutants can only be released to one medium (Young, 1993, p.60).

The final change of note was the creation of the National Rivers Authority (NRA) in 1989, which came about as a consequence of water privatization (see Chapter 8). The NRA has regulatory power over water pollution as well as responsibility for land drainage, fisheries, conservation and recreation. Prior to this, all aspects of water management – including sewage treatment and disposal and industrial emissions – was in the hands of ten Regional Water Authorities created by the Water Act 1973. By splitting water use from environmental responsibilities, however it came about, there is an assumption that water quality will improve, although there is only some evidence (see below) that this has actually occurred.

At the time of writing, the government has proposed to move the process of IPC one step further by combining the work of the NRA, HMIP and the waste regulation authorities in a new Environmental Protection Agency, to be established by January 1996 with a combined budget of £528 million (*Guardian*, 14 October 1994). This was the only domestic environmental commitment in the 1992 Conservative manifesto. Details of the government's intentions were announced in September 1994 but, despite the fact that the original proposals were later modified to meet some of the concerns expressed by environmentalists, weaknesses in the proposals were still evident (see below).

Pollution control debates

The preceding sketch of Britain's pollution control system raises a number of issues which we shall now consider. In the first place, there is a consensus among environmentalists, and increasingly governments too, that a move towards *integrated pollution control* is a key part of the ecological modernization strategy (Weale, 1992, p.96). We need here, then, to explain what is meant by the concept, what advantages are claimed for it and how far Britain has moved towards it.

Integration, of course, can be contrasted with fragmentation. Fragmentation in the environmental sphere occurs in two dimensions. First, there is the fragmentation which occurs because a number of government departments are responsible for policy action or inaction impacting on the environment. One form of integration (often called 'external integration'), therefore, refers to the attempt to incorporate an environmental dimension into all relevant policy areas – transport, energy, agriculture, and so on. External integration occurs, therefore, as Weale and Williams (1993, p.46) point out: 'when decision-makers in other policy sectors take into account environmental consequences in the making of their decisions and make suitable adjustments to their plans and the execution of those plans when environmental implications are recognised'. Following Jordan (1993, p.407), this form of integration is 'comprehensive, precautionary and preventative' in nature in that it seeks to deal with environmental problems at source (through, for instance, promoting public transport or prohibiting the use of certain substances) rather than dealing with pollution once it has occurred.

Another form of fragmentation occurs when a number of separate agencies are responsible for regulating emissions into the air, water or soil. Another form of integration (often called 'internal integration'), therefore, refers to the attempt to combine under one authority the responsibility for regulating all emissions into all mediums, whether it be air, water or soil. Again following Jordan (1993, p.407), this form of integration is 'reactive' in nature in that it seeks to deal with waste once it is produced.

The advantage of IPC is that it is more in accord with the nature of the problem. As Jordan (*ibid.*, 1993, p.406) points out:

> One of the inherent failings of environmental management systems in many countries has been the fundamental mismatch between the complex and holistic nature of environmental problems and the fragmented and sectorised institutions that have been created to deal with them.

Thus, in the case of internal integration, a fragmented regulatory system is not only inefficient, requiring a number of visits and separate authorizations, but also tends not to produce an optimal distribution of emissions (or pollution in the round) since an overall perspective is difficult to arrive at and pollution tends merely to be displaced from one medium to another (Dryzek, 1987, pp.10–13; Weale, 1992, pp.93–5). Likewise, in the case of external integration, the ability of the DoE to deal with environmental problems is limited if those departments and agencies responsible for policy areas having an impact on the environment do little or nothing to incorporate an environmental perspective.

When discussing the extent to which Britain has moved down the integration road, it is important to recognize that integration is an ideal type which does not exist anywhere in the world. Some countries – Sweden and the Netherlands, say – have, though, come closer than most (Weale, 1992, pp.94, 98, 125–52). In Britain the creation of HMIP was guided by the principle of internal integration and the Environmental Protection Act formally recognized the principle through the adoption of the BPEO operational criteria (Bradbeer, 1994, p.124), which was designed, as the RCEP pointed out, to provide 'the most benefit or the least damage to the environment as a whole' (O'Riordan and Weale, 1989, p.289).

There is some cause for concern, though. The resources of HMIP are limited, the agency having a deficit of £3 million in 1991–2 (Jordan, 1993, p.415), hampering its ability to attract qualified staff able to undertake the complicated task of fulfilling IPC. Furthermore, IPC is not being introduced very quickly. It took four years from its creation for HMIP's powers to be made available (in April 1991) and even then not all processes were to be subject to the BPEO procedure. A rolling programme is envisaged whereby it is hoped that all those processes producing more 'difficult' wastes (estimated to be about 5,000) will be subject to IPC by 1996 (*ibid.*, p.414). This, of course, leaves many processes uncovered by IPC. Some are to be regulated by HMIP in the traditional single medium fashion, local authorities still have responsibility for a great deal of air pollution and, for the time being at least, the NRA is a separate agency operating independently from, albeit closely to, HMIP.

As we pointed out above, the separation of the NRA and HMIP will not last much longer as the government has put forward proposals for the creation of an Environmental Protection Agency (EPA). The original draft proposals were criticized by environmentalists and opposition MPs. This was partly on the grounds that the powers to be given to the EPA are less extensive than the existing powers of its constituent elements. In the original proposals, the EPA was merely to 'have regard to the desirability of conserving and enhancing the environment' whereas the NRA is, at present, required to '*further* the conservation and enhancement' of the environment. Critics also pointed out that the clause which required the EPA 'to take into account costs which are likely to be incurred, and the benefits which are likely to accrue' from environmental measures would allow industry to avoid pollution control measures on the grounds of costs alone, taking court action, if necessary, to establish their case. Finally, the EPA is to have little independence from the government, its ten board members being chosen by the government, and will be largely under its control. Crucially, capital expenditure will require the full support of the Treasury. There will be no representation for environmentalists, local authorities, trade unions or the business sector (*Guardian*, 10,11 and 14 October 1994).

As a result of the criticisms, John Gummer, the Environment Secretary, announced in November 1994 that the wording of the legislation would be amended so that the EPA will have to 'further' conservation and the enhancement of the environment as opposed to just considering it. Additional clauses were also inserted. These will give the EPA powers to deal with contaminated land and overspill from abandoned mine workings (*Guardian*, 19 November 1994). One final point that should be made is that, although at present it is perceived that ministerial control of the EPA threatens its ability to exercise powers to protect the environment, such control could, at some point in the future, be used to force or encourage the EPA to act so as to maximize environmental protection.

If we turn our attention to external integration, it becomes clear that even less has been achieved. The White Paper, *This Common Inheritance* (Department of the Environment, 1990) did address this issue by advocating policy co-ordination across the whole range of government activities and, to reflect this concern for integration, the document was presented not just by the DoE but also by the DTI, the Departments of Health, Energy, Employment, Transport and Education as well as MAFF. The language of *This Common Inheritance* was impeccably integrationist. It sought to ensure that 'policies fit together in every sector; that we are not undoing in one area what we are trying to do in another; and that policies are based on a harmonious set of principles rather than on a clutter of expedients' (p.8). To this end, the White Paper proposed that the cabinet committee (chaired by the prime minister) responsible for drawing up the White Paper should continue for the purpose of co-ordinating the government's environmental approach. In addition, it advocated the creation of a committee of ministers to draw up an energy efficiency programme and it recommended that each department has to nominate ministers responsible for environmental issues in their departments (Weale, 1992, p.124).

There is little evidence, however, that these proposals have amounted to very much and some commentators have suggested that the then Environment Secretary Chris Patten's original intentions for the White Paper were considerably watered down through the intervention of the Treasury and the Department of Transport (Bradbeer, 1994, p.126). In some ways, the White Paper was a 'milestone' since it did represent the first comprehensive statement of Britain's environmental policy (Flynn and Lowe, 1992, p.33). The reaction of the press was probably closer to the mark – the *Independent*, for instance, called it 'as feeble as it is lengthy' (it ran to 296 pages). Most of the 350 measures listed had already been implemented or announced and there were very few new commitments.

As far as the move towards external integration goes, it is true that at least some of the development-oriented departments have taken on a greener hue. MAFF, for instance, now emphasizes the conservationist role of agriculture far more than it used to, and even the Department of Transport has cut its road building programme. These are, however, still minor concessions. Farmers are not subject to many compulsory environmental controls (see above and Chapter 8) and the recently announced cuts in the road building programme owe more to the pressure on public spending than to environmental considerations (see Chapter 8) (*Guardian*, 30 November, 20 December 1994). As for the cabinet committee, Weale (1992, p.124) revealed that ten months after its creation was announced it had not met once!

Environmental standards

Another debate that has emerged in recent years concerns the choice between the traditional pragmatic British regulatory system involving negotiation, compromise and a case-by-case approach on the one hand, and the imposition of rigorous uniform standards on the other. The advantages of the latter is that it avoids the dangers of what has been described as an implementation deficit whereby the regulators 'go native' by becoming too close to the regulated (Weale, 1992, pp.17, 87; see also Sandbach, 1980, p.56). On the other hand, the enforcement of uniform standards may well lead to greater corporate resistance and much time-consuming and expensive litigation. David Vogel's comparative study of regulatory practices in Britain and the United States, for instance, revealed that:

> Britain's emphasis on voluntary compliance has not proved any more or less effective in achieving its objectives than the more adversarial and legislative approach adopted by policy makers in the United States. American regulatory policy has been more ambitious, but as a result it has produced greater resistance from business. British regulatory authorities demand less, but because their demands are perceived as reasonable, industry is more likely to comply with them. (Vogel, 1986, p.23)

It is true that setting strict emission standards for particular substances is likely to satisfy public opinion far more than a system based on consensus, informality and confidentiality. It may be the case, however, that the latter offers greater advantages on environmental grounds since it allows for the kind of cost-benefit, cross-media analysis not available to a more rigid system (Weale, 1992, p.115). It is important to remember here that the emission of a potential pollutant is not a problem (that is, it does not become a pollutant) until it damages targets (humans, animals and plants) in the environment (Haigh, 1990, p.13). It is not necessary, therefore, to restrict emissions of potential pollutants completely and, furthermore, one particular medium may be able to absorb far more of a potential pollutant, without damage being caused, than another. Finding the right balance would be far more difficult with a rigid system of environmental standards. Moreover, a more open system of pollution control, which is likely to accompany a system of rigid standards, would probably result in public pressure (and environmental campaigns) for zero emissions into certain media although this would not necessarily be the best environmental option.

On the other hand, administering a system of fixed uniform standards may be easier than assessing the quality of, say, water. It is a relatively simple task to determine whether a particular emission has exceeded the standard set than to try to find out which discharges are responsible if water quality objectives have been breached (Haigh, 1990, p.21). Quality standards and varying authorizations, though, do allow the flexibility required to protect particularly vulnerable parts of the environment and do prevent unnecessarily restrictive standards being set where the environment needs less protection.

There has been increasing pressure on Britain to replicate the uniform standards applied in other European countries, such as Germany, the Netherlands and Denmark, particularly since the European Union has adopted this idea. In recent EU Environmental Action Programmes, environmental objectives have been advocated whereby uniform emission standards are set as stringently as available technology allows, irrespective of the cost – the so-called BAT approach (O'Riordan and Weale, 1989, pp.290–1). Subsequently, this was amended to 'best available technology not exceeding excessive costs' (BATNEEC) which was incorporated into the Environmental Protection Act 1990 (Jordan, 1993, p.417). This amendment, of course, is crucial since what constitutes excessive cost is contentious and can only be resolved by negotiation on a case-by-case basis. British governments have consistently resisted the idea of uniform emission standards, insisting, instead, on meeting environmental quality objectives which allow for the varying of authorizations depending on the capacity of particular media to absorb pollutants (Haigh, 1990, pp.17–21). While the arguments in favour of this approach stand, it should also be noted that there is an element of economic self-interest in Britain's reluctance to accept uniform emission standards decided in the Council of Ministers. Britain has short, fast-flowing rivers, which would require less stringent emission standards than other rivers in Europe (Haigh, 1990, p.22).

Of all the agencies responsible for pollution control, the NRA has come closest to adopting a more rigid system. Its approach is still based on statutory water quality objectives, set by government, rather than uniform emission standards, but the NRA has aggressively sought to enforce water quality objectives, through the courts if necessary (Jordan, 1993, p.412; Pickering and Owen, 1994, pp.137–8). In addition, while negotiation remains a central aspect of HMIP's work, the process of applying for an authorization is now much more formal and there is much more distance between regulators and the regulated than existed previously (Jordan, 1993, pp.414–5).

Economic instruments

The final debate we shall consider in this section concerns the use of economic instruments as a means of replacing or supplementing regulatory standards. Those who advocate the use of economic instruments recognize that solving environmental problems requires that those who pollute should be made responsible for it, but they argue that regulatory standards are not the best way to internalize the externalities. Rather, they suggest that a system of incentives should be put into place to encourage good environmental practice.

The clearest example is a system of environmental taxes whereby companies or individuals are made to pay if they want to continue using a production method which causes pollution or to continue buying leaded petrol. In this way, what had previously been an external cost to the whole community is internalized, in so far as producers and consumers have to take the environment into account as an extra cost for themselves. A more elaborate system involves tradeable pollution permits. This is where pollution permits amounting in total to an acceptable level of emissions are allocated to waste generators in a particular area. Each individual firm can then decide whether to invest in cleaner technology and, if they do, they can sell their unwanted permit to other firms (Bradbeer, 1994, p.127). The aim of the system, of course, is to encourage cleaner technology because the costs of not doing so will be passed on to the consumer in the form of more expensive goods, which will reduce the competitiveness of the company.

Economic instruments are, at least superficially, an attractive proposition. In particular, they minimize the problems of implementation deficit and non-detection prevalent in regulatory approaches as well as being potentially much cheaper to enforce. There are, however, disadvantages. In the first place, environmentalists tend to be suspicious of economic instruments because although the aim is to discourage pollution, it appears at the same time to legitimize polluting activities (Bradbeer, 1994, p.127). Moreover, they are notoriously difficult to set at an optimal level and complex adjustments would be needed on a regular basis.

Taxes too raise problems for governments at both a political and an ideological level (Weale, 1992, pp.161–3). The recent imposition of VAT on domestic supplies of gas and electricity is a case in point here. The policy had a budgetary rather than an environmental objective but it was little different from a carbon tax aimed at encouraging energy conservation, so the problems associated with it are applicable to the environmental field. The major problem is that such a tax would hit the poorest hardest, raising questions not just of fairness but also of votes. The political problem may be alleviated by compensating the poorest but this is barely adequate in environmental terms since the incentive for conserving energy disappears for those receiving it (Weale, 1992, p.163). Finally, there is little to suggest that an extensive system of policing would not still be required to ensure that the economic instruments are enforced. At best, then, they only constitute a supplement to traditional regulatory practices.

In Britain, there has been much talk but little action over economic instruments. The idea was intrinsically attractive to Thatcherites who were hostile to regulatory bureaucracy. In addition, when Chris Patten became Environment Secretary in the late 1980s he appointed David Pearce, a noted advocate of environmental taxes, as his adviser (Pearce *et al.*, 1989). Despite this, economic instruments have not played a large role in government environmental policy. The introduction of lead-free petrol is one notable exception, as is the NRA's strategy of charging fees for discharges up to a certain level beyond which prohibition occurs (Young, 1993, p.69). Road pricing too seems a possible future development. Beyond these instances, the focus still remains strongly on the traditional regulatory approach.

In conclusion, our survey of the development of environmental policy in Britain reveals an incremental and cautious pattern with occasional periods of heightened activity. In the early 1980s, the government showed little interest in environmental issues and the general consensus was that Britain was lagging behind many of her European partners. By the late 1980s, this situation had changed with the government's greater interest reflected in the creation of HMIP, the passage of the Environmental Protection Act and the publication of *This Common Inheritance*. Even now, though, there is little cause for environmentalists to celebrate. Progress towards integrated pollution control remains slow, there are significant gaps in the planning system and enforceable standards are too often overlooked in favour of exhortation and encouragement.

This applies particularly in the area of transport policy, where little has been done to reduce reliance on the private motor car. Action here is especially urgent because of the potential problem of global warming. Any effective solutions to global warming, and to many other environmental problems, however, require an international response. It is to the international politics of the environment that we now turn.

Further reading

Introductory accounts of environmental legislation and decision-making in Britain can be found in McCormick (1991), Young (1993), Flynn and Lowe (1992), Blowers (1987), Ward (1990) and Bradbeer (1994). An indispensable study of the development of environmental controls in Britain and the United States is Vogel (1986). Hawkins (1984) is also useful. An up-to-date coverage of the planning law is provided by Rydin (1993) and a fascinating case study of the planning system in action can be found in Blowers (1984). The integration of pollution control policy is the main theme of Weale (1992), Jordan (1993) and O'Riordan and Weale (1989), while Pearce (1989; 1993) promotes ecological modernization and the use of financial incentives. *This Common Inheritance* (Department of the Environment, 1990) is the chief guide to the British government's commitment to integration and environmental policy in general.

6

THE INTERNATIONAL POLITICS OF THE ENVIRONMENT

The politics of the environment is increasingly being fought out at the international level and, even though this book is primarily about environmental politics in Britain, the importance of the international dimension demands a separate chapter on the subject. Clearly, what Britain does in environmental terms is now crucially dependent on agreements reached at the supra-national level. Equally importantly, it is widely recognized that the most critical environmental problems can only be tackled internationally. Standing head and shoulders above the others is the issue of Third World development, which is discussed in a separate section, but also provides the backdrop to much of the material in this chapter.

The drive towards internationalism

International agreements concerning the environment are not new. It has long been recognized that pollution does not respect national boundaries but requires co-operation between states to deal with it. This need has increased markedly in the last two to three decades. This is partly because environmental problems have worsened in terms of the rates of resource depletion and population growth, and these problems are now inextricably linked with

Third World development and the world economy. Indeed, the global environment has the potential to become a major source of conflict between North and South (Hurrell and Kingsbury, 1992b, p.39). In other words, it is now impossible to separate the issues of environment and development and, as a reflection of this, the term 'sustainable development' has entered the language of international environmental politics.

The international dimension of environmentalism has also become more prominent because of the identification of genuinely global problems, such as global warming and ozone depletion. Only global co-operation can hope to solve these problems. Because of these developments, what were originally national or regional problems have now taken on a global character. The contribution of deforestation to climate change, for example, makes it a far more important issue to the West (Hurrell and Kingsbury, 1992b, pp.2–3). Similarly, a decline in biodiversity has such far-reaching implications in terms of ecological stability and the medicinal potential it offers that it ceases to be a local issue.

Some areas of environmental damage do not have a transnational character but international agreements may still be necessary or desirable in the interests of trade competitiveness. Thus, one obstacle to the development of stringent national environmental laws is the pressure that is likely to be applied by business organizations, which see themselves being economically disadvantaged since they have to pay the costs of environmental protection while their competitors in other countries do not. As we shall see below, one of the major justifications for the European Union's intervention in environmental matters was precisely on the grounds of harmonizing national laws rather than any specific interest in environmental protection *per se* (Simpson, 1990, p.29).

The nature of international environmental regimes

An initial distinction we need to make is between international treaties and permanent international organizations. Some in both categories are directly concerned with the environment, others may have been designed for different purposes but have, or could have, a significant impact on the environment.

International organizations

Included in the list of international organizations performing a specific environmental function are, most notably, the United Nations Environment Programme (UNEP), the International Union for the Conservation of Nature and Natural Resources (IUCN) and the European Union (EU). UNEP was established in 1972 following the UN Conference on the Human Environment in Stockholm. The aim was that the UN should become 'the principal centre for international environmental cooperation' (Thacher, 1992, p.186). In reality, the UNEP's primary role has been in environmental assessment activities (monitoring, research and information exchange), particularly through its global assessment programme 'Earthwatch', rather than actually doing something about the problems it identifies (p.187). The one crowning achievement of the UNEP was its role in placing the link between environment and development on the political agenda, the fruits of which were seen in the Bruntland Report (World Commission on Environment and Development, 1987) and the organization of the Rio Summit (see below).

The IUCN consists of government agencies and NGOs and, although it has no executive powers, its reports are regarded as authoritative and influential (see below and Chapter 4). The European Union is unlike other international agreements and treaties because of the degree of authority it has over its member states. Since its foundation in 1957 the EU has dabbled with environmental issues, but it was not until the 1970s that it began to focus seriously on the environment and not until the Single European Act 1986 that it had any legal competence to do so. Because of the EU's authority, its increasing propensity to issue environmental measures, and the large impact they have had on Britain, its role is considered in more detail below.

As well as those international organizations with a specifically environmental remit, it is also worth mentioning the World Bank, the International Maritime Organization, the Organization for Economic Co-operation and Development, the International Monetary Fund and even the Catholic Church. Clearly, these bodies play very different roles but they all in one way or another impact on the global environment. The World Bank, for instance, lends money to developing countries and, by attaching environmental conditions to loans – as it is pressured by NGOs to do – can have a determining role in promoting sustainable development (Piddington, 1992). Likewise, failure to do so can have severe environmental consequences (see *Guardian*, 9 January 1995).

International treaties

Agreements between nations in the form of treaties constitute the most common form of supra-national environmental action. As with international organizations, some treaties – such as the General Agreement on Tariff and Trade – are not specifically designed for environmental protection but can have a crucial positive or negative impact on the environment. In addition, there is a wide variety of agreements which fall short of formal treaties. These can occur in a number of forms such as the enunciation of general principles, the adoption of internationally recognized guidelines and the setting of standards by international technical bodies (Susskind and Ozawa, 1992, p.154). One example is the *World Conservation Strategy* jointly presented by the IUCN and the World Wide Fund for Nature. Although having no legally binding force, the document serves not only as a guide for the parties entering into conservation treaty negotiations, but also as a 'battering ram' for change by indicating the urgency for action (see Chapter 8).

The most common form of treaty-making on environmental issues involves the use of conventions and protocols. As Susskind and Ozawa (1992, pp.144–5) demonstrate, this approach involves several stages. First, before a treaty or convention is signed, it is necessary for a problem to be identified and acknowledged by the nations who can do most to tackle it. The role of the international scientific community here can be crucial (see Weale, 1992, ch.7). Once enough nations are convinced, negotiations can begin on a convention. At this stage, general principles and objectives only are established and sometimes, in addition, the administrative machinery is set in place in the form of a secretariat whose function is to arrange for meetings of the parties and monitor the workings of the convention. Following this, there is then an often extensive period when the convention is ratified by the signatories. Only when a specified number of states have done this will the treaty come into force. Only at this point will thought be directed towards specific objectives, which will appear in protocols negotiated between the parties to the original convention and possibly other countries too.

One of the best examples of an environmental treaty following this pattern involved attempts to deal with ozone depletion (Ward, 1990, p.241; Haigh, 1992, pp.241–6; Thacher, 1992, p.199; Pickering and Owen, 1994, pp.97–9). Thus, in the early 1980s, UNEP provided the impetus for countries to negotiate a convention on the reduction of CFCs. The Vienna Convention, setting forth the general principle that controls on CFC production should be introduced, was eventually signed in 1985 and adopted by twenty-one states and the EU. This was followed, in September 1987, by more specific measures in the Montreal Protocol (signed by the original Vienna Convention countries plus six other states), which came into force on 1 January 1989. The Protocol froze CFC production at 1986 levels followed by a 50 per cent reduction by the turn of the century. By the end of the 1980s, however, new scientific evidence revealed more severe ozone depletion than had previously been realized and, at a conference organized by the British government in March 1989, the EU, the USA and Canada agreed to the phasing out of the most dangerous CFCs by the year 2000. A further twenty countries signed the so-called London Amendment bringing the total number to fifty-nine, although three years later only just over half of these had ratified the revised version of the Montreal Protocol. Finally, in 1992, the timetable for phasing out CFCs was brought forward to 1996 in a further meeting of the parties in Copenhagen.

Another distinction worth making here is between treaties concerned with 'common pool' resources and those concerned with 'common sink' resources (Weale, 1992, pp.192–5). Common pool resources are those, such as the conservation of fish stocks and forests, which 'provide a source of benefit to those who have access to them'. These can be compared with common sink resources, such as the quality of seas or the atmosphere, which are 'pure public goods, either for the world at large . . . or for some portion of it'. The point of this distinction is that treaties concerned with the former are usually easier to conclude than those concerned with the latter. In particular, it is much easier to monitor the 'taking' of common pool resources and to allocate responsibility than it is to monitor, say, emissions into the sea or the atmosphere. Further, treaties based around common pool resources usually involve attempts to ensure the ability of the parties to continue gaining economically from exploitation. As such, there is a considerable incentive to conclude a treaty and comply with its provisions (see the example of whaling in Chapter 8). Considerable sacrifices, on the other hand, may be involved in treaties designed to limit the exploitation of common sink resources.

The difficulties of inter-state co-operation

The central problem of concluding international agreements is, of course, that the participants are all sovereign states with no higher legal force standing above them. In environmental terms, the problem is particularly acute because of the dichotomy between the interdependence of the world's ecology (and markets) which recognizes no political boundaries, on the one hand, and the fragmented nature of the world's political system consisting of 170 sovereign states on the other (Hurrell and Kingsbury, 1992b, p.4).

The 'realist' school of thought in the study of international relations sees no answer to the problem raised by this dichotomy (Morgenthau, 1962; see also Dryzek, 1987, ch.6). The natural condition of relations between sovereign states, according to this tradition, is one of anarchy. The world's political system is equivalent to Hobbes' state of nature with each sovereign state seeking to defend its own self-interests and being extremely suspicious of others. Thus, given that a world government is unrealistic (Ophuls, 1977), the prospects for effective international co-operation are bleak, even if the parties to them stand to benefit equally, because without a Leviathan – a body with power over the participants – there can be no guarantee, as in the critique of the Green emphasis on decentralization discussed in Chapter 2, that some 'free riders' will not try to enjoy the benefits without paying the costs (Weale, 1992, p.189).

There is no question that political sovereignty is a severe problem but the evidence suggests that the 'realist' perspective exaggerates the difficulties and underestimates the achievements of international co-operation. It does not, for instance, sit well with the number of international agreements which have been made. In the environmental field the UNEP lists 152 multilateral environmental agreements up until 1990, the vast majority of which have been concluded in the last two decades (Hurrell and Kingsbury, 1992b, p.10). This is not to say, of course, that all these agreements have been effective in achieving their objectives although some no doubt have done better than others. In order to assess them we need to look at some of the practical difficulties in more detail.

First, there is the problem of scope – what and who should be included? Environmental problems tend to be multi-causal and the more factors to consider, the more difficult it is to reach agreement. This goes a long way towards explaining why the treaty on ozone depletion exists and has been regarded as successful, whereas a long-term agreement on cutting CO_2 emissions has been much more difficult to arrive at (see below). In the former case, as a unicausal phenomenon – CFCs are known to be overwhelmingly the main culprit – it was relatively easy to focus on what needed to be done. Compare this with global warming where there are great uncertainties about the role played by numerous complex factors – fossil fuel combustion, the thorny issue of car use, the contribution of forests and oceans as carbon sinks, and so on – to take into account (Richardson *et al.*, 1992, pp.166–8).

A related factor is the sacrifices required. In the case of CFCs, alternatives are now readily available and are relatively cheap. Phasing out CFCs, then, does not raise question marks against continued economic growth in the West and economic development in the Third World. Financial assistance from the West for developing countries to adjust to CFC alternatives was willingly given (Connolly and Norris, 1991–2, p.99). The sacrifices required for other agreements, and particularly one involving global warming, would be considerable and financial aid from the West prohibitively expensive. As a consequence, arriving at a fair and workable distribution of sacrifices is so much more difficult. As Beckerman (1992, p.281) remarks: 'The prospects of China or India making sacrifices of current standards of living or immediate growth prospects in order to improve the standards of living of the world in 100 years' time are virtually non-existent.'

Given the difficulties identified above, it is hardly surprising that reaching binding agreements is problematic. This is why conventions are often couched in terms of vague commitments, general principles or guidelines rather than specific, meaningful obligations. The choice is often between attracting as many signatories as possible and adopting obligations which only a few are willing to accept. Had the Vienna Convention, for example, insisted on specific reductions in CFCs, it is unlikely at the time that Britain, France and Italy would have signed (Ward, 1990, p.241). Not all treaties are so vague. Two of the major wildlife conservation treaties, the Convention on the International Trade in Endangered Species (CITES) and the International Convention for the Regulation of Whaling (ICRW), impose stringent obligations on the signatories. In order to maximize the number of countries involved, however, both treaties allow for some flexibility, CITES enabling countries to record a reservation allowing them to continue trading in a particular species and the ICRW allowing some whaling to be conducted under the guise of scientific research (see Chapter 8).

Many treaties, though, do seek to maximize the number of participants through avoiding, at least initially, specific commitments. A classic case of a 'lowest common denominator' agreement designed to incorporate as many countries as possible is the 1989 Basel Convention concerned with controlling the movement and disposal of hazardous wastes. Hazardous waste, it says, should be disposed of in an 'environmentally sound manner', but not defining what is meant by the term is tantamount to maintaining the status quo since each country can decide for itself how to interpret it (Susskind and Ozawa, 1992, p.147).

The difficulties of negotiating binding agreements is also well illustrated by the UN Conference on Environment and Development (the Earth Summit) held in Rio de Janeiro in June 1992. Of the five official agreements signed there, only two (on biological diversity and climate change) are legally binding. Even so the US President George Bush refused to sign the former, although since then his successor Bill Clinton has done so. Even these two, though, have few specific commitments and provide no new sources of finance, thereby failing to address the issue of North/ South conflict (C. Thomas, 1993, pp.2, 24). The Convention on Climate Change, agreed at the Summit, seeks a reduction in three greenhouse gases (CO_2, CH_4 and nitrous oxide) to their 1990 levels by the end of the century. Only fourteen states have so far ratified the treaty, however, and there is no agreement beyond the year 2000 (Pickering and Owen, 1994, p.101).

This is not to say that the Summit was a complete failure. Persuading 160 countries to sign a convention on climate change, even if so few have so far ratified it, was a major achievement. In addition, each signatory of the Rio Declaration agreed to provide a national plan indicating how it will implement Agenda 21, the name given to the action plan for sustainable development emanating from the Summit. In addition, following the Summit, a new UN Commission (on Sustainable Development) was set up to monitor the progress of the national Agenda 21s (Young, 1993, pp.44–5). As Young (*ibid.*, p.46) points out, the Summit 'was a useful first step, a pause for further thought akin to a driver on a snow-bound motorway thinking about slowing down to a safer speed'. Whether first steps are, at this late stage, an adequate response is an open question.

As if the difficulties identified above are not enough, three additional weaknesses related to problems of implementation and enforcement can be briefly stated. In the first place, few sanctions exist for non-compliance although international publicity and diplomatic pressure can be applied. In this respect, the role of environmental groups can be crucial in publicizing non-compliance and, in addition, their expertise can be invaluable for governments genuinely seeking to comply with their treaty obligations. One increasingly used method is to enforce treaties through domestic legal systems by obliging signatories to enact treaty provisions in national legislation, as EU directives do (Hurrell and Kingsbury, 1992b, pp.28–9). Hence, for instance, endangered species which CITES prohibits trade in are protected by law in Britain. The only problem here is the problem mentioned earlier, that the greater the stringency of both the content of a treaty's provisions and the enforcement mechanism the fewer countries are willing to commit themselves.

Second, even if a treaty's enforcement mechanism is reasonably effective, assessing the effectiveness of the provisions themselves is extremely problematic. Not only is it expensive and time-consuming to gather the relevant information, but interpreting it is fraught with difficulties. The complexity and interdependence of the world's ecology is such that one can never be totally sure of cause and effect. Environmental degradation may not be an indication of a failure to enforce a treaty since a new factor not covered by it may be responsible. Equally, mere evidence of environmental improvement does not mean that the treaty was responsible. A decline in SO_2 emissions, to give one example, may have been caused by the recession rather than any direct action by a particular government (List and Rittberger, 1992, p.106). The final point is that enforcement of treaty provisions is often difficult for weak states. Factors such as civil unrest, ethnic strife, lack of financial resources and general economic problems are common and make it imperative that the stable developed countries offer economic and political assistance (Hurrell and Kingsbury, 1992b, p.30).

The European dimension of environmental politics

As was pointed out earlier in this chapter, the European Union is a unique international organization because it is the only one 'with the power to agree environmental policies binding on its members' (McCormick, 1991, p.128). The ceding of sovereignty by member states means that legislation emanating from the Council of Ministers does not have to be ratified by national legislatures although scrutiny does take place before the decision is made. The powers exercised by the European Union are not, however, equivalent to those of a nation-state. Member states have the legal right to secede and, even while remaining members, they are relied on to implement and enforce directives. Despite these limitations, the European Union has had a significant impact on environmental policy in Britain and other member states. Almost 300 items of environmental legislation have been adopted since 1957 and the scope of these has gradually increased (Haigh, 1992, p.235).

The history of EU environmental policy

Following Hildebrand (1992), it is possible to identify four main periods in the development of the EU's concern for the environment. First, the period 1957–72 was marked by minimal involvement. The Treaty of Rome made no reference to the environment and although legislation was introduced (a total of nine directives and one regulation) this 'cannot be regarded as adding up to any sort of proper and coherent policy' (*ibid.*, p.19). Indeed, the Treaty of Rome provided no legal competence for the EU to be involved in environmental issues and most of the measures carried were justified (under Article 2) on the grounds that the commitment to raising the standard of living incorporated the idea of environmental quality, and that they promoted the harmonization of laws throughout the Union, thereby providing parity for economic competition. Article 36 (providing a justification for restricting imports and exports on the grounds of morality or the protection of humans, animals and plants) and Article 235 (a catch-all enabling action to achieve the objectives of the Treaty for which no powers are clearly granted) also provided some, albeit obscure, justifications for environmental policy (Hildebrand, 1992, p.17; Wurzel, 1993, pp.181–2).

The second period, 1973–85, was marked by greater involvement in environmental issues. In 1973, the first Environmental Action Programme (since followed by four successors) was produced by the Commission, setting out the policy direction which it thinks the EU should follow. These programmes are accepted by the Council of Ministers as guides to EU policy and so they are not committed to every proposal in them (Haigh, 1990, p.11). Despite the fact that no legal competence yet existed, the first Action Programme established the principle that the EU had the authority to act in environmental matters 'whenever real effectiveness is attainable by action at Community level' (Hildebrand, 1992, p.20), a phrase vague enough to justify the considerable intervention which did occur. In this period, there was a significant increase in EU environmental legislation – 120 directives, 27 decisions and 14 regulations – covering a wide range of issues such as the quality of bathing and drinking water, air quality and the disposal of hazardous waste (*ibid.*, pp.27, 42).

The Action Programmes in particular, and greater EU involvement in general, came about for a number of reasons (*ibid.*, pp.24–5; Wurzel, 1993, p.180). The decision to introduce Action Programmes was taken at a Summit Conference of heads of member states held in Paris in October 1972. The Summit was convened at a time when environmental concern was near the top of the political agendas of many countries, when the survivalist *Limits to Growth* report had just been published and after the UN Conference in Stockholm. The internationalist emphasis of much contemporary environmental discourse was bound to focus attention on the EU as an already existing international body with considerable powers. In addition, it was becoming increasingly apparent that, as countries such as Germany and the Netherlands were adopting more stringent environmental regulations, they were being disadvantaged in terms of trade with other member states.

Crucially, it was as much business interests – which have considerable political clout – as environmentalists within these countries
who were calling for action at a European level. Finally, a series of
industrial disasters – notably at Flixborough in England in 1974
and Seveso in Italy in 1976 – helped to reinforce the need for the
continuing development of EU environmental policy.

The third period, between 1986 and 1992, was marked by the
establishment of the EU's legal competence to deal with environmental issues. This came about because of the Single European
Act (SEA) of 1986, a significant amendment to the Treaty of
Rome, which added an environmental dimension to the EU's responsibilities in Title VII. As Hildebrand (1992, p.29) points out,
this addition was not, for most, a priority when the revisions were
being made. Indeed, the environmental commitment was eventually tacked on at the end of the process as a belated recognition
that the creation of a single market and the hoped-for economic
growth would have environmental consequences.

As a consequence of the introduction of a formal legal framework for environmental policy, the environment has a much higher
status within the Commission and DG XI (the directorate-general
responsible for environmental policy) can seek, with greater authority, to influence other, particularly economic, aspects of the EU's
work. Thus, the fourth and fifth Action Programmes have made
external integration (see Chapter 5) a much more explicit objective (Weale and Williams, 1992, p.46). In addition, the SEA introduced new institutional structures which have increased the EU's
capacity to adopt environmental measures (Judge, 1992). The SEA
introduced qualified majority voting for environmental measures
designed to harmonize national laws in the process of completing
the single market (under Article 100a of the new treaty). It is thus
more difficult for a small number of member states to block
environmental proposals in the Council of Ministers. Further, decisions taken by qualified majority voting are subject to the co-
operation procedure which gives more influence to the European
Parliament, a body which tends to be greener than the Commission and the Council of Ministers. Although the European Parliament cannot reject environmental measures passed to it by the
Council of Ministers, it can significantly delay them through the
requirement that the European Parliament has a 'second reading'
before the Council of Ministers eventually makes a decision. The

passage of time also allows the environmental lobby to mobilize support for or against a measure.

Britain, Europe and the environment – an assessment

The fourth period, from 1992, in the historical development of the environmental role of the EU has been marked by considerable uncertainty. The latest Action Programme moves further down the integration road but the Maastricht Treaty (1992) raised the issue of subsidiarity and the prospect that at least some environmental problems will once again be decided at the national level (Wurzel, 1993, p.190). In Britain, the continuing dispute within the governing Conservative Party about the degree of European integration also raises doubts about the long-term future of European-wide environmental solutions.

There have been other problems too. For instance, despite the desirability of external integration and the emphasis placed on it in the Action Programmes, the 'implementation of integration has been a faltering and haphazard affair, without serious resonance in the central policy activities of the EC' (Weale and Williams, 1992, p.49). Thus, at an intellectual level, debates over the single market reflected the dominance of a form of neo-classical economics largely ignoring the environmental consequences of economic growth. Further, at an organizational level, DG XI remains small compared to the development-oriented parts of the Commission, and the transport and agricultural lobbies remain very powerful (*ibid.*, pp.53–7). Finally, Jacques Delors, as President of the Commission, was not noted for his enthusiasm for environmental measures and tensions existed between him and DG XI (Wurzel, 1993, p.189).

Perhaps the biggest obstacle to effective EU environmental policy is the difficulty of enforcement. The EU has no agents of its own to ensure its policies are implemented and enforced and therefore has to rely on the member states to do it (Haig, 1990, p.1). This has led to considerable problems. Infringement of EU measures can occur either through partial compliance (whereby national measures do not fully incorporate EU law), non-notification (which essentially means that the measure has not been implemented at all) and incorrect application (where the measure has been introduced but wrongly) (Collins and Earnshaw,

1992, p.216). A Commission report revealed that up to the end of 1989, there had been no fewer than 362 infringements (90 for partial compliance, 60 for non-notification and 213 for incorrect application) and infringement proceedings brought by the Commission had increased from 16 in 1982 to 217 in 1990 (*ibid.*, pp.219, 216).

Solutions to this problem have been varied (*ibid.*, pp.235–46). The creation of an EU inspectorate has been mooted but is widely thought to be financially prohibitive and politically unrealistic. Further suggestions have included a rationalization of national reporting requirements, greater access to national courts and a greater use of fines which could be imposed by the European Court of Justice. One positive step was the creation of the European Environment Agency in 1990 whose remit is to gather and analyze environmental information, which can then be used to aid improved enforcement.

The major drawback with these suggestions is that they assume the reason for failure to implement and enforce EU measures is related to political expediency. While this does play some part, the evidence suggests that expediency is not the only, or even the main, factor. Germany and the Netherlands, for example, are justly regarded as having a high awareness and concern for environmental protection. Yet, in the figures mentioned above, neither country has a particularly good record: both come near the bottom of the table of member states for partial compliance, with only France and Spain performing worse. Thus, we need to look at a variety of factors – the problem of reconciling EU legislation with existing laws and regulations, the complexity of the administrative machinery (a problem particularly apparent in federal systems such as Germany) and the level of consultation with interested parties allowed for – to explain the enforcement failures (Collins and Earnshaw, 1992, pp.217–18).

As far as Britain is concerned, the record of implementation and enforcement is not as bad as one might expect given the unfavourable publicity Britain often receives. Far from being a 'laggard state' (McCormick, 1991, p.133), Britain finished about half way up the league table of member state infringements (Collins and Earnshaw, 1992, p.219). It is true that a significant number of complaints are made to the Commission about Britain's record of compliance, but this may well reflect the strength of the British environmental lobby and a tradition of political protest rather than providing an objective measure of non-compliance (*ibid.*, pp.232–3).

It is rare for Britain to adopt environmental measures which run ahead of EU thinking, although in some areas of agricultural policy this is the case. In other areas, the UK government has had to be brought into line under protest – most notably over action to combat SO^2 emissions implicated in acid rain, demanded by the large combustion plant directive (McCormick, 1991, p.140), and the creation of the National Rivers Authority in 1989 (see Chapter 8). EU directives also provided much of the impetus for the Wildlife and Countryside Act in 1981 and the Environmental Protection Act in 1990 (Young, 1993, p.49).

The biggest impact that the EU has had on British environmental policy concerns the challenges to the traditional British style of policy-making (Liefferink *et al.*, 1993). As we saw in Chapter 5, the conflict between the voluntarist, consensual and pragmatic approaches (favoured in Britain) and the imposition of rigid uniform standards (favoured in much of Europe) has led to previously unknown levels of debate in Britain and some legislative movement from the former to the latter. One of the effects of this has been a trend towards greater centralization of policy-making in Britain. In the area of air pollution, for instance, the EU has placed an obligation on the UK government to ensure that specified standards are enforced for concentrations of smoke, SO^2, lead and nitrogen oxide. This in turn has led to increased direction of local authorities and the potential for much future direction of HMIP (Haigh, 1986).

Third World development and the environment

Much of what we have discussed in this chapter relates to what, in many ways, is the key issue in the international politics of the environment. Put simply, this issue concerns the reconciliation of economic development in the Third World with the objective of environmental protection. The potential for environmental damage due to Third World development is truly frightening and yet this development is, in some ways, both inevitable and desirable. For most people, therefore, the search is for sustainable means of achieving this growth, a principle which was put on the

UN agenda in the 1970s. Before we move on, it should be noted briefly here that there are some who argue that the ideology of sustainable development has been imposed on the Third World over the heads of indigenous societies whose own preference is for alternatives to development (Latouche, 1993).

For most, however, a quick glance at the gap between North and South is enough to appreciate the inevitability and desirability of Third World development (see Hurrell and Kingsbury, 1992b, p.39). At present, the developed world utilizes about 70 per cent of the world's energy supplies and yet constitutes only about 5 per cent of the world's population (Simpson, 1990, p.8; Pickering and Owen, 1994, p.185). The population gap is also set to widen. One study estimates that the world's population may reach 10.5 billion by 2050 (over double its present figure) and the vast majority of this increase will take place in the developing world (Pickering and Owen, 1994, pp.282–3).

It is futile to imagine, therefore, that economic growth will not take place at a significant rate in the developing world and, obviously, this growth could be catastrophic for the world's ecology. A massive increase in greenhouse gases is one major concern as is the depletion of non-renewable resources. In addition, the increase in population and urbanization will put stresses on the food production sector and the threat of shortages will encourage ever-intensive agricultural practices causing further environmental damage. Under threat are some of the most species-rich regions on the planet, and just as increasing levels of pollution have consequences for the developed world, so does a decline in biodiversity.

But if development is inevitable, it is also desirable to alleviate the poverty and deprivation many peoples of the developing countries endure. Even though, as we saw in an earlier chapter, there is a strong justification for environmental protection on the grounds that we owe a moral obligation to future generations, it is equally the case that we also have an obligation to people alive today (Shue, 1992). One of the major criticisms of environmentalists is that they are essentially engaged in a selfish, class-based exercise which seeks to deprive the less affluent peoples of the world of the standard of living they themselves enjoy (Martell, 1994, p.39). On the other hand, an essential idea behind the principle of sustainable development is that without taking environmental considerations into account, economic growth cannot be sustained for very long (Thacher,

1992, p.188). The choice, therefore, is not a completely stark one between present and future generations. As the Bruntland Report pointed out, sustainable development is about meeting 'the needs of the present without compromising the ability of future generations to meet their own needs' (World Commission on Environment and Development, 1987, p.8). In addition, environmentalists have also been loud in their criticism of the developed world's exploitation of the Third World (see, for instance, Porritt, 1984, pp.96–8, pp.188–90). Indeed, there is a school of thought which argues that environmental degradation in developing countries is in large part a product of their dependence on the West (the following account of this position is based on the excellent discussion in Yearley, 1992, pp.149–81).

Dependency on investment from the developed world, for instance, often leads Third World countries to relax environmental standards in order to attract multinational companies, which can then avoid the more rigorous standards applied in their home countries (in addition to taking advantage of cheap labour and the availability of raw materials). Likewise, some Third World countries, particularly in West Africa, are willing to accept the income generated by the dumping of hazardous wastes which no developed country will accept. The consequence of this drive for income is often excessive pollution and sometimes, as in the disaster at the Union Carbide pesticide plant in Bhopal, an immediate and devastating impact on human life and health.

Agricultural development in the Third World, too, is designed to meet the demands of the developed world. As a consequence, the needs of local people are ignored, many not being able to afford to buy the food produced, and the imported intensive methods employed cause environmental damage. Thus, forests are cleared for cattle grazing and environmental regulations are relaxed so that many products banned in the developed world are used.

An additional factor is the loans which developing countries have incurred to industrialize. It was rare for environmental conditions to be attached and too often the capital was used to invest in large projects, such as dams, which had dire environmental consequences. The environmental consequences of dependency have worsened with the onset of the debt crisis in the 1980s. As world trade slumped, developing countries found it increasingly difficult to repay the interest on the massive debts they had been encouraged to take out by the banks. As a consequence, in a desperate attempt to find the resources to meet their financial commitments, concern for the environment became an even lower priority.

Whoever is to blame, the environmental consequences of Third World development are, and will remain, acute. The concept of 'sustainable development' is much easier to promote in general terms than to put into practice. Crucial questions still remain. How much and what forms of development, for instance, can be justified on ecological grounds? What is the balance to be struck between environmental protection and the needs and demands of indigenous peoples? Such questions go to the heart of the modern politics of the environment and, indeed, the very future of the human race depends on finding adequate answers to them.

Further reading

An excellent volume of articles covering a variety of international environmental topics is Hurrell and Kingsbury (1992a). There are also useful chapters in Young (1993), McCormick (1991) and Weale (1992). Thomas (1993) contains a valuable collection of articles on the Rio Summit. The standard text on European environmental policy is Haigh (1990). See also the overviews in Haigh (1992) and Wurzel (1993) and a special edition of the journal *Environmental Politics* (1 April 1992), which contains the articles by Hilderbrand, Weale and Williams, and Collins and Earnshaw. On the issue of Third World development, Hurrell and Kingsbury (1992a) contains a number of useful articles. There is also an excellent discussion in Yearley (1992).

7

ENVIRONMENTALISM AND POLITICAL PARTIES

This chapter considers the party political dimension of environmentalism. Of obvious importance is the emergence and development of the Green Party, a party specifically designed to place environmentalism on the party political agenda. In British terms at least, the history of the Green Party is largely one of failure and a main task is to explain why the party has been unable to expand into a mass movement and why its share of the vote in elections, with the notable exception of the 1989 European Parliament elections, has been derisory. The second part of the chapter charts the development of environmental awareness within the major parties, examining the reasons for it and exploring its limitations. The relationship between environmentalism and the major parties is particularly important in Britain. In the first place, political parties are peculiarly central to government and politics in Britain. Elections are contests between candidates chosen and financed by the parties, Parliament is organized along party lines and, of course, single-party governments, supported by a majority in the House of Commons, are the norm (Garner and Kelly, 1993, ch.1). Second, the ability of the major parties to co-opt at least part of the environmental agenda may well help to explain why the Green Party has made such limited progress.

The Green Party

Green parties now exist in many countries. The Values Party, formed in New Zealand in 1972, was the first Green party in the world and the forerunner of the British Green Party was established, as the People Party, a year later to become the first of its kind in Europe (Rainbow, 1992). In some countries, although not in Britain, Greens have succeeded in achieving representation in national and state legislatures, two Swiss Greens elected in 1979 being the first to be elected at the national level, as well as the European Parliament. In some countries Greens have also occupied governmental posts. Most notable has been the German Green Party (Die Grünen), which secured increasing levels of support throughout the 1980s. Between 1983 and 1987, the party held the balance of power in the Hesse Parliament when it formed a coalition with the SPD. Greens have also held the balance of power in Liège in Belgium in 1982–88 and Tasmania in 1989–91 (Young, 1993, p.40).

Early historical development

The People Party was founded in a Coventry estate agent's office in February 1973 by a group of professional people who had been influenced by the growing environmental threat as represented in the survivalist literature of the time. Edward Goldsmith's *Blueprint for Survival* was, and still remains, a key text for British Greens and Paul Ehrlich's work on population was equally influential (Rudig and Lowe, 1986, p.266; Parkin, 1989, pp.217–18; McCulloch, 1992, pp.425–7). The first few years of the party's existence were hardly auspicious. After fighting a small number of seats in the two 1974 general elections (see Table 7.1), most of the founding members left and the party came close to folding (Rudig and Lowe, 1986, p.272).

That the party did survive was due to the emergence of a new set of national leaders including, most notably, Jonathon Tyler, Jonathon Porritt and David Fleming. In 1975, the People Party was renamed the Ecology Party and in the 1979 general election the brave decision was taken to fight fifty seats, the minimum necessary for a party to be entitled to a 5-minute election broadcast. Although the party's electoral support remained stubbornly low,

Table 7.1   Green Party electoral record

General elections	Seats fought	% of vote	% in seats fought	Total vote
Feb. 1974	5	–	1.8	–
Oct. 1974	4	–	0.7	–
1979	53	0.1	1.5	–
1983	108	0.2	1.0	54,077
1987	133	0.3	1.4	89,354
1992	253	0.5	1.3	173,008

European elections	Seats fought	% in seats fought	% of vote
1979	3	3.7	–
1984	16	2.6	0.6
1989	79	14.9	14.9
1994	84	3.2	3.2

Sources: Young (1993, p.37); *Guardian*, 25 June 1994.

the extra publicity did attract new members and the Ecology Party entered the 1980s an established party in reasonably good health. In 1985, another name change took place and the present name was introduced in place of the rather neutral and sterile 'Ecology' label.

Organization

There have been organizational disputes within most Green parties and in Britain they have been particularly acute. These disputes have not occurred by accident. They reflect the perennial strategic problem facing radical organizations seeking to make fundamental changes to society. The choice facing the Green Party has been to adopt one of two strategies. In Germany, the labels 'realos' and 'fundis' have been used to describe the advocates of these two positions, while in Britain the terms 'electoralists' and 'radicals' have been in more common usage, but the distinction remains essentially the same (see McCulloch, 1992, pp.419–20; Doherty, 1992b, pp.94–8).

The realos or electoralists advocate the adoption of a traditional hierarchical organization with a relatively autonomous leadership working within the existing political framework, fighting elections and being prepared to make electoral compromises and, if necessary, striking deals with other parties. The fundis or radicals, on the other hand, argue that Green parties should seek to maintain ideological purity by refusing to compromise their principles for electoral expediency. Organizationally, the creation of a decentralized, democratic organization with tight controls placed on those occupying leading positions is necessary. This is partly to protect against a leadership becoming deradicalized and compromising the party's principles in search of electoral success and partly because a hierarchical organization is anathema to the Green emphasis on decentralization and egalitarianism. In addition, this alternative strategy would mean being prepared to engage in extra-parliamentary action in support of environmental objectives and other social movements – anti-nuclear and road protestors, the feminist movement and so on – when their interests coincide.

The split identified above has been particularly evident in the British Green Party and the radicals have usually had the edge over the electoralists. This is partly because British Greens, unlike the German Greens, have never had to tackle the difficult decisions faced by parties making significant electoral and representational progress (see Doherty, 1992b, pp.107–8, for details of the internal disputes within Die Grünen). It is also, however, related to the fact that British Greens have been much more strongly influenced by radical ecocentric views than Greens in the rest of Europe (see, for instance, Dodds, 1989). Such views, of course, put the Greens at odds with both the prevailing ideology of the main parties, making compromises unthinkable, and with the political system itself.

The divisions within the Green Party (then the Ecology Party) began in the early 1980s when a growing membership brought an increasing number of radicals committed to the 'fundi' position into the party (Rudig and Lowe, 1986, p.275). At the same time, the electoralists within the leadership wanted reforms to transform the party into a conventional electoral organization. The affair came to a head in the mid-1980s. At the 1986 conference, amendments to achieve the electoralists' objective were put forward and rejected. As a result, leading electoralists, such as Tyler and Ekins, discussed setting up a parallel organization (a party within a party) called Maingreen to campaign for the electoralists' point of view putting forward, for instance, a slate of candidates for the party council (Parkin, 1989, pp.226–7). A passage from Tyler's paper for the Maingreen meeting illustrates the electoralist viewpoint nicely. 'Organisation, image, leadership: these are the substance and backbone of real-world politics,' he wrote. 'We may wish they were not', he continued, but 'our reward for continuing to pretend they are not will be eternal marginality' (quoted in Robinson, 1992, p.213). When news of the attempt to organize this organization filtered through to the party council, however, the move was roundly condemned and, feeling disillusioned about the prospects of ever changing the party, a number of leading electoralists, including Ekins and Tyler, resigned (Doherty, 1992a, p.294).

The departure of leading electoralists left the radicals in a very strong position, but this was not the end of the matter. In the late 1980s the dispute re-emerged (the following account is based on Doherty, 1992a). This time, a new set of electoralists containing some of the best-known figures in the party, including Caroline Lucas, David Bachelor, Jean Lambert and Alec Pontin, formed a party faction called Green 2000. The aim was to capitalize on the Green vote in the 1989 European election by creating the conditions, through reform of the party's decentralized structure, for major electoral success and Green participation in government early in the twenty-first century.

At the autumn 1991 conference, Green 2000 got the changes they wanted passed by the necessary two-thirds majority. This was achieved by using the proxy votes of the more passive party members who did not attend the conference. Thus, just as Neil Kinnock had reduced the influence of left-wing activists in the Labour Party by appealing over their heads to ordinary, more moderate, party members, Green 2000 were able to dilute the influence of the more active fundi by utilizing the less committed members (Rudig, 1993).

The reforms achieved were as follows. Although the conference remained the supreme authority in the party, the original Party Council, which had overall political and organizational authority, was replaced by two new bodies, a Political Executive and a Regional Council. The former, consisting of eleven members, elected by an annual, secret ballot of the membership, became the dominant institution with the Regional Council, consisting of twenty-eight members elected from Area Parties, performing only an advisory role. Moreover, the principle of rotating offices – a central Green device to prevent a party hierarchy developing – whereby no one person was permitted to serve in office for more than three consecutive years, was abolished.

The success of the Green 2000 campaign was revealed in the first elections to the new party bodies in January 1992. Supporters of Green 2000 took the vast majority of the positions on the Political Executive and Sara Parkin was elected to the Chair. Thus, a recognizable leadership was beginning to emerge with authority to direct the party in an electoralist direction. This did not, however, end the infighting. Poor election results, financial problems and a declining membership provided a stick with which the fundi, who dominated the Regional Council and had been alienated by the success of the Green 2000 strategy, could beat the electoralists. Only £50,000 was spent on the 1992 campaign (30 times less than the Natural Law Party), and by the autumn of 1992 the party's membership had fallen to 8,000 (from a high point of 20,000 in 1990) (*Guardian*, 10 September 1992). As a consequence, in 1992, after a disappointing general election performance, Sara Parkin and a number of other members of the Political Executive resigned, thus further weakening the party (Young, 1993, p.39).

Electoral support

As Table 7.1 reveals, the Greens have found it difficult to make an electoral breakthrough. In general elections, the gradual, albeit very slow, increased share of the vote, from 0.1 per cent in 1979 to 0.5 per cent in 1992, is almost entirely explained by the additional seats contested by the party (53 in 1979 and 253 in 1992) although the ability to contest more seats does itself indicate some growth. In addition, the highest share of the vote won in a particular constituency in each general election has hovered around the 3 per cent mark, with 3.9 per cent in Coventry North West in 1979 remaining the highest. Finally, the Greens have had some success in local elections where the party's lack of resources does not, perhaps, matter quite so much and where personalities and local issues have more of an impact. In 1989, for instance, the Greens won 1 county council, 11 district council and 90 parish council seats with an overall 4.1 per cent share of the vote. The share of the vote obtained by the party in the seats it contested was about 8 per cent and in parts of Avon and Kent the Green share was over 20 per cent (Rootes, 1991, p.41).

Only the 1989 European Parliament election result does not fit the pattern identified above and it is instructive to discuss this outcome in some detail. The 14.9 per cent share of the vote was the highest ever won by a Green Party in any national election in any European state. In addition, the party won over 20 per cent in seventeen constituencies, came second ahead of Labour in six and failed to come at least third in only two (Rootes, 1991, p.39). Despite this impressive showing, the general consensus, with which the present author agrees, has been that this result was an abberation, reflecting not so much an emerging environmental conscious- ness as a series of special circumstances unlikely to be repeated (the following account is based on Rootes, 1991; and Rudig and Franklin, 1991; see also Curtice, 1989).

The obvious evidence for this interpretation is that the Green vote was much lower before, and has declined since, the 1989 election. This is not, however, sufficient evidence for our claim. It may be that the 1989 result reflected the heightened concern for environmental issues quite clearly emerging in the late 1980s, in which case the subsequent decline in the Green vote may simply reflect the fact that since 1989 the environment has been relegated due, perhaps, to the recession and the re-emergence of economic issues at the forefront of voter concerns.

Certainly, the period immediately preceding the 1989 election was one in which the environment had played an unprecedented role in British politics. It does not automatically follow, however, that the Green Party would be the major beneficiary of this height- ened concern, particularly as the major parties had sought to adapt to it (see below). A more persuasive argument for the Green Party surge in 1989 is that, as Rootes points out, it was made possible by a change in the balance of political competition among British parties. Thus, the election was held during the mid-term of a Con- servative government which is often the occasion for a protest vote, particularly in an election which is not concerned with choos- ing a government. Moreover, the Conservative government in 1989 was particularly unpopular due largely to the introduction of the poll tax and the general economic malaise. Added to this was the extremely negative campaign run by the Conservatives in the European election itself.

The unpopularity of the Tories does not explain why it was the Greens who were the beneficiaries of the protest vote, however. Here, two factors were at work. First, the natural repository of a protest vote by disillusioned Conservatives is the party or parties of the centre. At the time, however, the Liberal Democrats had just been established as a result of the rather acrimonious merger of the Liberal Party and the Social Democratic Party. The new merged party was therefore not in a position to fight an effective campaign. Second, the whole trend of this argument depends on the accuracy of the added assertion that Green votes tended to come from disillusioned Tory or Alliance voters and this indeed was the case. Thus, an NOP poll in July 1989 revealed that 29 per cent of those who voted Green in 1989 said they had voted Conservative in the preceding general election compared to 27 per cent Alliance and only 18 per cent Labour. Furthermore, the Green vote was heavily skewed towards the South, where the vast majority of seats were held by the Conservative Party. Finally, where another minor party had campaigned strongly – such as in Scotland, Wales and the South West – the Greens polled less effectively.

If the preceding analysis is right, one would expect the Green vote to be very fragile. The subsequent decline in support for the Greens provides some evidence for this but as we pointed out above, this is not sufficient. Evidence from a sample of the electorate who voted in 1989, undertaken by Rudig and Franklin, reveals the true state of long-term Green prospects. They found that under a third of 1989 Green voters identified strongly with the party, that just under a third of Green voters said it was highly improbable they would ever vote Green again at a future European election and, finally, that virtually no one in their sample who voted for a party other than Green in 1989 was prepared to switch to the Greens at any future election. Thus, not only was Green support extremely fragile, but there was no sign of future support coming from elsewhere.

Explaining the weakness of the Green Party

There are a number of possible explanations for the Green Party's failure to make a significant impact on British politics. The most obvious of these, although not necessarily the most important, is the electoral system (Rudig and Lowe, 1986, pp.277–8). As is well

known, Britain's first past the post system has the effect of penaliz-
ing smaller parties with evenly spread support (unlike the national-
ist parties in Scotland and Wales). Thus, under a 'pure' system of
proportional representation, the Greens would have won 19 per
cent of the British allocation of European Parliament seats in 1989.
In Germany, a hybrid system combining elements of first past the
post and the party list system operates, whereby each member of
the electorate has two votes, one in a constituency contest and one
additional vote for a party. It is significant that all Greens elected
at the national level in Germany have been elected by this second
vote rather than in constituency contests (Yearley, 1992, p.89).
Thus, in 1983, twenty-seven Green delegates were elected to the
Bundestag on an overall 5.6 per cent share of the vote and forty-
four were elected on a 8.3 per cent share in 1987. Under varying
proportional systems, Greens have also been elected to national
parliaments in Sweden, Italy, Belgium, Switzerland and Austria
with relatively small shares of the vote (Callaghan, 1990, p.2).

There are a number of additional factors relating to the British
electoral system which are also worth mentioning. In the first
place, the requirement that each electoral candidate has to put
down a substantial deposit, which is not returned if the candidate
fails to win at least 5 per cent of the vote, puts a significant financial
strain on small parties. In a similar vein, there is no state funding
for political parties in Britain which benefits Labour and Conservative financial links with trade unions and business respectively.
Second, it may be that the first past the post system discourages
voters from choosing the Green Party because many feel it is a
wasted vote. Reluctantly, in such circumstances, voters may decide
it is preferable to vote tactically for one of the major parties to
prevent the other one from winning.

Finally, there is the broader constitutional distinction between
unitary and federal structures. In the latter type of system Greens
can gain media publicity and political experience by participating
in state elections and governments with considerable executive
power. This can be enormously useful in building a national party.
Thus, when Die Grünen held the balance of power in Hesse after
1982, the experience of government and the media coverage that
followed it was indispensable (Parkin, 1989, pp.116–17). In Britain,
by contrast, local politics, particularly after the reforms in the
1980s reduced the power of local authorities still further, is a much

more peripheral activity. Thus, it is not widely known that the Green Party has polled reasonably well in local elections in some areas of the country and has sitting councillors in a number of them.

The Green Party's performance cannot be explained merely by the particular electoral system it has to work within. Even if we were to assess the Green Party in narrow electoral terms, it should be remembered that the existence of an alternative electoral system is unlikely to have made much difference to the party's position. In Germany, the share of the vote won by Die Grünen in the 1980s (5.6 per cent in the 1983 general election and 8.3 per cent in 1987) was far higher than the British Greens have ever managed in equivalent elections. Indeed, under the 5 per cent barrier operating in Germany, the British Greens would still have won no seats. The Greens were seriously handicapped by the electoral system in 1989, of course, but one wonders what impact the election of Green MEPs from Britain would have had given the European Parliament's limited powers and the lack of interest accorded in Britain to the institution.

It should be noted too that other Green parties in Europe, including Die Grünen, have not done dramatically well in electoral terms despite more favourable electoral systems. Where many of them have outshone their British counterpart is in the degree to which they have become the focal point of mass environmental movements, influencing the direction of environmental campaigns and lobbying as well as seeking electoral success. The failure of the British Green Party to achieve this is worth exploring.

It was implied in the preceding paragraph that an important dimension of Green Party politics in Britain has been the *indifference of the environmental movement* towards the Green Party. This has, indeed, been the case. Despite repeated efforts by the latter to encourage co-operation with the former, these have largely fallen on deaf ears. There are a number of explanations for this (Rudig and Lowe, 1986, pp.269–70, 278–9). In Britain, environmental groups have felt it worthwhile, with some justification, to focus on conventional pressure group lobbying. Many of the older, more moderate, groups have a long history of respectable and moderate advocacy and, as a result, have the kind of access to decision-makers denied to similar groups in other European countries, such as France. For these groups in Britain, it is regarded as simply unnecessary to support a separate Green Party. For those who do not have effective access, there is still a great deal of outsider activity to focus on and sufficient hope of gaining access to decision-makers at some point in the future. For both, being associated too closely with a radical Green Party may risk alienating them from centres of influence and may also alienate supporters or potential supporters who vote for other parties.

The Green Party, unlike other European Green parties, has also failed to forge links with major new social movements such as those concerned with gender and race politics, peace campaigners, and those opposed to nuclear power in addition to the older and more established labour movement. Of particular importance has been the weakness of the anti-nuclear movement in Britain. Again unlike other European countries and particularly France, Britain has not been exclusively reliant on the nuclear option and, when the government has gone down that route, as in the case of Sizewell, it has allowed for an extensive consultation procedure – however biased towards the nuclear industry – thus enabling protest to be channelled in a safe direction. Local opposition to the siting of power stations has also not materialized, primarily because the locations were carefully chosen, more often than not to ensure that the provision of employment opportunities took precedence over the safety fears (Ward, 1983, p.184). As a consequence, the Greens have not been able to capitalize on the potential for concentrated support (Rudig, 1985, pp.67–8; Rudig and Lowe, 1986, p.279). In addition, the opposition to nuclear power that did exist in the 1980s was absorbed by the Labour Party (Ward, 1983, pp.186–7). By the time Labour had softened its anti-nuclear approach, nuclear power, for reasons explored in Chapter 8, was no longer a major part of the government's energy strategy.

A further weakness of the British Greens has been their *inability to attract the support of the broad Left*. The 'watermelon' label – green on the outside and red on the inside – attached to the German Greens indicates the Left's substantial contribution to the development of that particular party. Thus, the majority of Green supporters in Germany are recruited from the Left (Hulsberg, 1987) whereas, as we have seen, British Green support in electoral terms tends to come from disillusioned Right of Centre voters. There are a number of possible explanations for this. In particular, the British Left has not been tinged with Green to the same degree that the Left in many other European countries has (Weston, 1986). It is notable, for example, that the majority of the participants in the recent spate of protests against road building and the export of live animals, for instance, have been drawn from either the 'respectable', Tory-leaning middle classes or from those on the periphery of society. On the other hand, the traditional preoccupation of the organized Left in Britain has been with conflicts relating to industrial relations or general economic issues (such as the poll tax demonstrations in the 1980s), reflecting the continuing importance of class-based politics in Britain. Moreover, as was illustrated in the case of nuclear power, successive governments have been careful enough to avoid provoking conflicts over environmental issues which might have drawn in a variety of groups on the Left (Rudig and Lowe, 1986, pp.280–1). Finally, in so far as the Left has been concerned with environmental issues, the Labour Party has been a broad enough church to accommodate them (see below).

It should be said, in addition, that the Green Party has not sought to encourage alliances with the Left. The ideology of British Greens, influenced by Goldsmith's particular variety of deep ecology, has emphasized the view that the Green approach goes beyond the 'old' divisions between Left and Right (Porritt, 1984, pp.43–4; Doherty, 1992b, p.105). This in turn has been reinforced by the Green leadership which has tended to be middle class and moderately Left of Centre. Jonathon Porritt, for instance, threatened to leave the Green Party if the views of Green 2000 did not prevail, but the party he threatened to defect to was not Labour but the Liberal Democrats!

Greening the major parties

Any account of the impact of the environment on political parties must also consider the extent to which the issue has been adopted by the major parties, not least because this might provide an additional explanation for the Green Party's lack of success. Furthermore, it is useful to consider the limitations of the main parties as vehicles of environmental concern since it provides pointers to the likely future development of environmental policy in Britain.

The decade of the environment

It is certainly the case that all the main parties became increasingly interested in the environment as the 1980s progressed, although there was little inkling at the end of the 1970s that this interest would become so intense. In the 1979 election neither the Labour nor the Conservative Party allocated much space to environmental issues. It was the Liberal Party that 'gave by far the most comprehensive and enthusiastic coverage of the topic' (Robinson, 1992, pp.20–1). A radical faction within the modern Liberal Party had traditionally sought to move the party towards an anti-nuclear position and an emphasis on local community politics where the quality of the environment was often a issue. This radical environmental strand, however, was constrained by two factors. First, it was moderated by the party's leadership, which was concerned with the public's image of the party as little more than a coalition of fringe groupings, a perennial problem for a party which had been out of office for so long. Thus, there was never any chance that the decision reached by the 1979 Liberal Assembly in support of an end to the search for sustained economic growth would be accepted by the leadership (Lowe and Flynn, 1989, pp.14–15). Second, after the merger with the newly formed Social Democratic Party in the early 1980s, the Liberals' inherent radicalism was submerged. David Owen, the leader of the SDP and, in most people's eyes, the dominant force in the Alliance, regarded Liberal radicalism on environmentalism in general, and on nuclear issues in particular, as electoral handicaps and succeeded in diluting environmental commitments in both the 1983 and 1987 elections (Garner and Kelly, 1993, ch.8).

By 1983, environmentalism had become a more important part of the programmes of the two major parties but, as Robinson points out, although it was 'now firmly established within party agendas' it 'was nothing more than a "token" decoration, there to look good, but achieving little' (Robinson, 1992, pp.24–5). It was only after 1983 that a more substantial 'greening' of the major parties took place. This can be seen partly in the increasing number of conference resolutions and party publications on the issue (*ibid.*, pp.25–6; N. Carter, 1992a, pp.121–7). The environmental proposals published by Labour in 1986, for instance, were 'warmly welcomed' by environmental groups (Porritt and Winner, 1988, p.66). These included the creation of a new Ministry of Environmental Protection, a new Wildlife and Countryside Act, an

extension of planning controls to cover agriculture and strength-
ened regulations to deal with air and water pollution. Most of
these proposals, though, were omitted from Labour's 1987 general
election manifesto (*ibid.*, p.68). Of course, far and away the most
important party in the 1980s were the Conservatives and any assessment of the Conservative Party's environmental position is
inextricably linked to the record of successive Conservative governments since 1979 and with the attitude of Mrs Thatcher, who
was such a domineering figure in those governments.

Seen in this way, the pivotal development in the greening of the
major parties was Mrs Thatcher's dramatic *volte face* on the environment. It was not that she had been indifferent to the case for
environmental protection. Rather, she appeared to be positively
hostile to it and to those who advocated action. A Cabinet leak in
the early 1980s revealed, for example, that the intention of the
government was to 'reduce over-sensitivity to environmental considerations' (Flynn and Lowe, 1989, p.12). Likewise, at the time of
the Falklands War, the prime minister directly compared the ex-
citement of the conflict with the 'humdrum' nature of issues like
the environment (quoted in McCormick, 1991, p.58). Yet, in a low-
key address to the Royal Society on 28 September 1988, Thatcher
outlined the nature of environmental problems, announced that
her government espoused the concept of sustainable development
and talked about the need for the environment to be nurtured and
safeguarded. This was followed by her keynote speech to the Conservative Party Conference in October of the same year when she
focused on the environment, arguing that the Conservatives were
'not merely friends of the Earth' but also 'its guardians and
trustees for generations to come' (*ibid.*, p.60). This, and the Conservative government's subsequent actions (see below), were to
place the environment firmly on the political agenda. The other
parties were forced to respond, and did so by producing lengthy
policy statements of their own (the Liberal Democrat document
was called *What Price our Planet?* and Labour's was titled *An
Earthly Chance*) (Carter, 1992a, pp.126–30).

Pressure and intentional explanations

Having briefly outlined the increasing interest shown by the major
parties in the environment, we should now turn in search of

explanations. Robinson (1992) usefully suggests two opposing viewpoints here which we can utilize. One the one hand, the greening of the major parties can be explained in terms of a reaction to external pressure applied by the environmental movement, the media and public opinion. This is consistent with an 'economic' approach to political competition which sees parties merely as vote maximizers which, just like producers in a market economy, will shift their position in order to attract votes (Downs, 1959). Alternatively, we can explain it in terms of 'internal factors relating to the actions and positions of key personalities, and to ideological developments within the parties' (Robinson, 1992, p.4).

It is worthwhile initially discussing Thatcher's 'conversion' in terms of these two explanations. There would, on the face of it, seem to be enough evidence to suggest that this came about primarily as a result of external pressure. One can point, first, to the astonishing scale of the about-turn but more pertinent is the fact that her government's previous hostility to the pressure for greater environmental concern was consistent with the free-market ideology they were promoting. This was an ideology antipathetic to the regulatory framework most environmentalists regard as essential, a framework which would place obstacles to the wealth-generating capacity of the economy.

There is, not surprisingly, little conclusive evidence that electoral expediency was the primary motivation. It does appear, though, that Mrs Thatcher's change of heart dates back to 1984, when she became aware of the electoral strides being made by the German Greens, and that the Royal Society speech, far from representing a genuine recognition of environmental problems, was really an attempt to pre-empt Paddy Ashdown's intention to claim the environment for the Liberal Democrats in the first conference of the new party (Flynn and Lowe, 1989, pp.25–9). Finally, there is a suspicion that Thatcher's focus on global environmental issues revealed a greater concern for strengthening 'her position as an international statesperson' as opposed to any genuine interest in the environment *per se* (McCormick, 1991, p.65).

There is a more charitable view. There has been a suggestion that, as a scientist herself, Thatcher became convinced, when presented with the evidence, that severe global environmental problems did exist and that action was required to deal with them (*ibid.*, p.63). Furthermore, it might be argued that, even though external pressure was the main motivation, the greater emphasis placed by the Conservative government on environmental issues did produce some significant and beneficial results. As we have illustrated in earlier chapters, the Thatcher government did create Her Majesty's Inspectorate of Pollution, did reach agreements on CFC reductions and accept responsibility for acid rain, and did carry the Environmental Protection Act and publish the White Paper *This Common Inheritance*. Moreover, a significant step was the replacement of Nicholas Ridley (who had been consistently hostile to the case put by environmentalists) by Chris Patten as Environment Secretary in July 1989. Patten has been by far the 'greenest' Cabinet minister and the efforts he made while in office is an example of an internal party appointment having a significant effect on the direction of policy (Robinson, 1992, p.137).

Internal factors at work also become more apparent if we widen the discussion to consider both the non-Thatcherite elements within the Conservative Party and the influences operating within the Labour Party and the centre parties. On the first of these, it should be noted that Thatcher's concern was restricted largely to global environmental problems. Much closer to home the issue of land-use planning had been a considerable source of conflict within the Conservative Party almost from the beginning of Thatcher's first term as prime minister. This should be seen partly in terms of reacting to external pressure. Thus, particularly after the 1983 election, a number of Tory backbenchers representing rural constituencies primarily in the South East were uneasy about the electoral consequences of allowing further relaxations of development controls in the countryside (Flynn and Lowe, 1992, pp.18–19). As a consequence, while deregulation of planning controls was a feature of Tory policies towards urban areas, in the countryside not only did controls against development remained virtually untouched but (as we shall see in Chapter 8) the privileged position of the farmers was challenged for the first time since the Second World War (Blowers, 1987).

In addition to the electoral imperative, there was also an internal ideological justification for protecting the countryside. Throughout much of the 1980s, the traditional paternalistic or 'wet' tradition within the Conservative Party stood opposed to the free-market rational individualism represented by Thatcher, and this traditional Conservatism was invoked by those interested in protecting Britain's national heritage from the ravages of urban expansion. This was the main influence, for instance, behind the Conservative Ecology Group set up in 1977, and the conservation credentials claimed for the Conservatives from such 'wet' factions as the Bow Group. As one of their publications stated: 'Green voters and Conservative voters share an instinct for preserving what is good and fine and traditional around us. The nature conservationist is a natural Conservative' (quoted in Flynn and Lowe, 1992, p.20).

Likewise, while Nicholas Ridley's ideological guide had been Adam Smith, Chris Patten invoked Edmund Burke, the father-figure of traditional Toryism, in his first conference speech as Environment Secretary. Burke, he argued, reminds 'us of our duties as trustees for the nation, as good stewards of its traditions, its values and its riches' (Flynn and Lowe, 1992, p.31). William Waldegrave, the Minister for Environment, Countryside and Planning up to the 1987 election, also came from the wet wing of the Conservative Party, and the Burkean language in his comment that 'Most environmental disasters are the result of grand plans that somebody has imposed on others' is unmistakable (Porritt and Winner, 1988, p.83). From this it will be seen that the debate about the environment was inextricably linked with the wider debate about the direction of the Conservative Party – between the cautious, paternalistic and interventionism of the 'wets' and the free-market approach of the Thatcherites.

If we turn to Labour and the centre parties, similar internal factors become apparent. In terms of party groupings, the Socialist Environment and Resources Association has been particularly influential within the Labour Party. Established in October 1973, it now has consultative status within the Labour Party and its membership, which runs into the thousands, includes Labour MPs (Robinson, 1992, p.150). We have already noted the environmental credentials of the radical faction within the Liberal Party. The organizational vehicle for this was the Liberal Ecology Group founded in 1977. Those radical Liberals who survived the upheavals of the centre ground in the 1980s were also behind the creation of the Green Democrats and the Liberal Environmental Co-ordinating Group, the vehicles for environmental concern within the Liberal Democratic Party.

The Liberal Party's green tinge was, at least in part, ideologically driven by the concern for community politics and the threats to civil liberty posed by nuclear power. Similarly, Labour's environmentalism is filtered through its ideological and organizational commitment to the urban working class. Thus, the desire to improve the quality of life for the ordinary working-class family and the disadvantaged in general – through cleaning the inner cities, promoting public transport, improving access to the countryside and tackling Third World debt – is paramount (see, for instance, Labour Party, 1992, pp.21, 22, 27). There is also the role of individuals. In Labour's case, mention should be made of David Clark, for a time in the 1980s the party's spokesman on environmental protection, who has been passionately concerned about environmental issues and who has done a great deal to ease the fears of trade unions worried about the impact of environmental protection on employment prospects (Carter, 1992a, p.124). In the centre parties, too, a number of committed environmentalists have played important roles. Active in the SDP, for instance, were Tom Burke of the Green Alliance (see Chapter 4), David Astor of CPRE, and the academic Nigel Haigh (Robinson, 1992, p.135). In the Liberal Party and later the Liberal Democrats, Simon Hughes has consistently espoused Green causes, threatening after the 1987 election to stand in future as a joint Liberal/Green candidate because of his frustration with the Alliance's position on the environment. Des Wilson too, a noted environmental campaigner on issues such as lead in petrol, has been active and influential within the Liberal Party (Porritt and Winner, 1988, p.75).

Finally, it is also worth mentioning the cross-party support for animal welfare and wildlife conservation. Thus, the All-Party Parliamentary Group for Animal Welfare contains such diverse figures as Roger Gale, Janet Fookes and Andrew Bowden (Conservative), Elliot Morley and Tony Banks (Labour) and Simon Hughes (Liberal Democrat) (Garner, 1993a, pp.199–203). In addition, Richard Body, the Conservative backbencher and a farmer, has become a well-known critic of the environmental and animal welfare consequences of intensive agriculture (Body, 1982), and Alan Clarke, the former Conservative minister, is a well-known vegetarian and opponent of fox hunting. The Parliamentary Labour Party now has a researcher working full-time on animal welfare issues and paid for by the International Fund for Animal Welfare, and has also accepted money in the past from the League Against Cruel Sports because of the party's internally driven opposition to fox hunting.

The internal limitations of party greening

Just as there are external and internal factors accounting for the adoption of environmentalism by the major parties, there are also internal and external factors limiting the commitment to environmental concern. For despite the increasing interest in the issue documented above, the environment has not figured prominently in any general election. Thus, in the 1992 campaign, both major parties allocated it less than a page in their manifestos and, despite the Liberal Democrats' attempt to turn it into a major election issue, both they and the Green Party were submerged as the big parties fought the campaign on the traditional economic issues (Carter, 1992b). Thus, 'the sacred cow of economic growth has not been sacrificed' by the main parties and, indeed, remains their 'clarion call' (Robinson, 1992, p.217).

This situation can, in part, be explained by electoral constraints. No party is willing to adopt policies which will, at least in the short term, reduce the living standards of voters. The Conservative government led by John Major could (and did) claim with some justification that its recent proposal to increase VAT on fuel to 17.5 per cent would have environmental benefits. Despite offering a package excluding the poorer sections of the community from the charge, however, the government was defeated by Conservative backbenchers concerned about the electoral fall-out.

There are factors internal to parties which have also limited the greening of the major parties. We have already seen that party leaders such as Thatcher in the early 1980s at least, and Owen, constrained the development of environmentalism. Likewise, Neil Kinnock was 'barely interested' in the environment (Robinson, 1992, p.175). In addition, occupying key positions within their respective parties were Jack Cunningham, who, as the MP in whose constituency Sellafield nuclear power station is located, has a very good reason for fighting to retain the nuclear option in Labour's energy policy. Nicholas Ridley fulfilled a similar constraining role in the Conservative Party.

Finally, both major parties are financially dependent on economic interest groups. Labour's ties with the trade unions requires the party to place emphasis on economic growth in order to maximize employment opportunities. In the past, there was a general suspicion in the Labour Party, and in the labour movement generally, that environmentalism was a preoccupation of the middle classes, and some of this class-based hostility still no doubt exists (Carter, 1992a, pp.119–20). Similarly, the Conservatives' reliance on business interests including energy suppliers, farmers and house builders has obvious, if unquantifiable, consequences for the party's environmental policy (Robinson, 1992, pp.193–7). This may explain why the Liberals in their various guises, unencumbered by such vested interests, appear to be the greenest of the main parties. It also provides an additional environmental case for the state funding of political parties (Garner and Kelly, 1993, ch.10).

Political parties, of course, even when occupying governmental positions, are only one set of actors influencing policy outcomes. In this book, we have already looked at the role of pressure groups and the impact of supra-national decision-making. To focus on political parties alone, therefore, is to provide only a partial explanation for the direction of environmental policy. In the next chapter, therefore, an attempt is made to identify and examine the various influences upon the policy process in order to draw a more comprehensive picture which should enable us to explain environmental policy outcomes more thoroughly.

Further reading

The Green Party's development has not been the subject of a book-length study, although see Parkin (1989) for an insider's account of Green parties throughout the world. For the British Greens, it is necessary to plough through a number of articles. The main ones are Rudig and Lowe (1986), McCulloch (1992), Doherty (1992a; 1992b) and Rudig (1993). The electoral development of the Greens is covered convincingly in Rootes (1991). See also Rudig (1985), Rudig and Franklin (1991), Curtice (1989) and Carter (1992b). The reaction of the main parties to the rise of environmentalism is dealt with admirably in Robinson (1992). On the Labour Party, see Carter (1992a). On the Conservatives, see McCormick (1991) and Flynn and Lowe (1992).

8

THE POLITICAL PROCESS AND THE ENVIRONMENT

So far in this book we have focused mainly on two broad themes: questions concerning what ought and needs to be done to protect the environment on the one hand, and questions concerning what has been done at the national and supra-national level on the other. It should have become apparent that even from the perspective of the shallow or reformist environmentalist, and despite greater environmental awareness by decision-makers, there remains a gap between the is and the ought. In this chapter, through a series of case studies focusing on the politics of the countryside, pollution and wildlife conservation, the themes covered in previous chapters are further illustrated. The main purpose of this chapter though, particularly in the case of the examination of countryside and pollution issues, is to examine the political processes involved in producing policy outputs. In this way, we hope that a greater understanding will emerge of why the gap between 'is' and 'ought' exists. To provide a context for these case studies, we need first to consider various approaches to public policy which may help us to order the empirical evidence.

Approaches to policy-making

The process of policy-making is extremely complex, and disentangling the relative importance of the various influences on public

policy is notoriously difficult. Clearly, in Western liberal democracies, policy decisions come about as a result of the interaction
between elected politicians, bureaucrats working within public authorities, interest groups and public opinion. In addition, this interaction is mediated through the particular historical, social,
economic and political contexts within which policy decisions are
made. The situation is complicated, as we saw in Chapter 6, by the
fact that environmental policy no longer takes place primarily
within any one country, and the supra-national nature of policy-
making vastly increases the number of participants involved and in
turn the variables one has to take into account.

Students of policy-making are faced with a mass of empirical
evidence, and theory-building is a useful, albeit rather constraining, way of managing the information gathered. Numerous approaches from within the disciplines of political science and public
administration have been suggested, and agreement over typologies or the validity of competing approaches is very rarely
arrived at (compare, for instance, Greenaway et al., 1992, chs 1 and
2, with Ham and Hill, 1984; and see the case in Marsh and Rhodes,
1992, for the adoption of one particular approach). One recurring
problem is that the development of theory tends to run far ahead
of empirical application, a not surprising fact given the operational
difficulties – such as time and cost – involved with the latter.

It is hardly surprising, therefore, that there has not been a surfeit
of environmental studies which seek to relate empirical evidence
to theoretical perspectives, although, as this chapter will demonstrate, there have been some. One such example is Albert Weale's
(1992) account of pollution politics. In this work, Weale distinguishes between four idioms: rational choice theory, systems,
institutions and policy discourse. While this was an innovative
study, the choice of approaches was somewhat eclectic and Weale
himself finds it difficult, because of the paucity of research, to
relate them to actual cases of pollution politics.

A mention should be made of rational choice theory here (see
Weale, 1992, pp.38–46) since it would seem to help explain certain aspects of environmental policy. Rational choice theory
focuses on individual behaviour. It assumes individuals will make
rational choices designed to maximize their own utility. This individualistic approach seems to offer a convincing explanation for
the existence of a 'politics' of the environment. Thus, as we have

seen, governments have to intervene to clean up the environment because, as an externality, individual polluters, not otherwise economically affected by the damage they cause, will have no incentive to do so unless penalized by a public authority. Moreover, in a classic case of the 'prisoner's dilemma', those affected by the pollution will not, if left to their own devices, contribute towards cleaning it up since their individual contribution will make no difference to the outcome. They will benefit anyway if enough of the others in the community contribute, since cleaning up the pollution is a public good which cannot be restricted. Further, if an individual does contribute and not enough of the others do, then she would have done so for no benefit and at a possible cost if the contribution cannot be repaid.

Rational choice theory also offers an account of the character of environmental politics. Collective action problems, as Chapter 6 revealed, are rife in the concluding of international environmental agreements. We saw in Chapter 4, in addition, that Olson's theory of group mobilization, which derives from the rational choice school, seeks to explain why environmental groups are weak *vis-à-vis* those sectional interest groups with a vested interest in preventing or diluting environmental measures (Olson, 1965). Moreover, in Chapter 7, we saw that electoral expediency was at least one, albeit not the only or even the most important, factor in persuading the main parties to take environmentalism more seriously. This fits in nicely with the Downsian model of parties as mere vote maximizers, a theory which again can be accommodated within the rational choice tradition (Downs, 1959).

Pluralism and its critics

While not wishing to reject the rational choice approach entirely, it should be said that a great deal more importance has been attached to theories which seek to explain policy outcomes in terms of the power exercised by competing interests and, for better or worse, this chapter will focus on explaining environmental policy in terms of such theories. Again, stating the different perspectives is relatively straightforward while operationalizing them provides numerous methodological difficulties. The most appropriate way of beginning an examination of the enormous range of relevant material is to consider the pluralist approach.

The pluralist approach has been the dominant theory of the state in post-war Western political science (Dunleavy and O'Leary, 1987). It is particularly associated with the work of the American political scientist, Robert Dahl (1961; 1971). For pluralists, in all complex societies where no state repression exists, the formation of groups to represent interests which people have in common is a natural phenomenon. In turn, public policy-making is a product of the interaction between groups. For some pluralist thinkers, government is itself the neutral arbiter between groups, its decisions reflecting the balance of power between them. For others, the government has its own agenda and exists as one competing set of interests among the others. For all pluralists, the key feature of modern Western liberal democracies is that power is diffuse. This does not mean that all groups have an equal ability to achieve their objectives, but that no one interest or small set of interests dominates the decision-making process. Thus, the assumption is that if a group has an interest to promote, it will be able to gain entry to the political system and, further, that at some point it will achieve at least some of its objectives. The competition between groups thereby ensures that governments remain accountable to societal demands, and these demands are an on-going feature of the political process not merely occurring during election campaigns.

Now, the pluralist approach has been subject to a great deal of criticism from those (often operating from within a Marxist, elitist or corporatist perspective) who claim that pluralists seriously exaggerate the extent to which the political system is open to a variety of competing groups (Ham and Hill, 1984, chs 2 and 4). Central here is a critique of pluralist methodology. Pluralists, it is suggested, operate with what Lukes (1974) has called a 'one-dimensional' theory of power. Thus, a typical pluralist analysis of decision-making involves looking at what decisions have been made and comparing these with the preferences of the groups involved. If a group's aims are met, they are attributed with influence. This approach, of course, might lead to non-pluralist conclusions but, the argument goes, if the pluralist hypothesis is confirmed it may be unreliable and misleading because the methodology adopted cannot account for more subtle exercises of power.

The claim made by critics of pluralists, then, is that decision-making studies of the type described above do not tell the full story because they exclude the possibility that some decisions may not reach the decision-making arena or that, if they do, their resolution may not be dependent on the visible activities of particular groups. Thus, in what has been described as 'non-decision-making' (Bachrach and Barazt, 1962) or the 'second dimension' of power (Lukes, 1974), it might be possible to identify instances of covert grievances or concerns which are excluded from the political arena. This exclusion may occur for a variety of reasons (Dearlove and Saunders, 1984, pp.209–12). It could be the product of the use of force. Alternatively, it can come about through the use of rules or procedures so that, for instance, issues are referred to Royal Commissions where they can languish, or challenging groups can be co-opted and tamed. Finally, exclusion can occur through the law of anticipated reactions whereby the reputation for power of a particular interest may be such that a challenging group or groups may anticipate that it is not worth their while entering the political arena.

A variation on this non-decision making theme was provided by Charles Lindblom (1977). In this work, Lindblom, who had previously accepted the pluralist case, argues that business interests occupy a privileged position within the political system. This derives not just from the resources they can muster for conventional lobbying – which pluralist methodology would identify and take into account – but also, and most importantly, from their structural position in the economy. Thus, governments, he argues, will always take business interests into account, whether or not business organizations actually campaign openly for them, because the economic benefits business provides, in terms of employment and investment, and so on, is crucial for the re-election prospects of any government.

Pluralism and the environment

There have been some attempts to utilize the theories discussed above in environmental case studies. Most notably, Matthew Crenson's study (1971) of air pollution politics in two US cities in Indiana specifically adopts the non-decision-making approach. Thus he notes that air pollution regulations were introduced much later in one city (Gary) than in the other (East Chicago). His explanation was that in Gary, the economy was dominated by a single corporation (US Steel) whereas East Chicago had many steel companies. US Steel's reputation for power, Crenson argues, was so great that no environmental group thought it worthwhile to challenge its resistance to pollution controls. As well as the anticipated reactions involved in the reputation for power, there are elements of Lindblom's thesis here too. A major reason why US Steel could exercise such power was not because of its lobbying resources but because of the contribution it made to the local economy. Thus, there was an unstated assumption that any attempt to introduce more stringent pollution controls could result in US Steel relocating elsewhere. This would have been far more catastrophic for Gary, reliant on one major employer, than in other cities with a broader employment base.

One British study along similar lines was Andrew Blowers' account (1984) of the relationship between a Bedfordshire brickworks and the local county council in the 1970s and early 1980s. Blowers, who was himself actively involved in the events he describes as leader of the Labour group on the council and a member of the planning committee, argues that while a pluralist model makes sense of the initial period in the 1970s when air pollution became a political issue and environmental groups were successful in obstructing London Brick's application for further planning permission, the company's eventual victory cannot be explained in such terms. In the early 1980s, the initial objection by the planning authority was overturned and this came about, Blowers suggests, because of the changed economic climate which led to the employment opportunities offered by the company if planning permission was granted taking precedence over the alleviation of air pollution. Again, Lindblom's assertion – that business has a privileged position because of the economic clout it can exercise – would seem to have some relevance here. In this case, unlike the Crenson study, it did not prevent the issue of air pollution reaching the political agenda, but it did determine how the decision was resolved. On the other hand, the privileged position of London Brick only seemed to come into play at a particular (downward) point in the economic cycle. This suggests the position of business is weaker, as one would perhaps expect, during a period of relative economic prosperity, particularly if we add to the equation the assumption that at such times post-material values become more pronounced (see Chapter 4).

There is also a case for saying that a class bias is central to the British planning system. Superficially at least, the land-use planning system would seem to be consistent with a pluralist analysis. It allows for extensive participation and consultation, and, in the event of a public inquiry, the final decision rests with a neutral inspector and, ultimately, with a democratically elected minister. We have already observed, however, that the more affluent and professional classes are more able to take advantage of the system (see Sandbach, 1980, pp.132–3). Furthermore, developers have far more resources at their disposal compared to local or national environmental groups. The classic examples here were the nuclear inquiries (Windscale, 1977; Sizewell B, 1983–5; and Dounreay, 1986) where, despite marshalling their evidence effectively, the environmental lobby simply could not compete with the resources brought to bear by British Nuclear Fuels. BNF spent £750,000 in the Windscale Inquiry and £20 million in Sizewell B (Rydin, 1993, p.236). It is not just hard cash that hinders the environmental case. The quasi-legal character of inquiries also militates against local groups making their voices heard (*ibid.*, pp.236–7).

Such arguments would seem to suggest that the system works in favour of particular groups within society, allowing Pepper (1986, pp.180–1) to claim:

> At best the agencies and processes which are supposed to be neutral arbiters are heavily weighted towards and manipulated by the owners of capital. Through them, environmental protestors are put at immediate disadvantage when they try to make their cases in 'democratic' forums.

Here, environmental reformers could benefit from taking on board the radical ecocentric insistence on the relationship between environmental protection and political organisation. The argument – put most articulately by Dryzeck (1990, chs 6 and 7) – that effective resolutions to environmental problems must be accompanied by the democratization of policy-making is extremely relevant and is a point we shall come back to in the concluding chapter.

On the other hand, it should be said that while accepting that planning procedures are far from perfect, it is not clear that environmental conflicts can be reduced to class-based politics. For one thing, the building of nuclear power stations is a source of employment and, as we saw in Chapter 7, one of the reasons for the relative weakness of the anti-nuclear movement in Britain is the local support that has emerged for such developments. Furthermore, the opponents of development are themselves often (although by no means always) relatively affluent people adopting NIMBY attitudes. In this context, it might be said that at least some development is more beneficial to the working class and is prevented by those seeking to protect their relatively high standard of living (Blowers, 1984, pp.264–5).

Policy networks

One of the central claims of pluralism is that no one interest dominates decision-making in all areas of policy. It would indeed seem to be the case that policy-making in modern liberal democracies has become increasingly sectorized with a different set of actors operating within each sector. We have seen, for instance, that in the environmental sphere there is an acute problem of integrating an environmental perspective across a range of policy areas each centring on a distinct set of government departments and agencies. To take account of this policy sectorization, political scientists have developed the concept of policy networks which would seem to have considerable explanatory potential at least as far as environmental policy is concerned (Marsh and Rhodes, 1992; Smith, 1993).

Although there has been some dispute about the actual character of policy networks, a useful continuum has been developed, based on the degree of openness, complexity and competition (Marsh and Rhodes, 1992, p.249). At one end is the so-called policy community characterized by regular interaction between a small number of long-standing participants, usually a government agency and certain privileged interest groups, operating within a considerable degree of consensus and closed off both from competing groups not accepting the shared values and from other policy networks. At the other is the so-called issue network, characterized by a considerable degree of openness and flux, with a variety of competing groups able to gain access (Heclo, 1978). These are ideal types and most policy networks will lie between the two extremes. Different networks may, of course, be placed at different positions on the spectrum.

Once a particular network has been characterized, it is then possible to explain why it exists, what the policy output consequences are, and what are the prospects for change. Even if we accept that policy is made in distinct networks – a view that has been disputed (Hogwood, 1987) – it still does not necessarily result in confirmation of the pluralist position. For, if within a particular policy sphere, one set of unified interests continually gets its own way we are entitled to draw attention to it as an example of a structure which is more in accord with a corporatist or elitist model. Further, if, in the case of environmental policy, the objectives of the environmental lobby are continually thwarted by opponents within the different policy networks impacting on the environment, we are surely also entitled to say that there is a power bloc obstructing change. If this is so, we are able both to pinpoint the reason for the gap between the is and the ought, in addition to raising questions about the democratic legitimacy of this situation.

Agriculture, the countryside and the environment

The first of the case studies in this chapter considers the relationship between agriculture and the environment. It is hardly surprising that a study of countryside politics should focus on agriculture. Over 80 per cent of rural land is managed by farmers and, as McCormick points out, the threat to the countryside by modern farming methods is 'the most controversial and widely debated environmental issue of the post-war years – and perhaps of the twentieth century' (McCormick, 1991, p.69). We shall consider the issue in four parts corresponding to four specific questions. (1) Why is agriculture an important environmental issue? (2) How has agricultural policy traditionally been made, and by whom? (3) Why have the effects of agriculture on the countryside become a political issue? (4) How far has the respective influence of the National Farmers Union (NFU) and the environmental lobby changed?

The consequences of modern farming

Agriculture has become an environmental issue partly at least because there are now more people concerned about the condition of the countryside who do not have a vested interest in exploiting it. Without the objectively measured increase in environmental problems in the countryside, though, it is unlikely there would be a political dimension to the issue. When we consider the damage that has been done, farming methods are held to be largely responsible.

The countryside has been exploited for centuries and very little true wilderness now remains. For some deep ecologists this, by itself, would lead to condemnation even though human impact need not necessarily be destructive. The problem is that much modern farming *is* environmentally destructive. These modern agricultural practices date back to the Second World War when the development of intensive farming methods coincided with the desire for Britain to be self-sufficient in food. From this point on, the priority for most farmers was to increase the output and efficiency of their land. This was done with remarkable success. Thus, prior to the Second World War, nearly 70 per cent of Britain's food requirements were imported. By the mid-1980s, the position had been reversed with about two-thirds being provided by British agriculture to a population which had grown from 47 million to 56 million (Lowe *et al.*, 1986, p.21). This increase has involved arable and livestock farming. To take the latter case, increasing use of 'factory' farming methods has massively increased the availability, and therefore reduced the price, of meat and poultry, turning some products, such as chicken, from a luxury item into a common purchase.

The environmental costs of this increase in efficiency, though, were considerable (Body, 1982; Shoard, 1982; Lowe *et al.*, 1986, pp.64–80). The result was a disregard for ecologically important parts of the countryside such as hedgerows, forests and wetlands. Between 1946 and 1974, 25 per cent of the hedgerows in England and Wales disappeared and in a similar period half of the ancient woodlands in Britain were felled (McCormick, 1991, p.71). Likewise, in the past 30 years 95 per cent of lowland herb-rich grassland, 60 per cent of lowland heaths and 50 per cent of lowland fens and marshes have been lost (Lowe *et al.*, 1986, p.55).

Not only has this damage meant a loss of amenity for people to enjoy, it has also resulted in the extinction of a number of plant and animal species. Otters, badgers and bats have become so rare that it required legislation to protect them. Moreover, the application of fertilizers and pesticides used to increase yields, has had consequences not only for animal and plant species but also for human health (Carson, 1962). Finally, quite apart from the animal welfare implications of factory farming, the water requirements of intensive units can be phenomenal and, in addition, serious waste disposal problems occur, particularly as increasing specialization has resulted in the separation of arable and livestock farming and therefore, for many farming units, a natural outlet for animal wastes has been lost (Mason and Singer, 1990).

The agricultural policy community

So how has this come about? Why were farmers allowed to damage the countryside with so few apparent controls on their activities? In attempting to answer these questions, the policy network concept would appear to have a great deal of relevance. Indeed, agriculture would appear to be a classic case of a policy community with the NFU having a privileged position within the Ministry of Agriculture, Fisheries and Food (MAFF). This dated back to the period immediately after the Second World War. The Agriculture Act 1947 gave the NFU a statutory right to be consulted over agricultural policy and, since then, the NFU has had a very close relationship with the MAFF so that the department's and the farmers' interests have become indivisible.

As Smith (1990, pp.124–31) points out, the ideological glue which held the agricultural policy community together was based on a shared belief in agricultural expansion – that farmers should be encouraged to produce as much as possible as efficiently as possible. Any group of people, such as environmentalists or consumers, who did not concur with this were excluded from the policy community. So, for much of the post-war period, the environmental effects of intensive agriculture were excluded from the primary decision-making arena – a classic case of non-decision-making.

Indeed, for a large part of the post-war period, the expansionist ideology was so widely held that very few voices could be raised against it. Originally, there was a widespread assumption that farmers were the guardians of the countryside, so that there was no thought of protecting the countryside against them (Lowe *et al.*, 1986, pp.15–17). Crucially though, even when the opposition to intensive farming became more vocal, not least through the activities of environmental groups, the closed agricultural policy community still prevented these issues from being part of the mainstream policy agenda. Thus, in a classic instance, only the RSPB of the conservation community had any input into the Wildlife and Countryside Bill before it was put before Parliament in the early 1980s. Even the state conservation agencies were excluded. Numerous amendments were proposed during the bill's passage through Parliament but none of the successful amendments was opposed by the NFU (Cox and Lowe, 1983).

The assumption in the policy network literature is that the type of network will influence policy outcomes. In the case of the agricultural policy community, this would seem to be the case, with policies serving the NFU's interests predominating. Thus, the Agriculture Act 1947 introduced a system of guaranteed prices for all major agricultural produce. Since then, the farming industry has had subsidies far in excess of any other industry. Britain's entry into the European Union in 1973 changed the nature of the way these subsidies were paid to farmers – from consumers through guaranteed prices to taxpayers through direct subsidies – but the existence of substantial financial assistance remained (Smith, 1990, pp.147–7). In addition, as we saw in Chapter 5, the Town and Country Planning Act 1947 largely excluded farming from planning controls and farms were also exempt from paying rates.

Some scholars (Self and Storing, 1962; Wilson, 1977) have argued that the NFU's influence can be exaggerated – that the resources they can muster are not exceptional and that close contact with the MAFF produces the risk of imprisonment so that the NFU becomes fearful of openly criticizing government policy in case the MAFF turns against them. The evidence, however, does not really support this position and it might be the case that an analysis along these lines misunderstands the reasons why the NFU was incorporated into government in the first place. Two alternative explanations are pertinent here. The first is more consistent with pluralist methodology in that it suggests that the NFU became powerful because of the resources it could muster. These would include factors such as its all-inclusive membership, its considerable financial resources enabling it to lobby institutions in Britain and the European Union, its links with landowning interests in Parliament and the executive, the agricultural vote it can call on, and support from elsewhere in the industrial and financial community (Lowe *et al.*, 1986, pp.85–91; Grant, 1989, pp.102, 139; Smith, 1990, pp.147–77). This resource-based explanation is pluralist not because the role of the NFU fits the pluralist model. Indeed, exactly the opposite since the NFU/MAFF relationship is corporatist or elitist in nature (Cox, *et al.*, 1987). Rather, it is pluralist because it assigns to government a largely passive role. Government, according to this view, is merely reacting to the power of a particular group.

The alternative explanation emphasizes not the resources of the NFU but the historical, ideological and structural context within which the government and the NFU were operating. According to this view (associated, most notably, with Smith, 1990), the state itself played a positive role. Thus, the NFU was invited into government because it was functional for the government to do so. During and after the Second World War the major problem facing the government was the need to ensure a regular supply of food. This was the structural factor which established 'the limits of possibility' (Smith, 1990, p.38) within which governments and pressure groups had to operate. Once established in government, the dominant position of the NFU was maintained by the institutional framework which excluded other interests from emerging and the ideological promotion of expansionism which prevented alternative scenarios being raised. Thus, while the first resource-based explanation suggests that the close relationship between MAFF and the NFU is the *cause* of the adopted policy, the second, state autonomy, explanation suggests that the close relationship is the *result* of the policy adopted.

The politicization of agriculture

In recent years, the effects of intensive agriculture on the countryside has become a political issue and, as a result, the agricultural policy community is under threat. Why has this come about? There are a number of possible reasons. First, there is the increasing financial costs of agricultural policy which British people have become much more aware of since Britain joined the EU and the negotiations over the Common Agricultural Policy have taken place in a blaze of publicity (Grant, 1989, p.146). The emergency action to introduce milk quotas in the 1980s to forestall the bankruptcy of the EU is regarded here as a particularly crucial event

(Lowe *et al.*, 1986, p.52). Coupled with this was the free-market ideology of the Thatcher governments. The privileged position of the farmers was bound to sit uneasily with the antipathy of these governments both to subsidies and to corporatist relationships with interest groups. As a result, the NFU became much more vulnerable (Grant, 1989, p.146). Added to these factors was the campaigns of environmental groups which disseminated information about the environmental and animal welfare consequences of intensive agriculture.

Greater public awareness of, and concern for, the deteriorating state of the countryside was also a product of social and demographic changes (Grant, 1989, p.147; McCormick, 1991, pp.82–3). In particular, the mass ownership of cars has made the countryside more accessible. Further, many people have moved to rural areas taking advantage of changing work patterns and, as a result, farmers are being outnumbered by middle-class escapees from the cities who have no vested interest in farming and many of whom may indeed be concerned about the protection of the countryside.

As a consequence, it should be seen that the original problem – lack of self-sufficiency in food – which gave rise to the policy community has disappeared. Food shortages have become a thing of the past and the expansionary ethos has been successfully challenged. By the 1980s, new problems – food safety, healthy foods, animal welfare and the effects of intensive agriculture on the environment – had emerged to which government had to find solutions. Far from being a solution to the problem, the farmers had become a problem themselves (Smith, 1990, p.212).

The break-up of the policy community?

How far, then, has the agricultural policy community begun to fragment, as one would expect if we accept the state-autonomy explanation for its formation? The short answer here is, not very much. Clearly, the very fact that the impact of agriculture on the environment has become a political issue demonstrates some weakening of the NFU's position. Farmers have lost their ideological privilege and, because of this, they may be in danger of losing their institutional privilege (Smith, 1990, p.190). As a result, the NFU has to engage in much more conventional pressure group lobbying in order to justify its activities to a more sceptical public.

The NFU now emphasizes conservation as an important concern of farmers (Lowe *et al.*, 1986, p.102). Likewise, MAFF has at least to appear to reconcile the interests of farmers with the interests of those concerned about the countryside and the welfare of animals. Compare, for instance, the 1975 White Paper *Food From Our Own Resources* (HMSO, 1975), which emphasizes the expansionist ethos and has little to say about the environment, with MAFF's *Our Farming Future* (MAFF, 1991), which devotes almost half of its 40 pages to countryside, animal welfare and food consumer issues.

Legislation seeking to intervene in farming activities has also been forthcoming. The Agricultural (Miscellaneous Provisions) Act 1968 dealt with farm animal welfare, and the Wildlife and Countryside Act 1981, the Agricultural Acts 1986 and 1988 and parts of the Environmental Protection Act 1990 focused on countryside issues. There is no doubt, too, that environmental groups now find it easier to get their voices heard within the MAFF (Smith, 1990, pp.200–1). Some conservation groups, such as the RSNC and the RSPB, were formally incorporated within the MAFF in the Farming and Wildlife Advisory Group founded in 1969 where, together with Ministry and NFU officials, conservation issues are discussed (Grant, 1989, p.149; McCormick, 1991, p.81).

Despite all this, however, it is doubtful if the changes represent the death throes of the MAFF/NFU policy community. Although environmental groups do have greater access to the MAFF now, the NFU's access is still quantitatively and qualitatively greater. Furthermore, it tends to be the moderate conservation groups who have been co-opted and not more radical groups such as Friends of the Earth. The intention here is to give the impression that MAFF is listening to conservation interests. To some extent this may be true, but the more moderate conservation groups are less likely to challenge the prevailing ideology within the policy community – that there is no fundamental incompatibility between conservation and intensive agriculture and that farmers should not be penalized for good conservation practice.

The legislation supports this interpretation since the measures introduced have essentially protected the interests of farmers. Thus, with the exception of the banning of stubble burning introduced in the Environmental Protection Act 1990, all the conservation schemes are voluntary and allow for compensation to be paid to farmers for carrying them out (Smith, 1990, p.193; Pearce *et al.*, 1993, pp.119–20). The Wildlife and Countryside Act, for instance, does not plug the planning gap as conservationists wanted (see Chapter 5). Likewise, the Environmentally Sensitive Areas scheme, introduced in the Agriculture Act 1988, pays farmers for managing landscapes for environmental purposes rather than to maximize food production (Young, 1993, p.62). In addition, it is hardly a sacrifice for farmers not to use land for food production when subsidies for production are diminishing anyway. In 1994 alone, English farmers were paid £124 million to allow their land to remain idle under the EU set-aside scheme (*Guardian*, 23 May 1994).

What we have, then, is a classic case of a policy community protecting its interests by managing change in directions which it can control. By itself, this represents some weakening of the MAFF/NFU relationship. It remains to be seen whether the continuing emphasis on environmental protection will eventually lead to a new institutional framework.

The politics of pollution

We saw in Chapter 5 that pollution control policy in Britain has gone through a period of change in recent years. The purpose of this section is to seek to explain why changes have occurred and, equally importantly, to explain their limitations. Providing the context here is the notion of integrated pollution control (IPC) in its internal and external manifestations (see Chapter 5). It is widely recognized that IPC provides the most appropriate mechanism for environmental protection and, as such, it provides a benchmark against which we can measure the depth of the changes introduced.

Explaining pollution control reform

When examining the changing nature of British pollution control policy, it becomes apparent that a number of factors were at work. In the case of the creation of Her Majesty's Inspectorate of Pollution, for instance, an important determining factor was the role of ideas. Thus, the case for integrating the various pollution control agencies had been advocated in the 1970s by the Royal

Commission on Environmental Pollution and, by the 1980s, the necessity for internal integration had become the accepted view among environmental experts (Weale, 1992, pp.96–7, 102–3). This would support the 'policy discourse idiom' identified by Weale since it suggests that problem-solving and the role of research, argument and discussion was, in this case, an important determinant of policy outcomes.

Government, though, took a long time to be persuaded of the value of an integrated inspectorate. Indeed, it took the British government six years even to reply to the proposal, and then it was rejected (Weale, 1992, p.104). The RCEP called again in 1986 for the creation of HMIP but its eventual creation in 1987 owed more to additional factors. Most importantly, there was the embarrassment caused by the revelations that the existing regulatory machinery had failed to prevent discharges from Sellafield. Also of importance was the support for the reform from the Environment Minister William Waldegrave (*ibid.*, p.105). It was the environmental movement which drew attention to the problems at Sellafield but, other than that, it played little part in this central environmental reform.

Likewise, the environmental movement was only partly responsible for the creation of the NRA. Indeed, the debate about water pollution in general, and the quality of Britain's drinking water in particular, came about largely as an unintended consequence of water privatization (McCormick, 1991, pp.96–8). In the original White Paper published in 1986, the government announced its intention of transferring environmental responsibilities from the Regional Water Authorities to the private water companies. The European Commission was made aware of this plan, largely due to the scrutiny of the Council for the Protection of Rural England, and informed the government that it was illegal under EU law to place pollution controls into the hands of private companies. As a result, the White Paper was discarded and, after the 1987 election, plans to create an independent NRA with pollution control responsibilities were announced (Richardson, 1992).

The privatization of electricity had environmental consequences too. As a result of pressure from the environmental lobby, it led, first, to the creation of a new Office of Electricity Regulation (OFFER) which has responsibilities for environmental oversight of the electricity supply industry (McCormick, 1991, p.102). More importantly, electricity privatization has had severe consequences for the nuclear industry which for the vast majority of environmentalists has been a positive step.

In the early days of the first Thatcher government, there was considerable commitment to nuclear power and the plan was to build one reactor per year for a ten-year period beginning in 1982. This was not just a technical matter but reflected a political strategy designed to weaken the position of the miners who had all but brought down Heath's Conservative administration in 1974 (Greenaway *et al.*, 1992, p.130). By the end of the decade, however, this programme had been scrapped and there are now no future plans to build nuclear power stations in Britain.

It is difficult to pinpoint exactly why this turnaround occurred. The atmospheric and political fall-out from the Chernobyl disaster was clearly one factor and nuclear power was obviously opposed vigorously by the anti-nuclear movement (who did their best to publicize safety problems in the nuclear industry) and also (not so predictably) by the House of Commons Select Committee on Energy (Greenaway *et al.*, 1992, p.130). Thus, Michael Saward (1992) traces the development of the nuclear energy policy network and claims that it was transformed in the mid- to late 1970s from a closed policy community, dominated by the Atomic Energy Authority and its scientific experts, into a much more open issue network in which the competing manufacturers of nuclear reactors, the Central Electricity Generating Board and the anti-nuclear movement played an important role.

There is a suspicion that Saward's interpretation accords too much influence to the anti-nuclear lobby here. In general terms, as we intimated in the previous chapter, the anti-nuclear movement in Britain has been relatively weak. Saward (1992, pp.93–5) bases much of his claim on the participation of the anti-nuclear movement in the Windscale, Sizewell and Hinkley Point public inquiries. As Ward (1983) indicates, though, Friends of the Earth, who were heavily involved in the inquiries, could not compete with the resources of the nuclear industry (see above) and, despite marshalling a good case, their claims were largely ignored in the final reports. As for Chernobyl, the nuclear industry could, somewhat plausibly, explain it away by focusing on particular problems in the Soviet Union while denying claims about the inherent safety problems of nuclear power in general.

At the most, then, we can say that the anti-nuclear lobby has raised the issue of nuclear safety in particular and the wider issue of energy needs in general, thereby putting the nuclear industry and the government, which for so long had supported it, on the defensive. It still remains the case, however, that, ultimately, the role played by electricity privatization has been a crucial factor in weakening the case for nuclear power. Its major effect was to reveal the true costs of nuclear power (and the alternatives) by subjecting it to what, for true Thatcherites at least, is the real test of value – the market. Thus, the original intention, outlined in the 1988 White Paper on electricity privatization, was to divide the publicly owned CEGB generators between two private companies – PowerGen and National Power – with the latter being given responsibility for nuclear power generation. It soon became apparent, however, that nuclear power, when thoroughly accounted for separately from other sources of energy, was much more expensive than previously thought. Realizing that nuclear power constituted a poor investment, it was eventually removed from the public sale and put into the hands of a new public body, Nuclear Electric. As Greenaway *et al.* (1992, p.138) point out, then, 'Both the public and its representatives in Parliament play a peripheral role in the story of nuclear power.'

Explaining the limits to British pollution control

So far, we have attempted to explain why changes occurred in the character of pollution politics in Britain. In Chapter 5, we also noted that these changes have only gone so far down the road towards integrated pollution control (IPC). One possible explanation for this focuses on policy styles and, in particular, on the disjointed way in which decisions tend to be made in all Liberal democracies and Britain in particular (J. Richardson, 1982). This theory of 'disjointed incrementalism' or, as Charles Lindblom famously calls it, the 'science of muddling through', holds that the normal pattern of policy-making involves regular small and cautious adjustments to the existing framework. These adjustments are often accompanied by a low level of understanding and are more often than not reactions to events that unexpectedly arise (Lindblom, 1959).

For Lindblom, at least at the time, this was not just a description of the way in which policy was usually made, it was also in his view a prescription about how it *ought* to be made. Certainly, it is consistent with the pluralist framework, emphasizing the diffuse nature of power with a wide variety of actors able to influence policy outcomes leading to an outcome which satisfies at least some of the demands of the participants. In terms of pollution control policy, however, it arguably militates against the integrated approach which most environmentalists regard as crucial (Dryzek, 1990, pp.70, 122–3; Weale, 1992, p.100). For this to be achieved, a synoptic approach to policy-making is necessary, one which takes large steps, is proactive and involves a high degree of understanding.

An alternative explanation focuses not on the style of decision-making but on the power of those interests who oppose IPC. This power-based form of explanation, it seems to me, would seem to be more able to explain the failure to achieve external integration. As with agricultural policy, the notion of policy communities is particularly useful here. From this perspective, it can be argued that the major obstacle to external integration is the power exercised by economic interests occupying a privileged status within the development-oriented departments.

We have already considered the influence exercised by the NFU within the agricultural policy community. Equally if not more privileged are the constituent parts of the road lobby (within the Department of Transport), the power generators and suppliers (within the energy policy community) and a variety of business interests (operating within the Department of Trade and Industry). The policy community centring on the Department of Transport is a particularly pertinent area for study. For, despite the politicization of the transport issue – as the environmental consequences of more cars, more heavy goods vehicles and more roads have become well known – the policy emphasis of the Department of Transport – at least until recently – did not change. Thus, all forms of road traffic have grown as governments in the 1980s neglected public transport in favour of major road building programmes (Pearce, 1993, pp.150–1). As recently as May 1989, the government announced a more than doubling of expenditure on road building, from £5 billion to £12 billion, over a ten-year period (Ward, 1990, pp.232–3). This policy emphasis is clearly related to the influence of the road lobby. One only has to examine its constituent elements to recognize how formidable this lobby is. The umbrella organization is the British Road Federation, within which is contained the motor industry, the bus operators, road haulage firms, motorists' organizations, the road construction industry and the oil industry (Hamer, 1974; Pearce, 1993, p.191).

The recent cuts in the road building programme do reflect a weakening of the road lobby and, in part, a victory for the various parts of the environmental lobby, which has campaigned hard on this issue in recent years. Other factors have been equally if not more important, though. The government's desire to cut public spending is one. In addition, a growing consensus, accepted at least partly even by the road lobby, has emerged that building new roads is not the answer to road congestion, and other methods, such as road pricing and greater resources being directed at maintaining existing roads, need to be considered (*Guardian*, 26 October 1994). This would seem to be an example of the importance of ideas in explaining policy outcomes, and therefore provides some support for Weale's 'policy discourse idiom'.

To establish the exact nature of the relationships within these different policy areas requires detailed research for each of them, further demonstrating the vast scope of the subject matter of environmental politics. Here, we should repeat the point that there is evidence that the key White Paper *This Common Inheritance* was far less stringent than Chris Patten wanted; it did not, for instance, include his preference for a carbon tax, because of the pressure applied by development-oriented interests. Another example of the way in which development-oriented policy communities would seem to have had an impact was the case of the EPA proposal (see Chapter 5). Here, it has been suggested that the Environment Secretary's attempts to introduce stronger powers for the EPA were defeated by the pressure applied by the Treasury and the DTI (*Guardian*, 10 October 1994).

The politics of wildlife conservation

The issue of wildlife conservation raises a number of fundamental questions central to a study of environmental politics. The ethics of animal exploitation is obviously a central part of the debate but, unlike the treatment of domesticated animals which we have referred to on numerous occasions throughout this book, wildlife conservation on a global scale is inextricably linked with development issues and the North–South divide. In addition, an examination of the most important international treaties concerning wildlife provides a useful case study of the problems pertaining to the conclusion of supra-national environmental agreements, thereby enabling us to build on the material presented in Chapter 6.

Wildlife in one country – the British experience

The protection afforded to wild animals in Britain reflects a preoccupation with endangered species. Domesticated and 'captive' animals are legally protected against 'unnecessary suffering' under the Protection of Animals Act 1911. In addition, farm and laboratory animals have been given specific protection under the Agriculture (Miscellaneous Provisions) Act 1968 and the Animals (Scientific Procedures) Act 1986, respectively. The 'captive' clause in the 1911 Act, which could theoretically have provided much protection for wild animals, has been interpreted so narrowly that in effect non-endangered wild animals are not protected by the law at all (Sweeney, 1990, ch.2). Particularly contentious is the fact that there is nothing in the law which makes the hunting of foxes and stags as well as hare coursing illegal, or even subject to legal challenge.

The endangered category of wild animals receives much better protection than domesticated animals. The law here is not based on suffering but on the very existence of some species. The centrepiece of wildlife protection in Britain is the Wildlife and Countryside Act 1981. This legislation, which was introduced partly in order to implement the EU directive on the Conservation of Wild Birds, offers a hierarchy of protection. At one end of the spectrum, it is an offence to take, kill or injure those birds or mammals that are recognized as endangered in the Act's various schedules. At the other end of the spectrum, common species – such as crows, pigeons and sparrows – are not mentioned at all in the Act and therefore receive no protection by this or any other piece of legislation (Cooper, 1987, pp.121–31).

There are two main reasons for this preoccupation with endangered species. In the first place, the preservation of endangered species has more advantages from an anthropocentric perspective – in terms, for instance, of aesthetic and scientific value – than the protection of common wild or domesticated animals. Second, the anomaly in the law, by which some wild animals have extraordinary protection and others have none at all, is closely linked to the influence of the farming and country sports lobby. Attempts to plug the gap in the legislation, through either specifically prohibiting hunting or introducing a general anti-cruelty statute applicable to wild animals, has so far been resisted (Thomas, 1983).

Hunting has traditionally been regarded as a moral issue to which a free vote in the Commons can be attached, and the absence of direct executive involvement would seem to indicate the existence of an issue network where a wide variety of groups compete on a reasonably equal footing for the ear of MPs. Traditionally, though, the hunting lobby, consisting mainly of the British Field Sports Society, has had enormous influence within Parliament. Many MPs and peers are landowners themselves, and others represent rural constituencies where the support for hunting among farmers is crucial. In addition, pro-hunters have cleverly changed the focus of their argument, from justifying hunting on the grounds that it is an effective means of pest control (an argument popular with many farmers) to justifying it on conservation grounds – that without the hunting community there would be no incentive for landowners to preserve the habitats which the hunted animals rely on. This switch causes problems for the anti-hunting lobby because it divides the animal welfarists and rightists from many environmentalists whose ideological emphasis is on preserving endangered species and not protecting individual animals against cruelty (see Chapter 2). Thus, the very existence of a group calling itself the British Society for Shooting and Conservation is totally incomprehensible from an animal protection perspective but is less so from an environmentalist one.

There are signs, though, that the previously strong position of the hunting lobby is waning. Fewer MPs now represent rural constituencies and those that still do have to take into account the large number of new middle-class rural dwellers who are more hostile to hunting. As a result, recent votes on the issue have been much closer. For the first time, in March 1995, an anti-hunting bill was given a second reading in the Commons, although it was later emasculated in the committee stage. Given the relative ease with which private member's bills, without government support, can be defeated, the best hope for the anti-hunting lobby still remains the election of a Labour government. Labour has been traditionally hostile to hunting (as a reflection of this, the League Against Cruel Sports contributed £80,000 to the party's campaign fund in 1979) and their present policy is to allow time for an anti-hunting bill to pass through the legislative process.

International wildlife conservation

International co-operation is as important in the field of wildlife protection as it for other global environmental problems. Animals, and particularly birds, do not respect national boundaries so, at the very least, it is unfortunate if a particular species is protected in one country while being vigorously exploited in another. Moreover, live animals, and products derived from them, have become an important element of international trade and only supranational action can effectively constrain such trade if it represents a threat to a particular species or involves the infliction of a considerable degree of suffering, as it does in the case of exotic birds (Boardman, 1981, p.4).

Treaties designed to protect wildlife can be of several different varieties. Some, such as the International Convention for the Regulation of Whaling (ICRW), seek either to protect a species or group of species, while others, such as the Convention of Nature Protection and Wildlife Preservation in the Western Hemisphere, are concerned with conserving particular regions. Finally, there are what Lyster (1985, p.xxii) calls the 'big four' wildlife treaties, all dating back to the 1970s: the Convention on Wetlands of International Importance Especially as Waterfowl Habitat (known as Ramsar), the Convention Concerning the Protection of the World Cultural and Natural Heritage, the Convention on the Conservation of Migratory Species of Wild Animals (the Bonn Convention), and the Convention on International Trade In Endangered Species of Wild Fauna and Flora (CITES). To illustrate the character of wildlife treaties it is proposed now to look briefly at two of these treaties – whaling, and the trade in endangered species – in a little more detail.

Whaling

Whales serve a wide variety of commercial purposes and they have been hunted since the sixteenth century (Allaby, 1986, pp.146–7).

By the twentieth century, it was recognized that some control had to be exercised over whaling in order to preserve stocks and this led to the concluding of the ICRW in 1946. This set up a standing body, the International Whaling Commission (IWC), which calculates annual sustainable quotas for each species, which are then discussed and applied by a meeting of the parties to the treaty. If the numbers of any particular whale species were calculated to be low enough, a complete ban could be imposed.

The history of the ICRW reveals some features which are characteristic of international environmental agreements. In the first place, it should be noted that, as a device to conserve whales, the ICRW has been largely unsuccessful. As an agreement between sovereign states whaling nations are not obliged to join and although most have, this is primarily because the ICRW sought to encourage the widest possible membership. This was achieved through the introduction of a get-out clause which enables members who disapprove of a decision to register an objection within 90 days and thus not be bound by it. Furthermore, the treaty also allows nations to catch whales for scientific purposes irrespective of the quotas set and this is often used as a cover for continued commercial whaling (Cherfas, 1988, pp.118–19).

In reality, whale species have tended to be protected only once they have been hunted to the point of extinction. Thus, of the fourteen 'great' whales, all but the small minke have been exploited to danger levels. Most symbolically of all, the blue whale – the largest mammal ever to have existed on earth equivalent in size to twenty-five adult elephants – was not protected until 1963, by which time its numbers had dwindled to between 200 and 2,000 (*Guardian*, 13 July 1990). There is no precise way of determining how many whales in any particular species exist and thus what the quota should be. In consequence, political expediency has played a significant part in the IWC's deliberations. It is in the commercial interests of whaling nations to continue exploiting whale stocks to the point of extinction since they can then use the profits to invest in other projects (Cherfas, 1988, pp.200–3). On ecological and ethical grounds, of course, it is a different matter.

Since 1986, a moratorium on commercial whaling has been in place, although whaling for scientific purposes continues. The moratorium occurred, not primarily as a result of the desire of the whaling nations to conserve stocks, but because they were outvoted by non-whaling nations, such as Britain, who have over the years come to dominate the ICRW. Countries like Britain have no commercial interest in the continuation of whaling and every incentive, given the anti-whaling sentiments of the general public in these countries, to flex its muscle within the ICRW (Dryzek, 1990, p.105). Japan, Iceland, the USSR and Norway immediately invoked the get-out clause and registered objections to the 1982 decision, but have grudgingly accepted it (with the exception of Iceland which left the IWC in 1992 and plan to resume commercial whaling at some future point) mainly because of the sanctions threatened by the United States (Cherfas, 1988, p.114). With growing evidence that some whale stocks are now sufficiently large to justify a resumption in hunting (*Sunday Times*, 5 March 1995), the conflict between the original intention of the treaty as a means of managing whaling to increase its lifespan, and the animal cruelty and aesthetic justifications for continuing the moratorium will come to a head.

CITES

The international animal trade is big business. It becomes an environmental issue because of the threat the trade poses to endangered species on the one hand, and the suffering that is often inflicted on animals involved in the trade on the other. As a result of growing concern about the increasing popularity of fauna and flora as valuable trading commodities, the CITES treaty, which has now been adopted by some 110 countries, was concluded in Washington DC in 1973 and came into force in July 1975. As with the ICRW, the CITES treaty illustrates some of the major characteristics of international environmental agreements and, although CITES has been more successful than the whaling convention and, indeed, other treaties, it does share some common weaknesses.

The CITES convention is administered by a secretariat, based in Switzerland, and the parties meet every two years to discuss the allocation of species to various different categories offering different levels of protection. The main categories are Appendix I, containing 'endangered' species in which a commercial trade is completely prohibited and Appendix II containing 'threatened' species in which a commercial trade is restricted. Around 1,000 species are listed as endangered and 30,000 as threatened. Some trade for other purposes, including scientific research, is allowed in endangered species. For this, and for the commercial trade in threatened species, permits issued by member states are required (Cooper, 1987, p.171).

There are a number of familiar problems with the CITES treaty. In the first place, not all countries are members and some of those that are not, notably in the Far and Middle East, trade heavily in the products derived from endangered species. Second, countries are allowed to declare a reservation against a particular species when they join, and against any species added to Appendix I or II while they are members, thus exempting them from the provision (Lyster, 1985, p.9). These two weaknesses are linked to the general problem of enforcement. As with other treaties, CITES provisions have to be implemented in national law and enforced by member states. In some countries, minimal effort is made to enforce CITES provisions and added to this are the difficulties encountered by customs offers in determining the nature of the species being imported and the lenient penalties imposed on those who are convicted (*BBC Wildlife Magazine*, April 1991, pp.254–60). As a result of the failure to enforce the provisions of the treaty, the fact that some countries are not members of CITES and that others register reservations, smuggling and poaching is a serious problem.

The debate over sustainable use

Many endangered species of flora and fauna are affected by the weaknesses of CITES but a particularly high-profile issue is the ivory trade and the precarious existence of the rhino and the African elephant. Despite being included on Appendix I of CITES, the numbers of both species have continued to decline in recent years and this is almost exclusively the result of the vast profits that can be made in the ivory trade. The battle to protect the elephant from poachers provides the context for a crucial strategic and ideological debate in wildlife conservation (Garner, 1993a, ch.6). In simple terms there are two major camps. On the one hand, there are those who argue that there should be a complete ban on the trade in ivory and other products derived from elephants and rhinoceros, and on the other, are those who advocate a policy of 'sustainable use', whereby a restricted sustainable trade should be permitted.

There are strategic and ideological dimensions to this debate. In terms of strategy, it is argued by the sustainable use advocates that the only effective way to prevent poaching is to allow the exploitation of wildlife by the mostly poor rural people who have to co-exist with African game reserves. Only then will they see wildlife conservation as a source of income as opposed to a threat to their mainly agricultural livelihoods, and only then will they cease to turn a blind eye to poaching or cease to engage in it themselves. The opponents of this strategy argue that it will necessitate the reopening of the ivory trade (now banned in those countries who are members of CITES) and the consequent difficulties of determining 'legitimate' from poached ivory. Thus, while a restricted trade for elephant ivory was in operation between 1985 and 1989, the slaughter of the animals by the poachers continued unabated. In addition, although the strategy of complete prohibition will require some culling of elephants as their numbers increase, this regulated and managed culling activity is preferable to the arbitrary nature of poaching where the strongest and youngest members of the herd are just as likely to be killed as the old and the sick. Finally, there are other methods – and in particular eco-tourism – of enabling indigenous people to benefit from wildlife. Killing is not the only option.

At present, the prohibition on the ivory trade and indeed any trade in endangered elephants and rhinos continues. The pressure to adopt a sustainable use strategy, though, has been intense. Not only have a number of southern African states been practising a limited version of it, having exempted themselves from the CITES decision, but also the WWF and the IUCN have accepted the logic of the sustainable use argument in their last two major documents *World Conservation Strategy* (1980) and *Caring for the Earth: A Strategy for Sustainable Living* (1991). The WWF has not, though, turned this acceptance into a call for a return to a restricted ivory trade.

The reason for the WWF's reticence takes us nicely into the ideological dimension of the debate about sustainable use. As an ideology, sustainable use is based on the principle that wildlife conservation should not take precedence over the interests of humans. Clearly, the protection of endangered species can seriously affect the interests of humans – whether they be those who make their living out of whaling or those whose land is threatened by the incursion of elephants. For advocates of animal rights, of course, the exploitation of wildlife, whether endangered or not, is illegitimate (see Chapter 2) and there is no doubt that the influence of animal rightists and animal welfarists (appalled by the suffering inflicted on animals by poachers, trappers and whalers) on the conservation community has increased, making it difficult for groups like the WWF fully to support the sustainable use strategy in practice.

In reality, though, a great deal of emphasis is put on the protection of endangered species because of the human interest reasons – aesthetic, sporting, economic and ecological – for doing so. As a result, the protection of such species heavily promoted by Western governments and conservationists often results in sacrificing the interests of Third World peoples who stand to gain by exploiting them. This by itself is morally dubious but we must add to it the developed world's propensity to exploit animals when *they* find it valuable to do so, even to the point of overriding statutes designed to protect endangered wild animals, as in the case of gassing badgers suspected of carrying the tuberculosis bacillus which threatens cattle. In such circumstances, the moral case for allowing Third World peoples to exploit wildlife, irrespective of the consequences for endangered species, would appear to be unanswerable (Garner, 1994).

We have travelled a fair distance in this chapter, from the NFU's dominance in the politics of the countryside to the case for allowing the exploitation of wildlife in developing countries. This indicates the wide scope of environmental politics. It also indicates that explaining the nature of the environmental crisis and attempted resolutions of it involves above all a consideration of competing interests and the exercise of power, whether within one country or between different countries.

In terms of our first two case studies, what was most revealing is that the evidence does not seem to support a pluralist interpretation. Since 1945, agricultural policy has been made by a small group of actors seeking to defend the interests of farmers. Even when the environmental effects of agriculture became a political issue and a matter of public concern, environmentalists still failed to break into the policy community and, although attempts have been made to take account of the environmental damage agriculture has done to the countryside, policy is still geared to protecting the interests of farmers. In the case of pollution politics, the moves towards IPC did not occur primarily as a result of the environmental lobby's influence. Rather, change came about as a result of a variety of other factors – the technical case for IPC, the dynamic role played by state actors, the unintended by-products of government policy and the impact of the EU. Likewise, the limited move towards IPC can best be explained in terms of the veto exercised by powerful economic interests and their departmental allies.

The caveat we ought to introduce here is that it is by no means clear whether the decision-making structures described in our account of countryside and pollution politics can be said to challenge notions of democratic legitimacy. It might be argued, for instance, that more stringent controls on the sources of environmental problems would result in outcomes which most people would find difficult to swallow, and governments, when making environmental policy, are taking account of this as much as the pressure applied by vested economic interests. According to this argument, then, until the public are prepared to sacrifice their cars and use public transport, pay more for food and for products manufactured by companies shackled by more stringent environmental legislation, the present patchy response to environmental problems will continue. For environmentalists, and particularly those of the dark Green variety, this suggests that the route to a sustainable society must not merely focus on traditional lobbying in the hope that governments will take their ideas on board. Rather, it must explore a wide variety of strategies designed to overcome the obstacles to change. These we consider in the final chapter.

Further reading

General studies of policy-making approaches which might be applied to environmental issues are Greenaway *et al.* (1992), Ham and Hill (1984), Richardson (1982), Marsh and Rhodes (1992), Dunleavy and O'Leary (1987), Lukes (1974) and Smith (1993). There have been a number of attempts to apply decision-making theories to environmental issues. The most important are Crenson's study of pollution (1971), Blowers' (1984) study of a Bedfordshire brickworks and Sandbach's (1980) attempt to apply

Marxist theory. Weale (1992) also seeks to apply a number of theories in his study of pollution politics.

On the agricultural policy case study, McCormick (1991) and Grant (1989) provide useful introductions. Essential, book-length studies are Lowe *et al.* (1986) and Smith (1990). Essential to a study of pollution politics is Weale (1992). McCormick (1991) also has a useful chapter which goes beyond mere institutional description. Richardson (1992) provides details about the political context surrounding the creation of the NRA and Greenaway (1992), Saward (1992) and Ward (1983) are useful sources for the politics of nuclear power. Transport policy is covered in Hamer (1974) although this is now somewhat dated. See Pearce (1993) for more up-to-date information. There is no one volume which covers all aspects of wildlife conservation. See Garner (1993a; 1994), Warren and Goldsmith (1983) and Evans (1991) for an overview. Cooper (1987) documents British law relating to wildlife. Lyster (1985) is an unrivalled account of international wildlife treaties while on the specific issue of whaling see Cherfas (1988).

CONCLUSION
Towards a Sustainable Future

It is clear that the environmental record of governments across the world falls hopelessly short of dark Green or ecocentric objectives. Indeed, until relatively recently, many countries, including Britain, were governed according to a cornucopian ideology, which accepted the validity of unrestrained economic growth and an instrumental attitude towards the exploitation of the natural world, and was naively optimistic about science and technology's ability to come up with solutions to environmental problems (Pearce, 1993, pp.18–19). It is a mark of how far the world has come that, in rhetoric at least, few governments would now subscribe to this ideology. These two positions represent two extremes on a continuum and governments should be judged on how far they have moved from the one end to the other.

Faltering steps

What this book has suggested is that Britain has begun to adopt a more sustainable approach but that the steps taken so far have been short and faltering. Indeed, even from a very lightish green perspective, Britain's environmental record leaves a great deal to be desired. Whether because of the limitations of incremental decision-making, the power of economic interests or the perceived electoral consequences of more stringent environmental regulations, the governmental machinery in Britain remains fragmented and the main policy focus is reactive and voluntary, persuasion and compromise being preferred to compulsion. Making policy as a reaction to environmental problems is particularly constraining. It leads to a reliance on conclusive scientific evidence – what Porritt and Winner (1988, p.144) describe as the ' "Where is the pile of bodies?" school of environmental management' – which is rarely forthcoming.

Of course, the picture is not all bad. As John Gray (1993, p.155) points out: 'If time travel were possible, a visitor from an earlier period of industrial society . . . would most likely be astonished by the cleanliness and integrity of our environment, which early industrialism ravaged.' Over the last two decades, SO_2 concentrations in Britain have declined and national water quality surveys between the late 1950s and 1980 indicate marginal improvements. In addition, Britain was a key participant in the largely successful move to reduce the production and use of ozone-destroying chemicals and, likewise, Britain has ratified, and looks likely to comply with, the climate change and biological diversity conventions agreed at the Rio Summit (Pearce, 1993, pp.51, 68, 98–114). On top of this, as we saw in Chapter 5, significant moves have been made towards the greater integration of environmental policy so that Pearce *et al.* (1993, p.196) can claim that 'in comparison to many other states, the UK is still in the vanguard'.

All of this, of course, is only half the story. The institutional structure for internal integration took a long time to emerge and the resources available to HMIP have been limited. Furthermore, there is little evidence that the attempts to integrate environmental policy externally have been much more than cosmetic. At the very least, departmental secrecy makes it difficult to assess how far environmental costs and benefits have been taken into account in policy development. The examples of agriculture and transport policy do not suggest that much has changed. In the former case, the continuing exclusion of agriculture from planning controls and the lack of protection accorded to designated areas has resulted in the 'continual erosion of the UK's biological diversity' (Pearce, 1993, p.113). The environmental damage caused by present transport policies is even more stark. The continuing bias towards private cars and road freight and against public transport really does lead one to question whether the integrationist language of *This Common Inheritance* has been taken seriously by government.

Ecological modernization, sustainability and democracy

The reliance on conclusive scientific evidence of the causes and consequences of environmental problems is predicated, of course, on the assumption that action to protect the environment will have negative economic consequences. In this context, the theory of ecological modernization seems to offer an important way forward since its central argument, as we saw in Chapter 2, is that conflict between economic and environmental objectives is illusory. We have seen that a key obstacle to effective environmental policy-making is the lack of integration across a range of governmental activities. This, it was suggested, is primarily a product of departmental policy communities within which development-oriented interests have a dominating role. It might be thought that an acceptance of the ecological modernization ideology would remove the problem since if economic interests accepted that tougher environmental measures were not going to damage them they have no reason to object. Of course, it is not as simple as that. The argument is that, *overall*, the economy will not suffer from the adoption of sustainable policies. Some individual industries, however, will suffer from such policies, at least in the short term, and some of these (those, for instance, with a vested interest in the continuation of existing transport policy) are well placed within the decision-making machinery to fight their corner.

This situation clearly requires an effective political strategy, something which environmentalists have not been particularly good at developing. There has tended to be an assumption that once the public are informed about the seriousness of environmental problems, they will eventually come round to accepting the need to act (Dobson, 1990, pp.130–1). Such an assumption is naive, not least because it fails to recognize the power relations central to an understanding of decision-making. A strategy to 'sell' ecological modernization requires a number of elements (see Pearce, 1993, pp.12–13). First, industries that profit from environmental regulation should be encouraged, and the fact that the benefits of environmental regulation are economic in nature, as well as those connected with a general improvement in the quality of life, should be promoted.

More importantly, perhaps, the dominance of certain vested economic interests, which do stand to lose out through stricter regulatory regimes, can only be countered if there is a climate favourably inclined towards environmental protection. It is here that environmental reformists can learn from the ecocentric claim that environmentalism goes hand in hand with an active citizenry (see Dryzek, 1990). Thus, the move towards a sustainable future requires more than a top-down government response but also a major cultural transformation. Following Dobson (1990, ch.4), we can discuss the possible dimensions of this transformation in terms of lifestyle, communities and class.

Lifestyle changes

One seemingly effective way of promoting active environmentally aware citizens is in terms of encouraging individuals to adopt sustainable lifestyles. This can be in terms of our behaviour as consumers, as investors, as commuters and in the way we treat the animals we directly encounter. Encouraging green consumerism has been the major component of this strategy. Conserving energy and water through actions, such as better insulation and a more discriminate use of the toilet flush, is one form of this, as is recycling products bought, a practice which some local authorities have done a great deal to promote. The use of lead-free petrol, a product given a favourable tax regime, is another example, as are the local exchange trading systems (LETS), which now exist in over a hundred towns in Britain.

Most attention, though, has been placed on the green dimension of regular shopping. Superficially at least, this strategy – 'shopping for a better world', as it has been called (Porritt and Winner, 1988, p.193) – has been very successful. In the late 1980s, there was a huge increase in products claiming to be environmentally friendly – CFC-free aerosols, cruelty-free cosmetics, minimal and biodegradable packaging, 'dolphin-friendly' tuna and free-range eggs – as companies sought to compete with each other to satisfy the new green demands of the consumer. A book directing consumers to the best green products became a bestseller (Elkington and Hailes, 1988), and retailers specializing in providing such products, most notably the Body Shop and Beauty Without Cruelty, massively increased their market share. Industry has more generally recognized the marketability of environmental concern – witness Shell's 'Better Britain' campaign and Heinz's 'Guardians of the Countryside' programme. Industry too has contributed significantly to the funds of environmental groups, with 20 per cent of the WWF's income in 1987 coming from corporate contributions (Simpson, 1990, p.31).

The main advantage of the lifestyle strategy in general, and Green consumerism in particular, is that it focuses on what individuals can do, thereby encouraging participation which, in turn, may lead to an increased consciousness about wider environmental issues. Without wishing to belittle the importance of the consumer strategy, however, it should be noted that there are a number of problems with it. In the first place, the 'Green' claims made by some manufacturers are dubious and it is difficult, at least without legislative intervention, for consumers to interpret their competing claims. This lack of information provides an incentive for manufacturers to make misleading, or just bogus, statements. An infamous example here is the claim made by many manufacturers of washing up liquids that their products are 'phosphate-free'. True enough, but what they forgot to add was that phosphates had never been added to washing-up liquids in the first place! (Yearley, 1992, p.98). Similarly, what is a 'cruelty-free' cosmetic can vary from one manufacturer to another. For some companies, it is justifiable to make this claim if they themselves have not done any animal testing (even if the manufacturers of the ingredients have). For others, the label can be applied if products have not been tested for a five-year period. This problem can and has started to be overcome with the introduction of eco-labelling schemes, but this requires governmental action, which may not be forthcoming.

Second, it is doubtful if enough consumers can be persuaded to adopt Green lifestyles, particularly if not doing so is more convenient and/or less expensive. It is a strategy that appeals in particular to those who can afford to engage in substantial consumption. For those who cannot, the options are often limited to buying cheaper but more environmentally damaging products or, in other cases, not consuming at all. In both cases, the individual is locked out of the strategy completely, thus undermining its educative and consciousness-raising purpose. There is also a classic collective action problem here in that the environmental benefits of green consumerism will be available to all, irrespective of whether any one individual seeks to participate in achieving them. Third, the consumer strategy focuses on the finished product and not the nature of the whole production process. Important environmental questions, such as how the product was manufactured and how it is transported to retailers, are thereby avoided (Yearley, 1992, p.101).

While the consumer-oriented strategy is acceptable from a reformist perspective, from a dark Green perspective, of course, it is inadequate because even though it encourages green growth, it is growth all the same. Radical Greens emphasize the need to reduce consumption, whether it is environmentally friendly consumption or not (Dobson, 1990, pp.141–2). It is argued, therefore, that Greens would do far better to focus their attention on the spiritual dimension of what it is to be Green rather than seeking to promote 'grubby' materialism whether or not it has a green tint to it (Young, 1993, pp.105–6).

Communities and class

Another strategy to increase environmental consciousness is based on the creation of alternative communities working outside the dominant industrial and materialist paradigm (Dobson, 1990, pp.147–51). These communities, in the words of the German Green Rudolf Bahro, are 'liberated from the industrial system . . . liberated from nuclear weapons and from supermarkets. What we are talking about is a new social formation and a different civilization' (quoted in Dobson, 1990, p.146). Examples here would include self-sufficiency farms, some squats and workers' co-operatives and, in particular, mention should be made of the Centre for Alternative Technology at Machynlleth in Wales, the Findhorn community in Scotland and the Earth Centre educational project in South Yorkshire.

We can applaud the existence of such communities but as an agent of social and political change, they are surely very limited. Their success in this context will depend on how far they are able to persuade others to adopt similar lifestyles. Here, they have been a complete failure. This is partly because such communities tend to be 'outsiders' rather than 'oppositional' in that they represent opting out of society as opposed to deliberately setting themselves in a confrontational sense against the norms and values of industrial society (Dobson, 1990, p.147). Whatever the reason, and while laudable by themselves, they do not represent a convincing strategy for achieving a widespread raising of environmental consciousness.

A more promising strategy is the identification of a particular group or class in society who can be mobilized on behalf of environmental objectives. We saw earlier that the assumption of a simple link between a greater awareness of environmental problems and a desire to have them dealt with is inadequate. David Pepper (1986, pp.215–25) describes this as education *about* the environment in that it is a science-based response to the environmental predicament. Equally fallacious for Pepper is what he calls education *from* the environment. Although this approach introduces values to the debate by asking why we ought to protect the environment – something which, as Chapter 2 revealed, Greens have not been shy about – it is still inadequate because it assumes that environmental problems represent a common threat against which we should all pull together. The point here, then, is that environmentalists regularly fail to take into account the sociopolitical realities of environmentalism. For Pepper, writing from a Marxist perspective, it is the class-based power structure which has to be tackled if environmental degradation is to be reversed. The logic of this argument is that the working class are the obvious agents of any social transformation.

We need not accept Pepper's Marxist analysis to appreciate the point about the importance of identifying and mobilizing a collectivity in society who are more likely to lead a cultural transformation in favour of environmental protection. It is clearly the case, for instance, that the middle classes are not affected by environmental degradation to the same degree as the less affluent. As we have seen, the more affluent are able to escape from the grime of the inner cities and, when encamped in more salubrious locations, they can exercise considerable political clout through the party system and, moreover, are articulate enough to influence the planning system. As a result, they can ensure that their immediate environment remains reasonably good.

It might be argued, therefore, that the middle class, or at least a section of it, might be an effective green agency. This claim is reinforced by Inglehart's claim, discussed in Chapter 4, that post-material values are a product of affluence, and further evidence is the Green Party's support which, as we saw in Chapter 7, tends to be drawn from the more affluent sections of society. As Porritt (1984, p.116) points out:

> the post-industrial revolution is likely to be pioneered by middle-class people . . . such people not only have more chance of working out where their own *genuine* self-interest lies, but they also have the flexibility and security to act upon such insights.

On the other hand, the middle classes have, despite Hirsch's (1977) identification of the positional economy, benefited from, sometimes unsustainable, economic growth. Moreover, their adoption of a suburban or rural lifestyle is essentially shallow since it is based on material convenience and, in so far as the middle classes do engage in environmental campaigns, it is more often than not designed to protect their own privileges against encroachment by others.

If the middle classes are not a particularly likely agent for environmental change, does the working class fair any better? Arguably not. For one thing, in Britain at least, the working class has fragmented in recent years and it can no longer be regarded as a homogeneous bloc. The new, more affluent sections of the working class were seduced by the materialistic promises by the Thatcher governments in the 1980s, and are therefore unlikely to be a vehicle for environmental protection (Garner and Kelly, 1993, ch.9). Furthermore, the organized labour movement in Britain has always been 'labourist' in character, concerned, despite the strain of ethical socialism associated with such luminaries as William Morris and R.H. Tawney, with gaining for itself a larger slice of the capitalist pie rather than seeking to change the acquisitive and materialist nature of the system (Garner and Kelly, 1993, ch.6). Thus, it was noted in Chapter 7 that the trade unions have often provided a constraint on Labour adopting more radical environmental policies and, while their role in the Labour Party has been reduced, they still represent a significant obstacle to a Labour prime minister intent on carrying out more radical environmental policies.

Two other social groupings suggest themselves. The first is the women's movement. As we saw in Chapter 2, there has been an attempt to develop a feminist strand of ecology and part of this is concerned with explaining why women might be more likely than men to identify with environmental concerns. To talk about women as a homogeneous group, though, is problematic since, by virtue of their class position, they experience different lifechances. Furthermore, as Chapter 4 revealed, the empirical evidence suggests that affluence and occupation, rather than gender, provide important influences on the adoption of post-material values. On the other hand, support for environmental reforms is not dependent on holding such values and the life position of women (as, for instance, carers of children) may make them more likely than men to support some environmental initiatives, such as those relating to transport policy.

The final possibility is the unemployed, a social grouping which Andrew Dobson (1990, pp.163–9) suggests offers great potential as an agent of environmentalism (a view also advanced by Gorz, 1985). This is a group, he argues, which is 'not only relatively "disengaged" ' from industrial society but which 'also is already inclined towards the foundations of sustainable living'. Thus, in so far as 'the capacity of any group in society for Green social change' is determined by its 'distance from the process of consumption and the degree of permanence of this isolation', the unemployed would seem to fit the bill. In particular, the long-term unemployed have little stake in society and their predicament can be explained by the limits to growth in that unemployment is at least partly a product of the increasing price of scarce resources necessitating cuts in labour costs.

There are problems with according to the unemployed a role as the agents of social change, some of which are recognized by Dobson himself (1990, pp.167–9). Crucially, there is little evidence that the unemployed perceive their role as agents of such a change. The Green movement could attempt to make them more aware of their marginalized status and how it relates to the environmental crisis but, in the past, it has been notoriously difficult to mobilize the unemployed to campaign against their predicament. This is associated with the point that there is no necessary link between the marginalization of the unemployed and their rejection of the social and political institutions of unsustainable industrial society.

Indeed, British political history demonstrates that it was the non-unionized part of the working class – those at the bottom of the social scale working in casual jobs or not at all – who were more likely to be deferential towards the established order. This is why, historians argue, the Labour Party was not greatly concerned, before 1918, to achieve universal suffrage, since it would introduce into the electorate many of the poorest members of society who were more likely to vote Conservative (Pugh, 1982, ch.7).

The point, then, is that marginalisation is just as likely, without the introduction of any evidence to the contrary, to lead to a desire for inclusion rather than the development of an oppositional mentality. Finally, it is doubtful if the number of unemployed, and the poor in general, constitute a large enough group to make a significant impact. The Labour Party, for instance, has recognized that it needs to focus on attracting the votes of the better-off sections of the working class as well as middle-class, white-collar workers, if it is win a general election again.

The cultural transformation required to break the hold that certain economic interests have over environmental policy-making has a long way to go. The promotion of ecocentric values which challenge the dominant materialism of industrial society obviously has an important role to play in the development of a greater environmental consciousness. Equally if not more important is the ecological modernization claim that environmental protection and economic advancement can co-exist. Pursuing such an approach may not answer all the ecocentric questions but it is politically realistic and might just be enough to provide a viable future for the human species and the natural environment we depend on.

Above all, the preceding pages have demonstrated the dichotomy between, on the one hand, the widespread recognition of environmental problems and an environmental movement bristling with both scientific expertise and moral indignation at the present state of affairs and, on the other, the very slow progress that has been made towards changing people's attitudes and persuading public authorities to introduce more sustainable environmental measures. The spark that seemed to ignite widespread concern for the environment in the mid- to late 1980s has failed to keep the fire alight as we approach the end of the century, and yet the problems remain equally acute. As an important political issue and a subject worthy of study by natural and social scientists, however, the environment is here to stay. Those who despair at the absence of fundamental change should remember the old adage that the perfect should not be allowed to be the enemy of the good.

BIBLIOGRAPHY

Adams, C. (1990) *The Sexual Politics of Meat*, New York: Continuum.

Allaby, M. (1986) *Green Facts*, London: Hamlyn.

Ashford, N. (1989) 'Market liberalism and the environment: A response to Hay', *Politics* 9 (1), pp.43–4.

Atkinson, A. (1991) *Principles of Political Ecology*, London: Belhaven Press.

Attfield, R. (1983) *The Ethics of Environmental Concern*, Oxford: Blackwell.

Axelrod, A. and Phillips, C. (1993) *The Environmentalists: A Biographical Dictionary from the 17th Century to the Present*, New York: Facts on File Inc.

Bachrach, P. (1969) *The Theory of Democratic Elitism: A Critique*, London: University of London.

Bachrach, P. and Baratz, M. (1962) 'The two faces of power', *American Political Science Review* 56, pp.947–52.

Bahro, R. (1986) *Building the Green Movement*, London: Heretic.

Barry, J. (1994) 'The limits of the shallow and the deep: Green politics, philosophy and praxis', *Environmental Politics* 3 (3), pp.369–94.

Beck, U. (1992) *Risk Society: Towards a New Modernity*, London: Sage.

Beckerman, W. (1992) 'Global warming and international action: An economic perspective', in A. Hurrell and B. Kingsbury, *The International Politics of the Environment*, Oxford: Clarendon Press, pp.253–89.

Benton, T. (1993) *Natural Relations: Ecology, Animal Rights and Social Justice*, London: Verso.

Blowers, A. (1984) *Something in the Air: Corporate Power and the Environment*, London: Harper & Row.

Blowers, A. (1987) 'Transition or transformation? Environmental policy under Thatcher', *Public Administration* 65, pp.227–94.

Boardman, R. (1981) *International Organisations and the Conservation of Nature*, London: Macmillan.

Body, R. (1982) *Agriculture: The Triumph and the Shame*, London: Maurice Temple Smith.

Bookchin, M. (1962) *Our Synthetic Environment*, New York: Knopf.

Bookchin, M. (1971) *Post-Scarcity Anarchism*, Berkeley: Ramparts.

Boons, F. (1992) 'Product-oriented environmental policy and networks: Ecological aspects of economic internationalism', *Environmental Politics* 1 (4), pp.84–105.

Booth, N. (1994) *How Soon is Now? The Truth about the Ozone Layer*, Hemel Hempstead: Simon & Schuster.

Bradbeer, J. (1994) 'Environmental policy: Past and future agendas', in P. Savage, R. Atkinson and L. Robins (eds.), *Public Policy in Britain*, London: Macmillan, pp.116–36.

Bramwell, A. (1989) *Ecology in the Twentieth Century*, New Haven, CT: Yale University Press.

Callaghan, J. (1990) 'The greening of British politics', *Contemporary Record* 4 (2), pp.2–5.

Carson, R. (1962) *Silent Spring*, New York: Fawcett Crest.

Carter, A. (1993) 'Towards a green political theory', in A. Dobson and P. Lucardie (eds.) *The Politics of Nature Explorations in Green Political Theory*, London: Routledge.

Carter, N. (1992a) 'The "Greening" of Labour', in M.J. Smith and J. Spear, *The Changing Labour Party*, London: Routledge.

Carter, N. (1992b) 'Whatever happened to the environment? The British general election of 1992', *Environmental Politics* 1 (3), pp.442–8.

Cherfas, J. (1988) *The Hunting of the Whale*, London: The Bodley Head.

Clarke, P. and Linzey, A. (eds.) (1990) *Political Theory and Animal Rights*, London: Pluto Press.

Collard, A. (1988) *Rape of the Wild*, London: The Women's Press.

Collins, K. and Earnshaw, D. (1992) 'The implementation and enforcement of European Community environment legislation', *Environmental Politics* 1 (4), pp.213–49.

Connolly, J. and Norris, P. (1991–2) 'Making green policy: A guide to the politics of the environment', *Talking Politics* 4 (2), pp.96–100.

Cooper, M.E. (1987) *An Introduction to Animal Law*, London: Academic Press.

Cotgrove, S. and Duff, A. (1980) 'Environmentalism, middle class radicalism and politics', *Sociological Review* 28, pp.333–51.

Cotgrove, S. and Duff, A. (1981) 'Environmentalism, values and social change', *British Journal of Sociology* 32, pp.92–110.

Cox, G. and Lowe, P. (1983) 'Countryside politics: Goodbye to goodwill', *Political Quarterly* 54, pp.268–82.

Cox, G., Lowe, P. and Winter, M. (1987) 'Farmers and the state: A crisis for corporatism', *Political Quarterly* 58, pp.73–81.

Crenson, M.A. (1971) *The Unpolitics of Air Pollution*, Baltimore, MD: Johns Hopkins University Press.

Curtice, J. (1989) 'The 1989 European elections: Protest or green tide?', *Electoral Studies* 8, pp.217–30.

Dahl, R. (1961) *Who Governs?* New Haven, CT: Yale University Press.

Dahl, R. (1971) *Polyarchy*, New Haven, CT: Yale University Press.

Dasgupta, P. (1989) 'Exhaustible resources', in L. Friday and R. Laskey (eds.) *The Fragile Environment*, Cambridge: Cambridge University Press, pp.107–26.

Dearlove, J. and Saunders, P. (1984) *Introduction to British Politics: Analysing a Capitalist Democracy*, Cambridge: Polity Press.

Department of the Environment (1990) *This Common Inheritance: Britain's Environmental Strategy*, Cmnd. 1200, London, HMSO,

Dobson, A. (1990) *Green Political Thought*, London: Unwin Hyman.

Dobson, A. (ed.) (1991) *The Green Reader*, London: André Deutsch.

Dobson, A. and Lucardie, P. (eds.) (1993) *The Politics of Nature: Explorations in Green Political Theory*, London: Routledge.

Dodds, F. (ed.) (1989) *Into the 21st Century*, London: Green Print.

Doherty, B. (1992a) 'The Autumn 1991 Conference of the UK Green Party', *Environmental Politics* 1 (2), pp.292–8.

Doherty, B. (1992b) 'The Fundi–Realo controversy: An analysis of four European Green Parties', *Environmental Politics* 1 (1), pp.95–120.

Downs, A. (1959) *An Economic Theory of Democracy*, New York: Harper & Row.

Dryzek, J. (1987) *Rational Ecology*, Oxford: Blackwell.

Dryzek, J. (1990) *Discursive Democracy: Politics, Policy and Political Science*, Cambridge: Cambridge University Press.

Dunleavy, P. and O'Leary, B. (1987) *Theories of the State*, London: Macmillan.

Eckersley, R. (1992) *Environmentalism and Political Theory*, London: UCL.

Eckersley, R. (1993) 'Free market environmentalism: Friend or foe?', *Environmental Politics* 2 (1), pp.1–19.

Ehrlich, P. (1972) *The Population Bomb*, London: Pan.

Elkington, J. and Hailes, J. (1988) *The Green Consumer Guide*, London: Gollancz.

Enzensberger, H. (1974) 'A critique of political ecology', *New Left Review* 84, pp.3–31.

Evans, D. (1991) *A History of Nature Conservation in Britain*, London: Routledge.

Evans, J. (1993) 'Ecofeminism and the politics of the gendered self', in A. Dobson and P. Lucardie (eds.) *The Politics of Nature: Explorations in Green Political Theory*, London: Routledge, pp.177–89.

Flynn, A. and Lowe, P. (1992) 'The greening of the Tories: The Conservative Party and the environment' in W. Rudig (ed.) *Green Politics Two*, Edinburgh: Edinburgh University Press, pp.9–36.

Fox, W. (1984) 'Deep ecology: A new philosophy of our times', *The Ecologist* 14 (5), pp.199–200.

Frey, R.K. (1993) *Rights, Killing and Suffering*, Oxford: Clarendon Press.

Friday, L. and Laskey, R. (eds.) (1989) *The Fragile Environment*, Cambridge: Cambridge University Press.

Gamble, A. (1981) *An Introduction to Modern Social and Political Thought*, London: Macmillan.

Gamson, W. (1975) *The Strategy of Social Protest*, Illinois: The Dorsey Press.

Garner, R. (1993a) *Animals, Politics and Morality*, Manchester: Manchester University Press.

Garner, R. (1993b) 'Political animals: A survey of the animal protection movement in Britain', *Parliamentary Affairs* 46 (3), pp.333–52.

Garner, R. (1994) 'Wildlife conservation and the moral status of animals', *Environmental Politics* 3 (1), pp.114–19.

Garner, R. (1995) 'The politics of animal protection: A research agenda', *Society and Animals* 3 (1), pp.43–60.

Garner, R. and Kelly, R.N. (1993) *British Political Parties Today*, Manchester: Manchester University Press.

Georgescu-Roegen, N. (1973) 'The entropy law and the economic problem', in Daly, H.E. (ed.) *Towards a Steady State Economy*, San Francisco: Freeman, pp.37–49.

Goldsmith, E., Allen, R., Allaby, M., Davoll, J. and Lawrence, S. (1972) *Blueprint for Survival*, Harmondsworth: Penguin Books.

Goodin, R.E. (1992a) *Green Political Theory*, Cambridge: Polity Press.

Goodin, R.E. (1992b) 'The high ground is Green', *Environmental Politics* 1 (1) pp.1–8.

Gorz, A. (1982) *Farewell to the Working Class: An Essay in Post-Industrial Socialism*, London: Pluto.

Gorz, A. (1985) *Paths to Paradise/On the Liberation from Work*, London: Pluto.

Goudie, A. (1989) 'The changing human impact', in L. Friday and R. Laskey (eds.) *The Fragile Environment*, Cambridge: Cambridge University Press, pp.1–21.

Grant, W. (1989) *Pressure Groups, Politics and Democracy in Britain*, Hemel Hempstead: Philip Allan.

Gray, J. (1993) *Beyond the New Right: Markets, Government and the Common Environment*, Cambridge: Cambridge University Press.

Greenaway, J., Smith, S. and Street, J. (1992) *Deciding Factors in British Politics: A Case Study Approach*, London: Routledge.

Gribben, J. (1988) *The Hole in the Sky*, London: Corgi.

Griffin, S. (1978) *Woman and Nature: The Roaring Inside Her*, New York: Harper & Row.

Haigh, N. (1986) 'Developed responsibility and centralization: Effects of EEC environmental policy', *Public Administration* 64, pp.197–207.

Haigh, N. (1990) *EEC Environmental Policy and Britain*, 2nd edn, London: Longman.

Haigh, N. (1992) 'The European Community and international environmental policy', in A. Hurrell and B. Kingsbury, *The International Politics of the Environment*, Oxford, Clarendon Press, pp.228–49.

Ham, C. and Hill, M. (1984) *The Policy Process in the Modern Capitalist State*, Hemel Hempstead: Harvester Wheatsheaf.

Hamer, M. (1974) *Wheels within Wheels*, London: Friends of the Earth.

Hardin, G. (1968) 'The tragedy of the commons', *Science* 162, pp. 1243–48.

Hardin, G. (1977) 'Living on a lifeboat', in G. Hardin and J. Baden (eds.) *Managing the Commons*, San Francisco: Freeman.

Harvey, B. and Hallett, J.D. (1977) *Environment and Society: An Introductory Analysis*, London: Macmillan.

Hawkins, K. (1984) *Environment and Enforcement*, Oxford: Clarendon Press.

Hay, P.R. (1988) 'Ecological values and Western political traditions: From anarchism to fascism', *Politics* 8 (2), pp.22–9.

Heclo, H. (1978) 'Issue networks and the executive establishment', in A. King (ed.) *The New American Political System*, Washington DC: American Enterprise Institute.

Heilbroner, R.L. (1974) *An Inquiry into the Human Prospect*, New York: Norton.

Heywood, A. (1992) *Political Ideologies: An Introduction*, Basingstoke: Macmillan.

Hildebrand, P.M. (1992) 'The European Community's environmental Policy, 1957 to "1992": From incidental measures to an international regime?', *Environmental Politics* 1 (4), pp.13–44.

Hirsch, F. (1977) *Social Limits to Growth*, London, Routledge & Kegan Paul.

HMSO (1975) *Food from Our Own Resources*, Cmnd. 5254, London.

Hogwood, B. (1987) *From Crisis to Complacency? Shaping Public Policy in Britain*, Oxford: Oxford University Press.

Hulsberg, W. (1987) *The West German Greens*, London: Verso.

Hurrell, A. and Kingsbury, B. (1992a) *The International Politics of the Environment*, Oxford: Clarendon Press.

Hurrell, A. and Kingsbury, B. (1992b) 'The international politics of the environment: An introduction' in A. Hurrell and B. Kingsbury *The International Politics of the Environment*, Oxford: Clarendon Press.

Inglehart, R. (1977) *The Silent Revolution: Changing Values and Political Styles among Western Publics*, Princeton, NJ: Princeton University Press.

Inglehart, R. (1990) 'Values, ideology and cognitive mobilization in new social movements', in R.J. Dalton and M. Kuechler (eds.) *Challenging the Political Order: New Social and Political Movements in Western Democracies*, Cambridge: Polity Press, pp.43–66.

Johnson, L.E. (1991) *A Morally Deep World*, Cambridge: Cambridge University Press.

Jones, B. (1989) 'Green thinking', *Talking Politics* 2 (2), pp.50–4.

Jordan, A. (1993) 'Integrated pollution control and the evolving style and structure of environmental regulation in the UK', *Environmental Politics* 2 (3), pp.405–27.

Judge, D. (1992) ' "Predestined to save the earth": The environment committee of the European Parliament', *Environmental Politics* 1 (4), pp.186–212.

Kimber, R. and Richardson, J.J. (eds.) (1974) *Campaigning for the Environment*, London: Routledge & Kegan Paul.

Kitsuse, J.I. and Spector, M. (1981) 'The labelling of social problems', in E. Rubington and M.S. Weinberg (eds.) *The Study of Social Problems*, New York: Oxford University Press, pp.198–206.

Kriger, M.H. (1973) 'What's wrong with plastic trees', *Science* 179, pp.446–55.

Labour Party (1992) *It's Time to Get Britain Working Again*, London.

Latouche, S. (1993) *Post-Development*, London: Zed Books.

Lauber, V. (1978) 'Ecology politics and liberal democracy', *Government Opposition*, 13 (2), pp.199–217.

Leopold, A. (1949) *A Sand County Almanac*, Oxford: Oxford University Press.

Liefferink, D., Lowe, P. and Mol, T. (1993) *European Integration and Environmental Policy*, London: Belhaven.

Lindblom, C. (1959) 'The science of "muddling through" ', *Public Administration Review* 19, pp.79–88.

Lindblom, C. (1977) *Politics and Markets*, New York: Basic Books.

List, M. and Rittberger, V. (1992) 'Regime theory and international environmental management', in A. Hurrell and B. Kingsbury (eds.) *The International Politics of the Environment*, Oxford: Clarendon Press, pp.85–109.

Lively, J. (1975) *Democracy*, Oxford: Basil Blackwell.

Lovelock, J. (1979) *Gaia*, Oxford: Oxford University Press.

Lowe, P. *et al.* (1986) *Countryside Conflicts: The Politics of Farming, Forestry and Conservation*, Aldershot: Gower.

Lowe, P. and Flynn, A. (1989) 'Environmental politics and policy in the 1980s', in J. Moham, *The Political Geography of Contemporary Britain*, Basingstoke: Macmillan, pp.255–79.

Lowe, P. and Goyder, J. (1983) *Environmental Groups in Politics*, London: Allen & Unwin.

Lowe, P. and Rudig, W. (1986) 'Review article: Political ecology and the social sciences – The state of the art', *British Journal of Political Science* 16, pp.513–50.

Lukes, S. (1974) *Power: A Radical View*, London: Macmillan.

Lyster, S. (1985) *International Wildlife Law*, Cambridge: Grotius.

MacNeil, J., Winsemius, P. and Yakushiji, T. (1991) *Beyond Independence: The Meshing of the World's Economy and the Earth's Ecology*, Oxford: Oxford University Press.

MAFF (1991) *Our Farming Future*, London: Central Office of Information.

Mannion, A.M. (1991) *Global Environmental Change: A Natural and Cultural Environmental History*, London: Longman.

Marsh, D. (ed.) (1983) *Pressure Politics: Interest Groups in Britain*, London: Junction Books.

Marsh, D. and Rhodes, R. (eds.) (1992) *Policy Networks in British Politics*, Oxford: Oxford University Press.

Martell, L. (1994) *Ecology and Society*, Cambridge: Polity.

Maslow, A.H. (1954) *Motivation and Personality*, New York: Harper.

Mason, J. and Singer, P. (1990) *Animal Factories*, 2nd edn, New York: Harmony.

May, R. (1989) 'How many species?' in L. Friday and R. Laskey (eds.) *The Fragile Environment*, Cambridge: Cambridge University Press, pp.61–81.

Mazey, S. and Richardson, J. (1992) 'Environmental groups and the EC: Challenges and opportunities', *Environmental Politics* 1 (4), pp.109–28.

McCarthy, J.D. and Zald, M.N. (1977) 'Resource mobilization and social movements', *American Journal of Sociology* 82, pp.1212–41.

McCormick, J. (1989) *Acid Earth: The Global Threat of Acid Pollution*, London: Earthscan.

McCormick, J. (1991) *British Politics and the Environment*, London: Earthscan.

McCormick, J. (1992) *The Global Environmental Movement*, London: Belhaven.

McCulloch, A. (1988a) 'Shades of green: Ideas in the British Green movement', *Teaching Politics* 17 (2), pp.186–207.

McCulloch, A. (1988b) 'Politics and the Environment', *Talking Politics* 1 (1), pp.14–19.

McCulloch, A. (1991) 'Green pressure', *Contemporary Record* 4 (3), pp.10–12.

McCulloch, A. (1992) 'The Green Party in England and Wales: Structure and development: The early years', *Environmental Politics* 1 (3), pp.418–36.

McTaggart, D. (1978) *Greenpeace III. Journey into the Bomb*, London: Collins.

Meadows, D.H., Meadows, D.L., Randers, J. and Behrens III, W. (1972) *The Limits to Growth: A Report for the Club of Rome's Project on the Predicament of Mankind*, New York: Universe.

Meadows, D.H., Meadows, D.L. and Randers, J. (1992) *Beyond the Limits: Global Collapse or a Sustainable Society: Sequal to the Limits to Growth*, London: Earthscan.

Mellor, M. (1992) 'Ecofeminist, Ecofeminine or Ecomasculine', *Environmental Politics* 1 (2), pp.229–51.

Merchant, C. (1980) *The Death of Nature: Women, Ecology and the Scientific Revolution*, New York: Harper & Row.

Morgenthau, H.J. (1962) *Politics in the Twentieth Century*, Chicago: University of Chicago Press.

Myers, N. (1989) 'The future of forests', in Friday, L. and Laskey, R. (eds.) *The Fragile Environment*, Cambridge: Cambridge University Press, pp.22–40.

Naess, A. (1973) 'The shallow and the deep, long range ecology movement. A summary', *Inquiry* 16, pp.95–100.

Newby, H. (1988) *The Countryside in Question*, London: Hutchinson.

Nordliner, E. (1981) *On the Autonomy of the Democratic State*, Cambridge, MA: Harvard University Press.

Olson, M. (1965) *The Logic of Collective Action*, Cambridge, MA: Harvard University Press.

Ophuls, W. (1973) 'Leviathan or oblivion?', in H.E. Daly, *Toward a Steady State Economy*, San Francisco: Freeman, pp.215–30.

Ophuls, W. (1977) *Ecology and the Politics of Scarcity*, San Francisco: W.H. Freeman.

O'Riordan, T. (1976) *Environmentalism*, London: Pion.

O'Riordan, T. and Weale, A. (1989) 'Administrative reorganisation and policy change: The case of Her Majesty's Inspectorate of Pollution', *Public Administration* 67, pp.277–95.

Paehlke, R.C. (1989) *Environmentalism and the Future of Progressive Politics*, New Haven, CT: Yale University Press.

Parkin, S. (1989) *Green Parties: An International Guide*, London: Heretic Books.

Parsons, H. (1978) *Marx and Engels on Ecology*, Westport, CT: Greenwood.

Passmore, J. (1980) *Man's Responsibility for Nature*, 2nd edn, London: Duckworth.

Pateman, C. (1970) *Participation and Democratic Theory*, Cambridge: Cambridge University Press.

Pearce, D., Markandya, A. and Barbier, E.B. (1989) *Blueprint For a Green Economy*, London: Earthscan.

Pearce, D. *et al.* (1993) *Blueprint 3: Measuring Sustainable Development*, London: Earthscan.

Pepper, D. (1986) *The Roots of Modern Environmentalism*, London: Routledge.

Pepper, D. (1993a) *Eco-Socialism: From Deep Ecology to Social Justice*, London: Routledge.

Pepper, D. (1993b) 'Anthropocentrism, humanism and eco-socialism: A blueprint for the survival of ecological politics', *Environmental Politics* 2 (3), pp.428–52.

Pickering, K.T. and Owen, A.O. (1994) *An Introduction to Global Environmental Issues*, London: Routledge.

Piddington, K. (1992) 'The role of the World Bank', in A. Hurrell and B. Kingsbury, *The International Politics of the Environment*, Oxford: Clarendon Press, pp.212–27.

Porritt, J. (1984) *Seeing Green*, Oxford: Basil Blackwell.

Porritt, J. and Winner, D. (1988) *The Coming of the Greens*, London: Fontana.

Pugh, M. (1982) *The Making of Modern British Politics 1867–1939*, Oxford: Basil Blackwell.

Rachels, J. (1990) *Created from Animals: The Moral Implications of Darwinism*, Oxford: Oxford University Press.

Rainbow, S.L. (1992) 'Why did New Zealand and Tasmania spawn the world's first Green parties?', *Environmental Politics* 1 (3), pp.321–46.

Redclift, M. (1984) *Development and the Environmental Crisis: Red or Green?*, London: Methuen.

Regan, T. (1988) *The Case for Animal Rights*, London: Routledge.

Regan, T. (1991) *The Thee Generation: Reflections on the Coming Revolution*, Philadelphia: Temple University Press.

Regenstein, L. (1985) 'Animal rights, endangered species and human survival', in P. Singer (ed.) *In Defence of Animals*, Oxford: Blackwell.

Richardson, E.L. (1992) 'Climate change: Problems of law making', in A. Hurrell and B. Kingsbury, *The International Politics of the Environment*, Oxford: Clarendon Press, pp.166–79.

Richardson, J. (ed.) (1982) *Policy Styles in Western Europe*, London: Allen & Unwin.

Richardson, J. *et al.* (1992) 'The dynamics of policy change: Lobbying and water privatisation', *Public Administration* 70, pp.157–75.

Ritvo, H. (1987) *The Animal Estate: The English and Other Creatures in the Victorian Age*, Cambridge, Mass.: Harvard University Press.

Robinson, M. (1992) *The Greening of British Party Politics*, Manchester: Manchester University Press.

Rootes, C.A. (1991) 'Environmentalism and political competition: The British Greens in the 1989 elections to the European Parliament', *Politics* 11 (2), pp.39–44.

Rudig, W. (1985) 'The Greens in Europe: Ecological parties and the European elections of 1984', *Parliamentary Affairs* 38 (1), pp.56–72.

Rudig, W. (ed.) (1991) *Green Politics Two*, Edinburgh: Edinburgh University Press.

Rudig, W. (1993) 'Wilting greenery', *The Times Higher Education Supplement*, 17 September.

Rudig, W. and Franklin, M.N. (1991) 'Green prospects: The future of Green parties in Britain, France and Germany', in W. Rudig (ed.) *Green Politics Two*, Edinburgh: Edinburgh University Press, pp.37–58.

Rudig, W. and Lowe, P. (1986) 'The withered "greening" of British politics: A study of the Ecology Party', *Political Studies* 34 (2), pp.262–84.

Ryder, R. (ed.) (1992) *Animal Welfare and the Environment*, London: Duckworth.

Rydin, Y. (1993) *The British Planning System: An Introduction*, Basingstoke: Macmillan.

Ryle, M. (1988) *Ecology and Socialism*, London: Century Hutchinson.

Sagoff, M. (1988) *The Economy of the Earth: Philosophy, Law and the Environment*, Cambridge: Cambridge Univerisity Press.

Sale, K. (1980) *Human Scale*, New York: Coward, Cann and Geoghegan.

Sale, K. (1984) 'Bioregionalism – a new way to treat the land', *The Ecologist* 14, pp.167–73.

Sandbach, F. (1980) *Environment, Ideology and Policy*, Oxford: Blackwell.

Saward, M. (1992) 'The civil nuclear network in Britain', in D. Marsh and R. Rhodes (eds.) *Policy Networks in British Politics*, Oxford: Oxford University Press, pp.75–99.

Saward, M. (1993a) 'Green theory', *Environmental Politics* 2 (3), pp.509–12.

Saward, M. (1993b) 'Green democracy', in A. Dobson and P. Lucardie (eds.) *The Politics of Nature: Explorations in Green Political Theory*, London: Routledge, pp.63–80.

Scarrow, H.A. (1961) 'The impact of British domestic air pollution legislation', *British Journal of Political Science* 2, pp.261–82.

Schoon, N. (1990) 'Acid rain that earns Britain a black mark', *The Independent*, 26 March.

Schumacher, E.F. (1973) *Small is Beautiful: Economics as if People Mattered*, London: Blond & Briggs.

Self, P. and Storing, H. (1962) *The State and the Farmer*, London: George Allen & Unwin.

Shoard, M. (1982) *The Theft of the Countryside*, London: Temple Smith.

Shue, H. (1992) 'The unavoidability of justice', in A. Hurrell and B. Kingsbury, *The International Politics of the Environment*, Oxford: Clarendon Press, pp.373–97.

Simpson, S. (1990) *The Times Guide To The Environment*, London: Times Books.

Singer, P. (1983) *The Expanding Circle: Ethics and Sociobiology*, Oxford: Oxford University Press.

Singer, P. (1990) *Animal Liberation*, London: Cape.

Smith, D. and Blowers, A. (1991) 'Passing the buck – Hazardous waste disposal as an international problem', *Talking Politics* 4 (1), pp.44–9.

Smith, M.J. (1990) *The Politics of Agricultural Support in Britain: The Development of the Agricultural Policy Community*, Aldershot: Dartmouth.

Smith, M.J. (1993) *Pressure, Power & Policy: State Autonomy and Policy Networks in Britain and the United States*, Hemel Hempstead: Harvester Wheatsheaf.

Stone, C. (1974) *Should Trees Have Standing: Toward Legal Rights for Natural Objects*, Los Altos, CA: Kaufmann.

Susskind, L. and Ozawa, C. (1992) 'Negotiating more effective international environmental agreements', in A. Hurrell and B. Kingsbury, *The International Politics of the Environment*, Oxford: Clarendon Press.

Sweeney, N. (1990) *Animals and Cruelty and Law*, Bristol: Alibi.

Thacher, P.S. (1992) 'The role of the United Nations', in A. Hurrell and B. Kingsbury, *The International Politics of the Environment*, Oxford: Clarendon Press, pp.183–211.

Thomas, C. (1993) 'Beyond UNCED: An introduction', *Environmental Politics* 2 (4), pp.1–27.

Thomas, R. (1983) *The Politics of Hunting*, Aldershot: Gower.

Vincent, A. (1993) 'The character of ecology', *Environmental Politics* 2 (2), pp.248–76.

Vogel, D. (1986) *National Styles of Regulation: Environmental Policing in Great Britain and the United States*, Ithaca, NY: Cornell University Press.

Ward, B. and Dubos, R. (1972) *Only One Earth: The Care and Maintenance of a Small Planet*, London: André Deutsch.

Ward, H. (1983) 'The anti-nuclear lobby: An unequal struggle?', in D. Marsh (ed.) *Pressure Politics: Interest Groups in Britain*, London: Junction Books, pp.182–211.

Ward, H. (1990) 'Environmental politics and policy', in P. Dunleavy *et al.* (eds.) *Developments in British Politics 3*, Basingstoke: Macmillan, pp.221–45.

Ward, S. (1993) 'Thinking global, acting local? British local authorities and their environmental plans', *Environmental Politics* 2 (3), pp.453–78.

Warren, A. and Goldsmith, F.B. (eds.) (1983) *Conservation in Perspective*, Chichester: John Wiley & Sons.

Weale, A. (1992) *The New Politics Of Pollution*, Manchester: Manchester University Press.

Weale, A. and Williams, A. (1992) 'Between economy and ecology? The single market and the integration of environmental policy', *Environmental Politics* 1 (4), pp.45–64.

Weston, J. (ed.) (1986) *Red and Green: The New Politics of the Environment*, London: Pluto Press.

Williams, R. (1986) 'Hesitations before socialism', *New Socialist*, September, pp.34–6.

Wilson, G. (1977) *Special Interests and Policy Making*, London: John Wiley & Sons.

Wissenburg, M. (1993) 'The idea of nature and the nature of distributive justice', in A. Dobson and P. Lucardie (eds.) *The Politics of Nature: Explorations in Green Political Thought*, London: Routledge, pp.3–20.

World Commission on Environment and Development (1987) *Our Common Future*, Oxford: Oxford University Press.

Wurzel, R. (1993) 'Environmental policy', in J. Lodge (ed.) *The European Community and the Challenge of the Future*, London: Pinter, pp. 48–67.

Yearley, S. (1992) *The Green Case*, London: Routledge.

Young, S.C. (1992) 'The different dimensions of Green politics', *Environmental Politics* 1 (1), pp.9–44.

Young, S.C. (1993) *The Politics of the Environment*, Manchester: Baseline Books.

Index

acid rain, 6, 9, 17, 34
agricultural policy, 80–1, 96, 156–63
Agriculture (Miscellaneous
    Provisions) Act 1968, 88,
    162, 169
Agriculture Act 1947, 158, 159
Agriculture Act 1988, 162
Alkali Act 1863, 88, 97
All-Party Parliamentary Group for
    Animal Welfare, 145
alternative energy sources, 26–7
Animal Liberation Front, 84–5
animal protection movement, 47,
    63–4, 78
animal rights, 47, 58, 78, 84–5,
    175–6
Animals (Scientific Procedures)
    Act 1986, 88, 169
Ashdown, P., 142
Attfield, R., 45

Bachelor, D., 132
Bahro, R., 184
Banks, T., 145
Basel Convention, 117
Beauty Without Cruelty, 183
Beck, U., 9
Bentham, J., 55
biodiversity, 24–6, 111, 125

bioregionalism, 38
Blowers, A., 68, 95, 153
Body Shop, 72, 183
Body, R., 145
Bookchin, M., 59
Bowden, A., 145
Bramwell, A., 52
British Trust for Conservation
    Volunteers, 73–4
Brower, D., 66
Bruntland Report, 3, 6, 112, 126
BTCV, see British Trust for
    Conservation Volunteers
Burke, E., 52, 144

Carson, R., 5–6, 26
CITES, see Convention on the
    International Trade in
    Endangered Species
Civic Trust, 77
Clark, D., 145
Clarke, A., 145
Clean Air Act 1956, 17, 88, 97
Cole, G.D.H., 38, 58
Commons, Open Spaces and
    Footpaths Preservation
    Society, 63
Conservation Society, 70
Conservative Ecology Group, 144

Conservative Party
  and business interests, 147
  and elections, 134–5, 140
  and Europe, 122
  and land use planning, 91, 143
  and nuclear power, 165
  and Thatcher, M., 1–2, 141,
      142–4, 166
  manifestos, 100
Convention on the International
    Trade in Endangered
    Species, 117, 118, 171, 173–5
Cotgrove, S., 69, 70
Council for Environmental
    Conservation, 76, 77
Council for the Protection of
    Rural England, 63, 64, 70,
    71, 77, 164
Countryside Act 1968, 88
Countryside Commission, 93–4, 96
CPRE, *see* the Council for the
    Protection of Rural
    England
Crenson, M., 152–3
Cunningham, J., 146

Dahl, R., 151
Darwin, C., 37
decentralization, 38–41
deep ecology, 2–4, 9–10, 30, 49, 51,
    60, 84, 139, 179
  and anarchism, 59–60
  and animal rights, 47–9
  and conservatism, 52
  and decentralization, 38–41
  and fascism, 52–4
  and feminism, 58–9
  and liberalism, 54–5
  and Marxism, 55–8
  and science and technology,
      36–7
  and the economy, 30–1, 35–6
  and the inherent value of
      nature, 41–6
deforestation, 22, 24, 25, 94, 111,
    157
Delores, J., 122
Department of the Environment,
    74, 80, 90, 91, 92, 93, 95, 98,
    99, 101, 103

Descartes, R., 47
Dobson, A., 2, 46, 59, 60, 182, 187
Dryzeck, J., 154
Duff, A., 69, 70

Earth First!, 84
Eckersley, R., 3, 9–10, 42, 45, 59,
    60
eco-feminism, 58–9
eco-socialism, 55–8
ecocentrism, *see* deep ecology
ecological modernization, 4, 32–5,
    100, 181, 188
economic instruments, 107–8
Ehrlich, P., 54
electricity privatization, 164–6
English Nature, 92, 93, 96
environmental disasters
  Aberfan, 5
  Bhopal, 5, 126
  Camelford, 20
  Chernobyl, 5, 8, 27, 165
  Exxon Valdez, 5
  Flixborough, 121
  Seveso, 5, 121
  Three Mile Island, 5
  Torrey Canyon, 5, 20
Environmental Investigation
    Agency, 84
environmental movement
  and direct action, 83–5
  and issue concern, 77–8
  and Parliament, 83
  and the Green Party, 137–8
  classification of, 71–8
  explaining the rise of, 67–71
  membership of, 64–5, 81–2
  origins of, 62–4
Environmental Protection Act
    1990, 89, 93, 98, 102, 106,
    124, 143, 162
Environmental Protection Agency,
    100, 102–3, 168
environmentalism and social class,
    69–70, 185–8
European Environment Agency,
    123
European Environmental Bureau,
    76

European Union, 7, 18, 74, 76, 83, 106, 111, 112, 119–24, 159, 160, 163, 164, 169, 177
externalities, 33–4

factory farming, 18, 49, 157–8
Fleming, D., 129
Fookes, J., 145
Forestry Commission, 94
fox hunting, 169, 170–1
Fox, W., 49
Franklin, M., 135
Frey, R., 44
Friends of the Earth, 64, 65, 66, 70, 71, 74, 76, 77, 81, 162, 165

Gaia, 56
Gale, R., 145
General Agreement on Tariff and Trade, 113
global warming, 5, 6, 15, 21, 22–4, 95, 111, 116
Goldsmith, E., 30–1, 39, 129, 139
Goodin, R., 40, 45–6
Gorz, A., 187
Gray, J., 52, 180
Green Alliance, 76–7
green consumerism, 182–4
Green parties outside Britain, 129, 130, 136, 137
Green Party, 12, 128–39
    and elections, 2, 130, 133–5
    explaining the weakness of, 135–9
    historical development of, 129–30
    organization, 130–3
Greenpeace, 64, 65, 66, 76, 84
Gummer, J., 103

Haeckel, E., 3
Hardin, G., 53–4
Hay, P.R., 53
Her Majesty's Inspectorate of Pollution, 89, 98, 99, 100, 102, 106, 143, 163–4, 180
Hirsch, F., 36, 186
HMIP, see Her Majesty's Inspectorate of Pollution

Hobbes, T., 56, 115
Hughes, S., 145

industrial revolution, 13–14
Inglehart, R., 67–9, 70, 186
integrated pollution control, 100–4, 163, 166, 180–1
International Union for the Conservation of Nature and Natural Resources, 75, 112, 113, 175
International Whaling Commission, 25, 42, 76, 89, 117, 172–3
IUCN, see the International Union for the Conservation of Nature and Natural Resources
ivory trade, 174–6

Jordan, A., 101

Kinnock, N., 132, 146
Kropotkin, P., 59

Labour Party
    and environmental policy, 140–1
    and nuclear power, 138
    and the Green Party, 138–9
    and the trade unions, 146–7
    manifestos, 146
Lambert, J., 132
land use planning, 89, 90, 91–3, 94–6, 143, 153–4
lead-free petrol, 15, 16, 107, 182
League Against Cruel Sports, 78, 146
Leopold, A., 41, 44
Liberal Democratic Party
    and elections, 135, 146
    and environmental policy, 141, 142
Liberal Ecology Group, 144
Liberal Party, 135, 140, 144–5
Limits to Growth, 6, 14, 31–2, 120
Lindblom, C., 152, 153, 166
Locke, J., 56
Lovelock, J., 56

Lucas, C., 132
Lukes, S., 151
Lyster, S., 171

MAFF, *see* Ministry of
    Agriculture, Fisheries and
    Food
Martell, L., 35, 39, 41, 60, 67
McCormick, J., 62, 156
Mill, J.S., 55
Ministry of Agriculture, Fisheries
    and Food, 80, 81, 90, 92, 93,
    94, 103, 104, 158, 159, 160,
    162, 163
More, T., 38
Morley, E., 145
Morris, W., 58, 186

Naess, A., 3, 4, 41
National Antivivisection Society,
    78
National Farmers Union, 80, 156,
    158–63, 167
National Rivers Authority, 99, 100,
    102, 106, 108, 124, 164
National Society for Clean Air, 77
National Trust, 63, 64, 65, 73, 77
NFU, *see* National Farmers Union
NRA, *see* National Rivers
    Authority
nuclear power, 8–9, 23, 27, 72, 138,
    139, 140, 145, 146, 154–5,
    165–6

O'Riordan, T., 3
Olson, M., 72–3, 150
Ophuls, W., 54
opinion polls, 1, 65, 135
Owen, D., 140, 146
ozone depletion, 5, 7, 15, 21–2, 111,
    114, 116

Paehike, R., 54
Parkin, S., 133
Patten, C., 90, 104, 108, 143, 144,
    168
Pearce, D., 3, 108
Pepper, D., 37, 56, 60, 154, 185

pesticides, 16, 19, 26, 157–8
pluralism, 78, 150–2, 155, 156, 160,
    167, 176
policy networks, 155–6, 158, 159,
    161–3, 167, 170, 176
pollution, 14, 15–20, 110, 152–3
Pontin, A., 132
Porritt, J., 2, 39, 46, 56, 129, 139,
    180, 186
public inquiries, 93, 95, 154, 165

Ramblers Association, 63, 64
rational choice theory, 149–50
RCEP, *see* Royal Commission on
    Environmental Pollution
Regan, T., 45
resource depletion, 15, 26–7, 31,
    110
Ridley, N., 143, 144, 146
Rio Summit, 75, 112, 117–18, 180
Ritvo, H., 64
Robinson, M., 140, 142
Rootes, C., 134
Rousseau, J.J., 38
Royal Commission on
    Environmental Pollution,
    88, 98, 163–4
Royal Society for Nature
    Conservation, 63, 64, 71, 73,
    74, 162
Royal Society for the Prevention
    of Cruelty to Animals, 64,
    74, 76
Royal Society for the Protection
    of Birds, 63, 64, 67, 70, 73,
    74, 75–6, 77, 81, 159, 162
RSNC, *see* the Royal Society for
    Nature Conservation
RSPB, *see* the Royal Society for
    the Protection of Birds
RSPCA, *see* the Royal Society for
    the Prevention of Cruelty
    to Animals
Rudig, W., 135

Sale, K., 38
Saward, M., 46, 165
Schumacher, E.F., 35

Sea Shepherd Conservation Society, 84
Sierra Club, 66
Singer, P., 44
Smith, A., 144
Smith, M., 158
Social Democratic Party, 140
Socialist Environment and Resources Association, 144
Soil Association, 77
sustainable communities, 184–5
sustainable development, 3, 32, 33, 75, 95, 111, 124–6
sustainable lifestyles, 182–4

technocentrism, 30, 32, 36, 49, 51
Thatcher, M., 141, 142–3, 146
Third World, 7, 21, 24, 32, 53–4, 110, 111, 116, 124–7, 145, 175–6
This Common Inheritance, 89, 103–4, 143, 168, 181
Town and Country Planning Act 1947, 88, 91, 96, 159
trade unions, 146–7, 186
transport, 14–15, 34, 80, 90, 98, 104, 167–8, 180–1
Tyler, J., 129, 133

United Nations, 112, 114, 115–16, 117, 118

Vincent, A., 46, 53
Vogel, D., 95, 105
Waldegrave, W., 144, 164
Water Act 1989, 89
water privatization, 164
Weale, A., 10, 15, 32, 149, 168
whales, 25, 42, 171–3
wildlife
    extinction of, 24–5, 157
    in Britain, 169–71
    international conservation of, 171–6
    reasons for conservation of, 25–6, 48–9, 172–3
    sustainable use of, 174–6
Wildlife and Countryside Act 1981, 79, 81, 89, 124, 162, 163, 169
Wilson, D., 145
Wing Airport Resistance Association, 72
women's movement, 187
World Bank, 112–13
World Conservation Strategy, 75, 113, 175
World Wide Fund for Nature, 74, 76, 77, 113, 175, 176, 183
WWF, *see* the World Wide Fund for Nature

Young, S., 3, 6, 81, 95, 118